TEN BEST PRACTICES

TO MAKE YOUR SUNDAY SCHOOL WORK

KEN HEMPHILL AND BILL TAYLOR

LifeWay Press®
Nashville, Tennessee

ISBN 0-7673-9593-X

This book is a resource in the Leadership and Skill Development category of the Christian Growth Study Plan for course numbers LS-0048, LS-0052, LS-0066, LS-0090, and LS-0104.

Dewey Decimal Classification: 268.1
Subject Headings: SUNDAY SCHOOL \ RELIGIOUS EDUCATION

Cover design: Micah Kandros
Cover photography: Tony Stone

Unless otherwise designated, all Scripture quotations are from the Holy Bible, New International Version. Copyright ©1973, 1978, 1984 by International Bible Society. Used by permission.

Scripture quotations marked HCSB® are taken from The Holman Christian Standard Bible®, copyright ©1999, 2000, 2001, 2002, 2003 by Holman Bible Publishers.Used by permission.

To order additional copies of this book or other resources identified as available from LifeWay Church Resources, write LifeWay Church Resources Customer Service, One LifeWay Plaza, North, Nashville, TN 37234-0113; fax order to (615) 251-5933; phone 1-800-458-2772; order online at *www.lifeway.com*; or visit the LifeWay Christian Store serving you.

Printed in the United States of America

Leadership and Adult Publishing
LifeWay Church Resources
One LifeWay Plaza
Nashville, Tennessee 37234-0175

ten best practices

1234567891012345678

CONTENTS

MEET THE AUTHORS 4

INTRODUCTION 5

BEST PRACTICE 1: **COMMIT TO THE STRATEGY** 23

BEST PRACTICE 2: **ORGANIZE WITH PURPOSE** 59

BEST PRACTICE 3: **BUILD KINGDOM LEADERS** 79

BEST PRACTICE 4: **DEVELOP SOUL WINNERS** 121

BEST PRACTICE 5: **WIN THE LOST** 133

BEST PRACTICE 6: **ASSIMILATE PEOPLE** 155

BEST PRACTICE 7: **PARTNER WITH FAMILIES** 171

BEST PRACTICE 8: **TEACH TO TRANSFORM** 181

BEST PRACTICE 9: **MOBILIZE FOR MINISTRY** 209

BEST PRACTICE 10: **MULTIPLY LEADERS AND UNITS** 223

APPENDICES 237

AN OVERVIEW AND USE PLAN 270

INDEX 272

CHRISTIAN GROWTH STUDY PLAN 275

to make your
sunday school work

0123456789101234567

115351

MEET THE AUTHORS

Ken Hemphill is national strategist for the Southern Baptist Convention's Empowering Kingdom Growth initiative. A leading authority on church growth, Dr. Hemphill has been a long-time advocate for the value of Sunday School ministry as a strategy for doing the work of the Great Commission. His book *Revitalizing the Sunday Morning Dinosaur,* published by Broadman & Holman Publishers, lifts up the potential of Sunday School as a strategy for evangelism, assimilation, and discipleship based on his experience as pastor of First Baptist Church, Norfolk, Virginia. Some content from that book has been adapted for use in this resource. Dr. Hemphill also is developer of *gotlife?*™, a personal witnessing training resource. See page 270 for a brief description and ordering information.

Bill Taylor is the former director of the Sunday School Group, Lifeway Church Resources, Nashville, Tennessee. As a national spokesperson for Sunday School as the foundational strategy in a local church for evangelism and discipleship, Dr. Taylor draws from his own wealth of experience as a local church practitioner, conference leader, speaker, and writer to focus on the ten best practices of effective Sunday School ministry. Previous publications include *Sunday School for a New Century.* Some content from that book has been adapted for use in this resource.

10

1234567891012345678 ten best practices

A Different Way of Thinking About Sunday School

Sunday School is the foundational strategy in a local church for leading people to faith in the Lord Jesus Christ and for building on-mission Christians through open Bible study groups that engage people in evangelism, discipleship, ministry, fellowship, and worship.

Sunday School has a heritage that spans more than two centuries. It has been an important part of Southern Baptist churches for more than 100 years. Therefore, some people may consider Sunday School a relic of the past that served us well then but has nothing to offer us now. They doubt it can meet the demands of the third millennium. Such opinions not only are blinded to the current potential of Sunday School ministry but would appear to ignore the resiliency and adaptability that has characterized Sunday School throughout its history. Resiliency and adaptability are reasons Sunday School has survived. That is also why it has such great potential for the future. Sunday School can change—and has changed—with the times.

Changing with the Times

The Sunday School of Robert Raikes

Even if Robert Raikes did not start the first Sunday School, he still is regarded as the father of the Sunday School movement. In 1780, he sought to help the poor, working children of Gloucester, England, by launching a school on Sunday to teach them reading, writing, and religion. This British model of Sunday School, using the Bible as its primer, grew rapidly as a means of providing a basic education for children unable to attend regular schools.

to make your sunday school work
0123456789101234567

Sunday School Moved West

At least by 1790, Sunday School had become rooted in the New World. At first, Sunday Schools were patterned after the British model, providing basic education and other essentials to children in need. In time, this model faded into a uniquely American model characterized by volunteer teachers and an evangelical curriculum that focused on interpreting the Bible and seeking the conversion of the learner. As Sunday School moved westward across the American frontier, this evangelistic thrust became more intentional and prominent.

Even during this time, Sunday Schools still were not church schools. In fact, some of the staunchest opponents to the Sunday School movement were church leaders. Pastors questioned the effectiveness of lay leaders teaching and interpreting the Bible to the unlearned.

By the early 1800s, local interdenominational Sunday School unions were established to provide support and strength to the efforts of the movement. In 1824, a national Sunday School union was organized, which gave Sunday School an even stronger platform for doing its work. Thousands of new Sunday Schools were started, especially as the nation continued its western expansion. Some of these Sunday Schools eventually became churches.

Sunday School Embraced by Denominations

The Sunday School movement was not going away. American church denominations realized that; therefore, many denominations reached out to embrace Sunday Schools for a pragmatic reason. As children—and even youth and adults—were converted through Sunday School influence, the denominations not only more clearly saw the evangelistic potential of Sunday School, they became concerned about doctrinal purity and positions on moral issues. Each denomination moved to protect itself by developing materials to teach the unique theological and doctrinal perspective it espoused.

By the end of the 19th century and continuing throughout the 20th century, Southern Baptists played a major role in the denominationalization of the Sunday School movement and seized the potential inherent in the movement. The incredible growth in Southern Baptist churches between

1940–1960 paralleled the growth of Sunday School ministry. Even though Southern Baptist Sunday School enrollment generally flattened over the last quarter of the twentieth century, the strength of Sunday School among Southern Baptists can be seen in perspective by noting the drastic declines among nearly all other mainline denominations. Moreover, Southern Baptists continued to be a leader in providing Bible study curriculum materials for use in all-age, lay-led Sunday School Bible teaching ministries.

Some Constants Through the Ages

Even a brief summary of Sunday School history reveals how resilient Sunday School has been as it has grown from humble beginnings on the streets of Gloucester to being a significant presence in thousands of communities, towns, and cities across the North American continent and beyond; from being an independent movement of which some church leaders were skeptical to being a vital ministry that is embraced by virtually every evangelical denomination.

At least two constants have characterized Sunday School ministry throughout its history.
- The Bible has been the centerpiece of teaching.
- The teaching has been by lay volunteers.

Those elements continue to be key to effective Sunday School ministry.

When the American Sunday School has been most effective as a tool for helping a church do its work, it has had at least one more major characteristic: evangelism has been at the heart. The early architects of the Sunday School movement in America believed that the Sunday School must have a Great Commission focus. They did not believe that Sunday School could function properly without a clear and intentional strategy of evangelism. Furthermore, after persons were won to Christ, the Sunday School would nurture and train these new believers even as it helped to mature all believers.

The decline of Southern Baptist Sunday School enrollment and the corresponding decline in Southern Baptist baptisms during the last two decades of the twentieth century can be tied to a decreased emphasis on evangelism in Sunday School and to an increased emphasis on fellowship

and Bible teaching focused on believers. Fellowship and Bible teaching for believers are not bad within themselves, but they focus attention on those already gathered rather than on those who need to be gathered. Fellowship tends to focus more on "us" than "them." An emphasis on Bible teaching targeted at believers tends to be concerned more with learners being informed rather than being transformed.

This being the true, perhaps the problem is not with Sunday School after all; the problem is with the way we think about Sunday School and the way we do Sunday School. Sunday School does have something to offer churches of the third millennium. We need to develop a new way—or for some people, perhaps, recover the old way—of thinking about Sunday School if we are to tap its vitality for a new day. That is what this book is about—redefining and rethinking Sunday School. The content is built around ten best practices for implementing biblical and strategic Sunday School ministry in a local church.

Sunday School Ten Best Practices

1. **Commit to the Strategy**

2. **Organize with Purpose**

3. **Build Kingdom Leaders**

4. **Develop Soul Winners**

5. **Win the Lost**

6. **Assimilate People**

7. **Partner with Families**

8. **Teach to Transform**

9. **Mobilize for Ministry**

10. **Multiply Leaders and Units**

ten best practices

Introducing Sunday School Best Practices

Simply stated, best practices are essential actions for doing the work. They become ways of making the theoretical and philosophical practical. The best practices described in this book are rooted in the knowledge of how people and churches work, but foremost they come from observing effective work in a broad base of churches over an extended period of time.

Best practices is a strong phrase. It suggests that while there may be several ways of doing something, one way has proven to be better and more effective. The challenges of the new century will require the best. No longer can we be satisfied to crowd into the corridors of complacency or meander in the meadows of mediocrity. Instead, we must step forward with bold solutions. When you believe you have the solution, when you are convinced you know the best way, surely you want to share it with others.

These best practices are not independent actions.. They exist as part of the broad context for describing Sunday School ministry, moving from the philosophical to the practical. The various elements of that context may be seen in this relationship:

> *Kingdom Mission*
> > *Great Commission*
> > > *Church Functions*
> > > > *Biblical Foundations*
> > > > > *Sunday School Definition*
> > > > > > *Strategic Principles*
> > > > > > > **Best Practices**
> > > > > > > > *Local Church Actions*

Sunday School: On Kingdom Mission

To be on kingdom mission is to focus on the kingdom of God—the rule and reign of God. The kingdom of God and kingdom work are God's work. People enter the kingdom through repentance and faith in Jesus Christ. In that way, they are opening themselves to be ruled by God.

Sunday School is a strategy for a church desiring to be on kingdom mission. The focus is on the kingdom not the program or the institution. The church is an important part of the kingdom but is not to be equated with the kingdom. The church is God's agent in the world. The church's mission is to declare the good news of the kingdom of God. The Lord has called and

empowered His church for that mission (Matt. 28:18-20). People may never get excited about preserving the status quo, helping out the pastor, or otherwise going through the motions of "church work"; they will respond to the powerful call of God to join Him and His people on kingdom mission.

Sunday School and the Great Commission: "Make Disciples"

At its core, the Great Commission (Matt. 28:18-20) is a command to join Christ in His mission. It represents the overriding mandate—the driving force—to any New Testament church. That mandate is "make disciples."

The first step in making disciples is intentional evangelistic effort in which the gospel is presented and hearers respond in faith to the convicting power of the Holy Spirit. When Jesus gave His disciples the Great Commission, He knew they would be "going." After all, they would not be staying on the mountain (v. 16). Jesus wanted them to go with purpose, so He gave them one—"make disciples."

The Great Commission is not just biblical history. The commission to make disciples is contemporary to followers of Jesus in any era of time. Making disciples begins with proclaiming the gospel message of Jesus out of the deep conviction that "it is the power of God for the salvation of everyone who believes" (Rom. 1:16). Churches who realize that the Great Commission gives them their purpose and reason for existence look for an effective way to mobilize their members to intentional gospel presentation—the "going" aspect of the Great Commission.

Making disciples includes assimilating new believers into the life and ministry of the church. The salvation available in Jesus brings a person into the kingdom, not for rest but for service. Churches that take seriously the mandate to "make disciples" look for an effective way to assimilate new believers into the fellowship—the "baptizing" dimension of the Great Commission.

Making disciples includes teaching obedience to the commandments of Christ. And as we have seen, at least one command of Jesus is to "make disciples." Hence, teaching is aimed at cycling new believers into the life and mission of the church. Obedience becomes both a means to, and a sign

ten best practices

of, maturity in Christ. Therefore, churches that take seriously the mandate to make disciples look for an effective way to help new believers grow in obedience—the "teaching" dimension of the Great Commission.

Is there an effective strategy to help a church carry out the Great Commission to make disciples? A strategy that mobilizes people for gospel proclamation, assimilates individuals and families into the life of the church, and teaches believers through obedience to Christ to deepen their relationship with Him and be engaged in the ministry of the church? There is. Sunday School at work can be that strategy.

Sunday School and The Church

The Great Commission is the one great driving force for the growth of God's kingdom and the health of His church on kingdom mission. The objective is spiritual transformation through which people are made fit for the kingdom—both here and hereafter.

The church—consisting of those who have been and are being changed in Christ—is characterized by five essential functions. These functions grow out of the Great Commission and are evident in the New Testament church as seen in Acts 2:42-47. The five essential functions are:

• *Evangelism*—believers sharing the gospel with lost people;

• *Discipleship*—a process that begins after conversion in which the believer grows to become more Christlike in every area of life;

• *Ministry*—meeting another person's needs in the name of Jesus Christ;

• *Fellowship*—a oneness of believers that comes from their common relationship in Jesus Christ;

• *Worship*—encountering God in a meaningful, spiritual way and showing adoration and reverence for Him.

Four kinds of growth result when a church faithfully follows the mandate of the Great Commission and is engaged in those five essential functions.

• *Numerical Growth*—the numerical increase of the church measured in membership, baptisms, attendance levels, and ministry participation;

• *Spiritual Transformation*—God's work of changing a believer into the likeness of Jesus by creating a new identity in Christ and by empowering a lifelong relationship of love, trust, and obedience to glorify God;

- *Ministry Expansion*—as a church grows numerically and as people are transformed spiritually, the Holy Spirit opens additional doors of ministry;
- *Kingdom Advance*—God's daily work of extending His kingdom through the church.

Sunday School as strategy is driven by the Great Commission and focuses on the five essential functions of the church. Through Sunday School more people come to know Christ, believers grow in Christ, members are called out into service, and members are mobilized to share the gospel in their world and the whole world.

Biblical Foundations for Sunday School as Strategy

As a strategy, Sunday School also is built upon certain biblical foundations. Sunday School as strategy—

- *Affirms the Bible as God's Word and as the textbook for understanding truth and for fully integrating truth into life.*—God provided the Bible as the authoritative written revelation of Himself to humanity. He assigned to the Bible's message the power to bring people to faith in Christ and guide them to follow Him in obedience (2 Tim. 3:15-17).
- *Accepts the Great Commission as the mission mandate to God's people and becomes a way of fulfilling that mission as people are lead to obey Christ's commandments.*—Jesus commands His followers to acknowledge His authority over all things, to evangelize the world, to bring people into fellowship with God and one another, and to lead them to become His disciples (Matt. 28:16-20).
- *Recognizes God's active purpose of reconciling a spiritually lost world to Himself and provides a way for people to join Him in the work of intentional evangelism.*—God loves all people and desires that they hear the gospel and receive salvation through His Son, Jesus Christ (John 3:16; Rom. 1:16-17; 2 Pet. 3:9).
- *Affirms the Christian family as the primary institution for biblical instruction.*—God desires for parents to teach His Word to their children as an integral and natural part of daily living (Deut. 6:4-9).
- *Engages people in spiritually transforming ministry opportunities*

ten best practices
1234567891012345678

through Bible study groups that lead people to love, trust, and obey God.—
God urges His followers to worship Him by submitting their lives to His
leadership, allowing Him to transform their lives (Rom. 12:1-2).

• *Enables believers to be servant-leaders and offers them opportunities
to discover, develop, and use their spiritual gifts and abilities in service to
Christ and His people.*—Through the Holy Spirit, God gives Christians
spiritual gifts and empowers Christians to use those gifts in His service (1
Cor. 12—13; Rom. 12:1-8; Eph. 4:12).

• *Provides a structure that enables the largest number of God's people
to do the work assigned the church.*—God urges the church as the body of
Christ to be unified and to work in harmony to accomplish His purpose
(Eph. 4:1-6; 1 Cor. 12:12-27).

• *Requires leaders who are willing to be held accountable for calling
forth and equipping new leaders. It is a way in which all believers can be
involved actively in leading spiritually lost people toward faith in the Lord
Jesus Christ.*—God intends for Christians to be accountable individually and
collectively to develop new disciples (Matt. 25:14-30; 2 Tim. 2:1-2).

• *Leads people to be involved in Bible study that facilitates the
transforming work of the Holy Spirit in a person's life.*—God intends for
people to engage in Bible study that leads to transformational living (2 Cor.
3:18; 2 Tim. 3:16-17).

Definition of Sunday School
for a New Century

*Sunday School is the foundational strategy in a local church for leading
people to faith in the Lord Jesus Christ and for building on-mission
Christians through open Bible study groups that engage people in
evangelism, discipleship, ministry, fellowship, and worship.*

Simply stated, Sunday School is a strategy that guides people to come to
know Jesus and then begin to deepen their lives in evangelism, discipleship,
ministry, fellowship, and worship. Knowing Jesus and learning what it
means to follow Jesus is a transforming—life-changing—experience. That is
the goal of the teaching that takes place in the open Bible study groups that
are the vehicles for carrying out the Sunday School strategy.

The open-group concept will be explored in more detail in chapter 1, but some introductory comments are needed at this point. You may be wondering, *What is an open-group strategy, and how does it relate to Sunday School?* Consider the following definition. Note its similarity and relationship to the definition for Sunday School given above.

An open-group strategy exists to lead people to faith in the Lord Jesus Christ and to build on-mission Christians by engaging people in foundational evangelism, discipleship, ministry, fellowship, and worship through ongoing, evangelistic Bible study units of believers together with unbelievers in an atmosphere of compassion to share the gospel.

The open group is a foundational strategy that serves as an entry point into the church for unbelievers. An open group is primarily an evangelistic Bible study group or event comprised of an intentional mix of believers and unbelievers. An open group also emphasizes the "sending out" of people on mission outside the church and multiplying leaders of new groups for service in the church.

An evangelistic Bible study group is a group intentionally formed around the study of God's Word. This is different from a group that gathers for mutual support, fellowship, leadership training, or skill development that often requires requisite knowledge of the content being studied. Bible study groups that are designed *primarily* for reaching lost people are open groups. Bible study groups that are designed *primarily* for moving saved people toward spiritual maturity and transformation are closed groups.

Sunday School, as an expression of the open-group concept, is recommended as the best proven organizational framework for involving families and individuals in the evangelistic work of the church.

Strategic Principles for Sunday School for a New Century

If Sunday School is to fulfill its objectives as strategy, church leaders must champion and communicate the objectives in a clear, compelling manner. The following five strategic principles undergird Sunday School as strategy and represent priorities to be addressed through Sunday School as strategy. They will be valuable as primary messages that guide the effectiveness of Sunday School in a new century.

ten best practices

123456789101234567890

The Principle of Foundational Evangelism

Sunday School is the foundational evangelism strategy of the church.

1. Sunday School emphasizes ongoing open Bible study groups that reproduce new groups as the best long-term approach for building a ministry environment that guides preschoolers and children toward conversion through foundational teaching, encourages unsaved people to come to faith in Christ, assimilates new believers into the life of the church, and encourages believers to lead others to Christ.

2. Sunday School provides the most efficient churchwide evangelism training network to equip members to become passionate soul-winners.

3. Sunday School encourages Bible study in short-term groups and through special Bible teaching events as effective ways to promote outreach and evangelism and to address specific life concerns, spiritual issues, church functions, and doctrinal issues.

4. Sunday School creates a great center for missionary power as people tell and live the wondrous story of Christ's redeeming love.

The Principle of Foundational Discipleship

Knowing God through Jesus is the first step of discipleship. Sunday School is a seven-day-a-week strategy, and Bible study is a foundational step of discipleship for involving people in seeking the kingdom of God and fulfilling the Great Commission.

1. Sunday School provides the primary organizational framework for involving families and individuals in the comprehensive work of the church, including evangelism, discipleship, ministry, fellowship, and worship.

2. Sunday School provides foundational discipleship and encourages members to strengthen their Christian walk by participating in other discipleship opportunities.

3. Sunday School emphasizes that every member who is a believer must become accountable for the responsibility God has given him or her as a minister and missionary to the world.

4. Sunday School supports all church ministries and intentionally encourages its members to be good stewards, fully involved in the church's overall mission.

to make your
sunday school work

0123456789101234567

The Principle of Family Responsibility

Sunday School affirms the home as the center of biblical guidance.

1. Sunday School helps equip Christian parents, including single parents, to fulfill their responsibility as the primary Bible teachers and disciplers of their children.

2. The Sunday School encourages Christian parents who by word and deed guide their children to integrate the Scriptures into their lives, influencing how they think and act.

3. Sunday School involves families in the comprehensive work of the church.

4. Sunday School works to nurture sound and healthy families and seeks to lead non-Christian parents to Christ.

The Principle of Spiritual Transformation

Sunday School engages learners in the biblical model of instruction that leads to spiritual transformation.

1. Sunday School affirms that spiritual transformation is God's work of changing a believer into the likeness of Jesus by creating a new identity in Christ and by empowering a lifelong relationship of love, trust, and obedience to glorify God.

2. Sunday School champions the absolute truth and authority of the Word of God and compels believers to integrate a biblical worldview into their minds, hearts, and lives through ongoing, systematic Bible study.

3. Sunday School recognizes that Bible study is most effective when it occurs in the context of the learner's total life, especially family relationships, and when it considers the special needs, generational perspective, age and life-stage characteristics, and learning styles of the learner.

4. Sunday School addresses transcultural life issues common to individuals, churches, families, tribes, and nations regardless of geographic, ethnic, or language identity.

The Principle of Biblical Leadership

Sunday School calls leaders to follow the biblical standard of leadership.

1. Sunday School affirms the pastor as the primary leader in its ministry

10

123456789101234567891 ten best practices

of building on-mission Christians.

2. Sunday School calls leaders to a prophetic ministry, one in which they listen to God's voice, discover His message, integrate His message into their lives, and proclaim His truth through His church to the nations.

3. Sunday School recognizes that the leader is the lesson in that every leader is accountable for being an authentic example of Christianity in personal living and in producing new leaders for service through the ministries of the church.

4. Sunday School recognizes that planning is essential in implementing its strategy.

An Overview of Ten Best Practices

The best practices of Sunday School as strategy are presented here as ten brief, concrete, imperative statements. The bulleted statements under each best practice enlarge the meaning of the practice. Generally, the best practices are listed in the sequence in which they would be implemented, but the sequence should not be overemphasized. The best practices are not offered as a mechanical formula for success. The sequence, however, does identify and describe the process of designing and implementing an effective Sunday School strategy. So, in that sense the sequence has high value.

These best practices, as we have said, are based on observing churches that have effectively used Sunday School in a strategic way. Their effectiveness is realized in the commitment of the people to the mission of Christ, the willingness of people to work, and of course, the quickening power of the Holy Spirit. Apart from the Spirit, no lasting kingdom work takes place. The rest of this book focuses on each best practice and how it can be used in your church as you implement Sunday School as strategy.

1. Commit to the Strategy
We will commit to Sunday School as the foundational strategy in a local church for doing the work of the Great Commission by —
- developing an annual plan that supports the church's thrust to lead people to faith in the Lord Jesus Christ and build on-mission Christians.
- including as key elements of the plan ongoing and short-term open

Bible study groups and additional Bible study events, such as Vacation Bible School, that focus on foundational evangelism and foundational discipleship.

- providing the best-possible financial support to implement the strategic plans.
- implementing the plan through specific monthly and weekly actions.

2. Organize with Purpose

We will organize our Sunday School ministry to accomplish the objectives of leading people to faith in the Lord Jesus Christ and building on-mission Christians by —

- using the concept of age-graded, open Bible study groups as the primary organizing principle for Bible study groups.
- providing groups for all ages and generations, including preschool, children, youth, young adults, and adults.
- relying on sound learner:leader ratios proven to be effective for each age group in developing the age-group organizational structures.

3. Build Kingdom Leaders

We will build kingdom leaders who are committed to Sunday School strategy as an expression of faithfulness to Christ, His church, and the mission mandate He has given by —

- praying for God to call out leaders for kingdom service through Sunday School ministry.
- implementing a leader-enlistment approach that focuses on helping people respond to their personal call from God rather than an approach that is primarily concerned with filling church or organizational positions.
- enlisting leaders who themselves are committed to cultivating and multiplying new leaders.
- devoting major attention to leadership meetings that focus on the mission, on relationships, and on Bible study.
- providing training that equips leaders for their work and enhances the quality of their leadership.

123456789101234567 ten best practices 89

- calling out people who will give their lives to evangelizing the lost and who are willing to participate in ongoing evangelism training and multiplication of evangelism leaders.

4. Develop Soul Winners

We will lead leaders and members to become soul-winners and witnesses for Christ in all life settings, including the home, by —

- teaching members to view being a practicing soul-winner as the role of every believer.
- challenging members continually to be aware of the spiritually lost people they encounter daily.
- focusing attention on the responsibility of Sunday School leaders and members to lead people to faith in the Lord Jesus Christ.
- training leaders and members how to share the gospel through an intentional, ongoing strategy.
- providing regular opportunities for leaders and members to share the gospel as part of personal home visits.

5. Win the Lost

We will engage in evangelistic actions that result in winning the lost to Christ, as well as in other actions that target the unchurched and reclaim the spiritually indifferent, by —

- involving members in discovering individual and family prospects.
- maintaining up-to-date master and working prospect files and implementing an ongoing approach for making evangelistic prospect visitation assignments to members.
- providing regular, specific times for evangelistic, outreach, and ministry visitation.
- committing ourselves to witness for Christ in all life settings, including the home.
- teaching evangelistically, including foundational teaching, especially with preschoolers and children, that becomes the basis for a later conversion as the Holy Spirit brings conviction of sin.
- challenging unchurched or spiritually indifferent individuals and families to commit to living as followers of Jesus Christ.

6. Assimilate People

We will assimilate individuals and families into the life of the church and facilitate their growth as disciples of Christ by —

- encouraging new believers to identify with Christ and His church through baptism and church membership.
- emphasizing regular participation in systematic Bible study as the foundational step of discipleship.
- enrolling people anytime, anywhere in ongoing Bible study and other short-term Bible study groups.
- providing an atmosphere for building relationships with one another in an environment of grace, acceptance, support, and encouragement.
- encouraging all believers to strengthen their walk with Christ by participating in other discipleship opportunities.
- developing a system for tracking individual and family participation in ongoing Bible study and in discipleship groups.
- developing a system for tracking actions that serve as indicators of spiritual growth and personal spiritual vitality.
- providing opportunities for new Christians and church members, and their families, to discover how they fit into the life and ministry of the church.
- planning opportunities for individuals and families to pray together and to work together toward fulfilling the Great Commission.
- promoting systematic, biblical giving and the stewardship of life as the norm for believers.

7. Partner with Families

We will partner with parents and families to build the home as the center of biblical guidance by —

- providing an appropriate open Bible study group for every member of the family, including family members with special needs.
- providing training and resources to help parents fulfill their responsibility as the primary Bible teachers and disciplers of their children.
- developing family-oriented evangelistic and ministry strategies that help families to reach other families for Christ and the church and minister to their needs.

ten best practices

1234567891012345678

- building a leadership team that believes in and models the essential partnership of home and church in Bible teaching.
- providing Bible study and devotional materials that encourage and support family worship and Bible study in the home.
- exploring the possibilities for intergenerational ministries that enable the different generations to interact with each other rather than being isolated from one another.

8. Teach to Transform

We will engage individuals and families in the biblical model of instruction that leads to spiritual transformation by —

- preparing faithfully for the open-group Bible teaching session, including personal spiritual preparation and participation in leadership meetings.
- encountering God's Word in a Bible study group guiding learners toward spiritual transformation.
- continuing to guide learners toward spiritual transformation in daily living and family relationships.
- centering the transformational teaching-learning process around these Bible teaching elements: acknowledge authority, search the truth, discover the truth, personalize the truth, struggle with the truth, believe the truth, and obey the truth.
- preparing open-group lesson plans to teach in a variety of ways, including relational, musical, logical, physical, reflective, visual, and verbal approaches.
- looking for opportunities in other settings to both teach and model the message of the Bible.
- equipping parents to be the primary Bible teachers in their homes.
- choosing open-group Bible study curriculum materials that lead learners to explore the entire counsel of God during their life stages.
- providing the best-possible teaching resources that enable teachers to teach for spiritual transformation.
- providing the best-possible space and equipment as appropriate for age-group teaching and learning.

to make your sunday school work
0123456789101234567

9. Mobilize for Ministry

We will take deliberate actions to mobilize people to meet with compassion the needs of individuals and families by —

- remembering that the greatest need is to be in right relationship with the Lord.
- helping identify ministry needs and informing leaders and members about ministry opportunities.
- equipping individuals and families to minister to others in need in all settings.
- leading members and their families to be involved in ministry and mission projects as a continuation of Sunday School Bible study.
- involving the church family in supporting missionaries and mission work through prayer and giving.

10. Multiply Leaders and Units

We will develop and implement an intentional process for continually multiplying leaders and units by —

- communicating the key relationship that multiplication of leaders and units has to the overall mission of Sunday School as strategy.
- teaching every believer to be in service and on mission and to multiply themselves.
- developing a potential leader-training ministry that helps members explore their leadership potential and possibilities.
- making leader enlistment and multiplication of units an ongoing process rather than annual actions.
- encouraging and supporting the initiative of existing Bible study groups to reproduce themselves through new open Bible study groups that increase the opportunity to evangelize and disciple more people.
- encouraging and supporting the efforts of leaders to identify prospective leaders and guide them toward service for Christ and His church.
- engaging the church to start a new Vacation Bible School, start a new Sunday School, or help to plant a new church mission.

10

123456789101234567 89 ten best practices

BEST PRACTICE 1
Commit to the Strategy

"Whatever you do, work at it with all your heart, as working for the Lord, not for men, since you know that you will receive an inheritance from the Lord as a reward. It is the Lord Christ you are serving."
—Colossians 3:23-24

The two associates firmly clasped hands in a display of their commitment to each other, the plans they had developed, and the approach they would take to achieve them. With that affirmation they entered into what would become a successful venture.

In most any worthy endeavor the difference between succeeding and failing usually comes down to this: Were the people involved committed? What were they committed to? Would they willingly affirm that commitment?

Nothing worthwhile will be accomplished in a church without a deep-felt commitment to both the person and the teaching of Jesus Christ. Actually, the two cannot be separated. According to Jesus' own words, a true love for Him and relationship with Him—both of which are dimensions of commitment—issue in obedience to His commandments (John 14:15, 21-24; 15:10,15). So, we need to begin with a commitment, or recommitment as it were, to Jesus Christ as Savior and Lord.

As we established in the "Introduction," our whole focus for Sunday School is as a strategy for doing the Great Commission. We do the Great

to make your
01234567891101234567
sunday school work

Commission not so the church will grow but because we desire to obey Christ. Yes, growth will result, but it is not what we are about. Growth is God's work. His expectation for us is faithfulness to Him. So, we need a commitment to the Great Commission as our mandate for action because we want to be obedient followers.

It is important not only to be committed to the objective—which in this case is the Great Commission—but to the strategy that makes it possible. A strategy is a multi-faceted plan designed to reach an objective. Therefore, if Sunday School is a viable strategy enabling us to bring glory to Christ through obedience to the Great Commission, then it too deserves our commitment. The strategy will not work without a people who are committed to making it work. Commitment to the strategy calls for some intentional actions that give it life.

We will commit to Sunday School as the foundational strategy in a local church for doing the work of the Great Commission by —
- *developing an annual plan that supports the church's thrust to lead people to faith in the Lord Jesus Christ and build on-mission Christians.*
- *including as key elements of the plan ongoing and short-term open Bible study groups and additional Bible study events, such as Vacation Bible School, that focus on foundational evangelism and foundational discipleship.*
- *providing the best-possible financial support to implement the strategic plans.*
- *implementing the plan through specific monthly and weekly actions.*

Developing an Annual Plan

Resolutions, good intentions, visions, and dreams sometimes have gone unfulfilled because plans were never made to bring them to fruition. We know we need to plan, and we say we will plan. But when all is said and done, more has been said than done. We usually just do not get around to planning.

Annual planning is hard work. It takes time and energy. But the results will save time later and bring more long-term positive results sooner. Therefore, planning ways to implement the strategy turns out to be worth both the time and effort. Finally, developing an annual plan is one expression of our commitment to Sunday School as strategy.

Some Benefits of Developing an Annual Plan

Annual planning provides an opportunity to evaluate the relationship of what you are doing to what you want to accomplish. The annual plan is to help you achieve your purpose. It is possible to plan things for the year, but those plans may not be targeted toward the primary mission of leading people to faith in the Lord Jesus Christ and building on-mission Christians. Measure all your planning by what you want to accomplish. Eliminate what does not contribute to the mission, even if the action is a good thing. Focus all your resources on your mission.

Annual planning is an intentional design to close the gap between where your church is and where it wants to be. To do that, two essential questions need to be answered: *Where are we now? Where do we want to be when this year is over?*

Annual planning gives you the opportunity to solve potential problems. Some leaders are so absorbed in "putting out fires" that they cannot give attention to preventing them. During annual planning, you have the opportunity to "prevent fires" by directing your energies toward the mission.

Annual planning allows you to learn from the past, better understand the present, and move purposefully toward the future. The present may be better understood if it is viewed in light of the past. Current actions, based on lessons learned in the past and carried out in the context of the present reality, can successfully move the church toward mission accomplishment in the future.

Annual planning helps leaders to be more productive. Results that are planned for are more likely to occur. Energies and resources can be channeled to accomplish mission, vision, and goals.

Annual planning allows you to celebrate accomplishments. An annual planning event becomes an opportunity to celebrate the accomplishments of the past year. Look for ways to share the previous successes with the congregation so they too can enjoy the celebration.

to make your sunday school work

Annual planning helps you to anticipate future leadership and space needs. In planning for future growth, you can anticipate expanded leadership needs, including replacing leaders lost through attrition. Space needs and space adjustments also can be anticipated, avoiding having to react to crisis situations later.

Annual planning helps to bring about balanced work. Evaluate whether too much time and effort are being given to one area of work to the detriment of another. Unbalanced work eventually will deplete the strength of your strategy and the church.

Annual planning helps you to make the best use of resources. No matter how much or how little we have, we need to use our resources in the best ways possible. Planning can help us to be good stewards of resources.

Annual planning makes for fulfilled leaders. Annual planning brings a sense of purpose and direction to the work. When leaders feel part of something purposeful and can see direction and results in their work, they will feel a greater satisfaction and fulfillment in what they are doing.

Suggestions for an Annual Planning Event

Gather a Planning Team

Annual planning is done best by a team. In many churches, the team that develops the annual detail of the strategy—the strategic plan—may be called the Sunday School Planning Team. The composition of that team may vary depending on the size of the church and the organizational structure used in grouping people for Bible study.

If the church has age-group divisions, the team may consist of the pastor, educational staff, general officers, and division directors. If the church only has age-group departments, the planning team may consist of the pastor, educational staff, general officers, and department directors. In smaller churches or churches with a class structure, the team may include the pastor, Sunday School director, and a leader from each class. Some churches also include the Discipleship director on the team to assist in developing plans for carrying out the church's discipleship function.

Whatever the composition, this team leads out in the planning process and formulates details of the strategy. This may be done during an annual planning event. Here are some steps for preparing for that event.

Set the Date

Many churches do their annual planning in the spring for the church year that begins in the fall. Two factors will influence the time. First, do annual planning far enough in advance of the new year to affect organizational, space, and leadership needs. Second, prior to the annual planning event, complete the enlistment of leaders for the new church year so they can be involved in developing the plans they implement.

Determine the Schedule

Several schedules are possible for an annual planning event. Consider these options; choose the one most suitable for your situation. Better yet, create your own.

• Friday-Saturday Retreat

Friday

6:00 p.m.	Supper
7:00	Welcome
	• What We Hope to Accomplish
	• Agenda Review
7:15	Devotional on the Great Commission
	• Prayer for God's Leadership
	• Sunday School: Our Church's Great Commission Strategy
8:00	A Look At Where We Are—Evaluation
9:30	Dismiss

Saturday

8:00 a.m.	Breakfast
8:45	Devotional
9:00	A Look at What Our Evaluation Shows Us—Our Needs
10:30	Break
10:45	Setting Priorities and Determining Goals

12:00 noon	Lunch
12:45 p.m.	Building Action Plans
3:00	Committing Our Plans to God
3:30	Dismiss and Head Home

• All-day Saturday Retreat

8:30 a.m.	Continental Breakfast
9:00	Welcome
	• What We Hope to Accomplish
	• Agenda Review
9:20	Devotional on the Great Commission
	• Prayer for God's Leadership
	• Sunday School: Our Church's Great Commission Strategy
10:00	A Look At Where We Are—Evaluation
11:00	A Look at What Our Evaluation Shows Us—Our Needs
12:00 noon	Lunch
12:45 p.m.	Setting Priorities and Determining Goals
1:30	Building Action Plans
3:30	Committing Our Plans to God
3:45	Dismiss and Head Home

• Several Weeknights Option

Spread the agenda items described in the options above over a series of sessions meeting several evenings.

Secure a Location

Select a location that allows participants to avoid distractions, helps them to focus their thinking, and stimulates creativity. Some possibilities are:

- associational assembly or encampment
- local hotel or motel conference room
- state park accommodations
- vacation/recreation cabin
- neighboring church
- home of a member of the planning group

If none of those options are possible, your church building still can be a good planning location. In fact, there are some benefits to meeting at the church building, such as easy access to records and other materials and the opportunity to view space and equipment. If you choose to meet in your church facilities, find ways to add to the spirit and anticipation that the meeting will be something out of the ordinary.

Wherever you meet, provide an atmosphere that is conducive to good planning. Meeting around tables makes it easier to look at materials and to take notes. Participants will be sitting for a long time, so arrange for comfortable chairs. As the event leader, arrive early to finalize room arrangements and make sure that everything is in order.

Gather Resources

An annual planning event can be enhanced by having these resources on hand:

• *Planning Guide.* This book, annual Launch Event resources produced by LifeWay Church Resources, and other printed resources that treat Sunday School as strategy can provide direction for doing annual planning. The best practices described in this book are essential if they are to guide the implementation of the strategy.

• *Records.* Reviewing what your Bible study groups have accomplished during the past year specifically and the past several years generally is a valuable part of planning. Provide a summary of the enrollment and attendance records for each class and department in your Sunday School ministry. Gather other information that helps leaders answer these questions.

- What was the total Bible study enrollment at the beginning of the year? The end of the year?
- How many people were enrolled during the year? How many were dropped?
- What was the annual net gain or loss?
- What was the total average attendance for the previous year? What is the total average attendance for this year?
- What were the number of contacts reported for each class and department for the year?
- How many visitors were reported for each class and department?

to make your sunday school work

• Do you know of any deficiencies in record keeping by any classes and departments that may have affected the accuracy of the statistics?

Additionally, prepare a breakdown of the total enrollment, new people enrolled, people dropped from enrollment, and average attendance for the past 5 to 10 years. A visual presentation of this information as a graph or chart can help leaders see any trends that have developed.

Also, bring training records to the annual planning event. For example, a review of the church's Christian Growth Study Plan summary can provide helpful information in planning for training.

• *Calendars.* Obtain copies of the church calendar (dates committed to this point), associational calendar, state convention calendar, Southern Baptist Convention calendar, schedules for leadership development events at LifeWay Glorieta® Conference Center and LifeWay Ridgecrest® Conference Center. Pull dates from the calendars that may relate to your plans, and compile them on a sheet for distribution during the planning sessions.

• *Budget information.* During annual planning, you will begin formulating the budget needed to implement Sunday School strategy. Budget and expenditure information for the previous and current years will be helpful in budget development. Of course, the new budget needs to reflect the plans that are being made for the year, not be only an adjustment of what was allocated last year. Further help with budget development is offered later in this chapter.

• *Goals.* Review goals that were set for the current year. This evaluation can be helpful as you anticipate goals for the new church year.

• *Organizational information.* A major subject of discussion during annual planning will be the structure of the Bible teaching organization for the coming year. Use the list of current classes and departments along with the enrollment and average attendance figures and prospect information for each to help leaders determine which new departments or classes may be needed.

• *Prospect information.* The number of prospects and their status will be useful in projecting goals and in making plans related to evangelism, enrollment, leader enlistment, new units, budget preparation, and other such activities.

ten best practices

- *Evaluation instruments.* Use such items as the Sunday School Strategy check-ups (Appendix A) and the Sunday School Growth and Evaluation Plan (Appendix B) to evaluate the past year.

A 6-Step Process for Doing Annual Planning

Step 1.— Make Spiritual Preparation

Annual planning can be an administrative chore or a spiritual experience in knowing and doing the will of God. Most of us would prefer the latter. Here are some suggestions for making this a spiritual experience.

Read the Bible and pray for God's direction.

Consider what the Bible says related to God's mission for His church, spiritual vision, and planning. Read and talk about such passages as Proverbs 16:3,9; Psalm 20:4; Jeremiah 29:11; Ephesians 3:8-11; and Hebrews 11:1. Acknowledge that planning is a faith process. It is seeking to know where God is at work and how your church can use Sunday School as the strategy for joining Him in kingdom work and fulfilling the Great Commission.

To do that, seek God in prayer. Specifically ask God to reveal Himself to the planning team and to give them insight and guidance as they plan. Let prayer be a major part of annual planning, not just a way of opening and closing the meeting sessions.

Review the Great Commission.

The Great Commission, Matthew 28:18-20, forms a blueprint for the mission and ministry of the church. Discuss what it has to say to your church about its work and mission. Discuss how Sunday School as strategy relates to the Great Commission.

Ask God for a vision for your church.

Do not put limitations, barriers, or boundaries on the vision. Spend time as a planning team sharing the vision and asking God to reveal His direction for your church and how Sunday School ministry as your church's foundational strategy can contribute to bringing that vision to reality.

to make your sunday school work

Step 2.— Evaluate Present Work

Evaluation answers the question *"Where are we now?"* Work to keep the evaluation positive, but honest. Evaluation will reveal strengths and weaknesses. The discovery of strengths and weaknesses will help to clarify the direction the church needs to take in the new year.

Examine records for the past year. Review the records of enrollment, new members, losses, new units, baptisms, other changes in church membership, and leadership training. Compare that data to the same information for several previous years to identify any patterns or trends.

Evaluate the work of your church in light of the Great Commission and the purpose of Sunday School. Sunday School is the foundational strategy for doing foundational evangelism and foundational discipleship.

Evaluate the effectiveness of your Sunday School strategy in relationship to the functions of the church. For help in leading a discussion on the relationship of Sunday School ministry to church functions, see Appendix A, "Sunday School and Church Functions."

Evaluate the effectiveness of your Sunday School strategy in light of the best practices for making Sunday School as strategy work. The remaining chapters of this book will help at this point.

Step 3.—Identify Needs on Which to Focus Next Year

Build on the spiritual preparation made in Step 1 and the data gathered in Step 2. Identify the priority needs of implementing Sunday School as strategy in relationship to

- making a commitment to Sunday School as the local church strategy
- organizing to accomplish your purpose
- building kingdom leaders
- developing soul-winners
- winning the lost
- assimilating people
- partnering with families
- teaching to transform
- mobilizing for ministry
- multiplying leaders and units

List the need identified in each area. Be as specific as possible.

ten best practices

Step 4.—Determine Priorities

A thorough evaluation ordinarily will reveal more needs than can be addressed during a year. This may be true in your case. Do not be overwhelmed.

For that reason, the next step is prayerfully and carefully to review the list of discovered needs to determine priorities. Identify the needs that are most important, and specify what must be accomplished first. If possible, retain at least one priority for each best practice. Obviously, that means you will end up with at least 10 priority needs. Again, you may feel overwhelmed. Perhaps you will need to continue to fine tune this fourth step until you have something manageable for your situation. That is a judgment you and your leaders will need to make as they discern the will of God.

Finally, put the priorities in writing. Some examples are identified in the "Objective" statements in the sample Sunday School Strategy Plan Sheets on pages 36-37.

Step 5.—Set Goals That Will Fulfill the Priorities

Now that you have determined priorities to be addressed by your strategy for the coming year, you are ready to set goals. Goals should state the specific outcomes you want to accomplish by the end of the year (or during the year if a goal should and can be accomplished sooner). This step answers the question *"Where do we want to be when this next year is over?"*

In some cases, the goals will be numerical. Set specific numerical goals in enrollment, average attendance, baptisms, leader enlistment and training, organizational units, participants in evangelism, ministry, and so forth.

Not all goals will be numerical. For example, a goal based on a priority need related to leader enlistment might be: "To equip all leaders to enlist their co-leaders personally." Actions to accomplish this goal might include conducting a leader enlistment emphasis, providing leader enlistment training during Sunday School leadership meetings, and working with key leaders one-on-one.

Another priority need might be to lead individuals and families to establish a daily encounter with God through Bible reading and prayer. The goal might be: "To enlist 75 percent of all Sunday School leaders and members to commit to reading the Bible through by December 31, 20—."

This goal is measurable and specific. Actions can then be planned to accomplish it.

Goal statements are not intended to be action statements. Goal statements take priorities from the level of need to a desired outcome, which in turn takes you a step closer to mission accomplishment. How that outcome is achieved is the next step.

Step 6.—Plan Actions to Achieve Goals

The planning process is incomplete and will be ineffective unless it results in determining specific actions to be taken to achieve the goals. An action plan should be built for each goal. Following are some models for developing this phase of the annual plan. The plan should identify the actions, the persons responsible, and the dates by which the actions are to be completed. Action plans may include multi-detailed projects and emphases, but they may also be a specific, single action; for example, "Order appropriate-size chairs for the older preschool department."

Of course, planning does not end with simply developing action plans. The person responsible for the action must understand his or her responsibility for completing the action. The actions need to be monitored throughout the year. The Sunday School Planning Team in its monthly meeting assumes responsibility for monitoring action plans and making modifications as needed.

Give annual planning your best effort. Recognize that planning is a spiritual task, and commit each phase to God for His guidance, empowering, and wisdom.

Example of Strategic Plans

The Strategy Plan Sheets that follow are provided as examples only. They are not intended to be comprehensive. Use a separate sheet of paper to develop your own action plan for implementing each best practice.

Once the planning team has come to agreement on specific objectives and goals, consider asking your age-group leaders to follow a similar process. It is at this point that all leaders can buy into plans for the new year. As a planning team, leaders can resolve areas of overlap or repetition.

ten best practices

Remember:

- *objectives* are broad statements that declare the long-term intent of Sunday School ministry as strategy as it relates to the best practices—the priority needs identified in Step 3 of annual planning;
- *goals* are focused, short-term statements that can be used to track progress toward an objective;
- *actions* are specific, intentional steps toward accomplishing a goal.

Sunday School Strategy Plan Sheet: Develop Soul Winners

Objective

To provide, promote, and encourage members to be engaged in evangelism both as a matter of daily living and as part of an intentional church ministry process.

Goal

By August 31, 20—, have a minimum of _____ people participating in weekly evangelistic visitation using FAITH Sunday School Evangelism Strategy®* as our evangelism training and visitation process.

Actions

Discuss with the pastor the potential of the FAITH Sunday School Evangelism Strategy.
- Person Responsible
- Date to Be Completed

Enlist a minimum of one representative from each adult department to attend a FAITH Training Clinic with the pastor.
- Person Responsible
- Date to Be Completed

Work with appropriate leaders to choose a date and time for implementing FAITH that allows for the involvement of the largest number of people.
- Person Responsible
- Date to Be Completed

Enlist new leaders with the expectation they will participate in FAITH.
- Person Responsible
- Date to Be Completed

*FAITH Sunday School Evangelism Strategy® is a registered trademark of LifeWay Christian Resources of the Southern Baptist Convention.

ten best practices

Sunday School Strategy Plan Sheet: Mobilize for Ministry

Objective

To assist members in identifying and using their abilities in ministry to others.

Goal

Begin a "Helping Hand" ministry by May 1, 20--, that uses class/department ministry teams to help people who need assistance with household repairs but are not financially or physically able to care for those needs on their own.

Actions

Lead each youth or adult class or department to enlist a ministry leader if they do not have one.
- Person Responsible
- Date to Be Completed

Secure or develop and administer an abilities inventory in all youth and adult classes or departments.
- Person Responsible
- Date to Be Completed

Using the inventory results, work with ministry leaders to develop ministry teams in youth and adult classes or departments.
- Person Responsible
- Date to Be Completed

Develop and implement a process for discovering ministry needs and assigning teams to address them.
- Person Responsible
- Date to Be Completed

Monthly Sunday School Planning Team Meetings

All the planning required for effective, ongoing Sunday School ministry and its implementation as foundational strategy cannot take place at an annual planning event. Plans change. New situations arise that need to be addressed.

To stay apprised of new situations and to manage implementation of the plan, a monthly Sunday School Planning Team meeting needs to be set in place. This team usually will be made up of the same people as the annual planning team.

By meeting regularly, the Sunday School Planning Team positions itself to be proactive—addressing matters related to implementing the annual plan and purposefully looking ahead for other actions that can move the plan toward fulfillment—rather than reactive—addressing issues in the midst of crisis. Even so, the best annual plan needs to be flexible enough to accommodate unanticipated needs, issues, and problems.

Select an Appropriate Meeting Time

A regular Sunday School Planning Team meeting following the last Sunday of the month is ideal because statistical data for the month usually is available. The members of the team need to select a time most convenient for them. Usually about one hour is enough time to do the work.

Use an Agenda

A valuable tool for an effective monthly planning meeting is a meeting agenda. Some benefits of preparing and distributing an agenda in advance of the meeting are to

- remind participants of the time and place of the meeting;
- identify the focus of the meeting;
- provide a summary of the work to be completed;
- clarify who is responsible for various elements of the meeting.

Plan the Elements of the Agenda

A model plan sheet to help you develop an agenda is on page 40. A version of the plan sheet with monthly update information is provided in each issue of *The Sunday School Leader.* The plan sheet is built around these elements of the meeting:

* *Inspiration.*—Set the meeting within a spiritual context and relate the work to the commission of Christ and the mission of the church.
* *Information.*—Provide pertinent information that can help leaders improve the effectiveness of Sunday School.
* *Evaluation.*—Discuss the effectiveness of events that have been completed and consider ways they could have been improved.
* *Communication.*—Report on current activities or on upcoming events.
* *Preparation.*—Initiate efforts related to future or new projects.

Follow Up the Meeting

Send members a summary of the meeting. Absentees will know what occurred during the meeting, and those who attended will be reminded of assignments.

to make your
sunday school work

Suggested Monthly
Planning Team Meeting Agenda

Date of Meeting_____
Focus of Meeting_____

Preparing for the Meeting	**Person Responsible**

- Plan, prepare, and mail a copy of the agenda to all members one week before the meeting.

Sunday School director or minister of education

- Contact every member.

General secretary

Suggested Agenda

A Time for Inspiration
  Devotional
  Pray for:

_____

A Time for Information
  Review pertinent articles in
    other appropriate resources.

_____

A Time for Evaluation
  Discuss events and activities
    concluded.
  Consider how they could be
    improved and whether they
    should be repeated.

A Time for Communication
  Receive progress reports on
  - Evangelistic results
  - Church calendar
  - Age-group concerns
  - Leadership training
  - New units

_____

A Time for Preparation
  Schedule, plan, and assign
    responsibilities for future
    projects or emphases.

_____

After the Meeting

- Prepare a summary of the meeting; mail a copy to absentees.

General secretary

- Follow up on all assignments.

Sunday School director / minister of education

ten best practices

Key Element of Sunday School as Strategy

The vehicle for implementing Sunday School as strategy is the open Bible study group. These individual units are where the personal touch takes place. It is where people are mobilized for ministry.

In general, to be open means to be characterized by ready accessibility for a particular purpose; not shut or locked; having no enclosing or confining barrier. In the context of Sunday School ministry, open means both believers and unbelievers are invited to participate in a class, department, study group, or event that has an intentional evangelistic purpose.

That is key. An open group is an evangelistic Bible study group. Open does not simply mean that new people can join or enter the group at anytime, though they can do that. The key focus is that the group is open at anytime for unbelievers to join. An open group is a Bible study group centered on the study of God's Word with an intentional focus on teaching that guides people toward conversion and assimilates them into the local church.

The open Bible study group is intentionally formed around the study and living of God's Word. The primary question in these groups is, "What is God saying to us through the Bible text?" While there may be other books, tapes, and people, that serve as resources to the study, those resources are not the focus of the event. The Bible is the focus. This is the significant difference from groups that gather for support, fellowship, leadership training, skill development, and so forth. Such groups may study the Bible peripherally or as a part of the agenda, but Bible study is not the primary agenda.

While Bible study groups may be categorized in a variety of ways, nothing shapes the core nature of a Bible study group more than its primary target audience. From the church's perspective, there are two basic target audiences: lost people and saved people. Open Bible study groups that are designed primarily for reaching lost people are Sunday School groups. Bible study groups that are designed primarily for moving saved people toward spiritual maturity and transformation are Discipleship groups, or "closed groups."

Many churches claiming that Sunday School ministry has lost its effectiveness have been functioning with closed groups. An intentional open-group ministry design needs to be set in place to receive new believers and

encourage further evangelism. An open group may be an ongoing Bible study group, a short-term Bible study group, or a Bible study event.

Ongoing Open Bible Study Groups

Ongoing open Bible study groups have no specified end date. They focus on reaching the unsaved, building relationships, and promoting spiritual growth and have as an ongoing goal to multiply themselves by developing leaders and starting new Bible study groups. Ongoing Bible study groups are traditionally called Sunday School classes or departments. The terminology is not so important as the understanding that the group is defined by its purpose, nature, and function rather than by when and where it meets, the materials it uses, or any organizational labels.

Ongoing open Bible study groups offer a church a number of advantages.

- An ongoing open Bible study group ministry emphasizes the church's long-term obligation and commitment to spiritual transformation and biblical instruction.
- The initial focus of an ongoing open Bible study group tends to be on its purpose, members, and relationships rather than the topic of study or affinity need of the group.
- Ongoing open Bible study groups provide a long-term environment for building lasting friendships.
- The long-term curriculum study plans used with ongoing open Bible study groups tend to provide greater balance, stronger sequence, and more comprehensive scope.
- Ongoing open Bible study groups typically meet before or after the time for corporate worship, which is convenient for participants and reinforces the essential relationship between worship, evangelism, and discipleship.
- Ongoing open Bible study groups usually are easier for the church leadership to maintain. This is true for several reasons:
    - The groups tend to have a fixed location (usually in a public building), time, and facilities.
    - Leader enlistment for the groups typically is annual.
    - A fully age-graded ministry provides a stronger family ministry by offering substantive, age-appropriate Bible study for all family members.

- Materials are typically dated and ordered rather automatically.
- Most ongoing open Bible study group ministries are fully age-graded programs, solving a number of child-care issues.
- Record keeping is easier in a centralized location.

Furthermore, ongoing open Bible study groups that reproduce new groups provide the best long-term approach for building a ministry environment that

- guides preschoolers and children toward conversion through foundational teaching;
- encourages unsaved people to come to faith in Christ;
- assimilates new believers into the life of the church;
- encourages believers to lead others to Christ.

Sunday morning Bible study continues to be the way most Southern Baptist churches provide ongoing open Bible study groups. The historical hallmark of Southern Baptist Sunday School is evangelistic Bible teaching through ongoing Bible study classes that are always open for anyone to participate. Ideally, the leaders and members are dedicated to seeking, discovering, and inviting spiritually lost people to participate in open Bible study groups. A great threat to Sunday School's effectiveness has been the tendency to become closed groups, focused on the needs and interests of existing members to the exclusion of those who do not know Christ.

Short-term Open Bible Study Groups

Short-term open Bible study groups are started with a specified end date. They are defined by their purpose, nature, and function rather than by their resources, label, time frame, or location. Like ongoing open groups, short-term open groups focus on reaching the unsaved, building relationships, and promoting spiritual growth. They have an additional objective of transitioning participants into an ongoing Bible study group.

Short-term open Bible study groups offer several advantages:

- Short-term open Bible study groups usually meet in homes where a more informal and intimate environment can be created.
- Short-term open groups tend to appeal to unreached people who are reluctant to attend a group "at the church."
- The study content in a short-term open group can be selected to appeal to individuals with specific life needs.

- Short-term open Bible study groups are not limited by public building space.
- Leader enlistment and member participation may be facilitated by the shorter commitment of time.
- Short-term open Bible study groups tend to focus more intentionally and naturally on building relationships.

Several target groups may be identified for short-term open Bible study groups, including

- reached or unreached adults, youth, or children who may not respond to a Sunday morning approach to ongoing open Bible study or who may prefer or need Bible study in a weekday setting;
- unreached persons in apartment complexes, mobile home parks, retirement villages, low-income housing, community centers, businesses, homes, and so forth;
- persons in institutions in the community such as nursing homes and penal facilities;
- youth involved in equal access Bible clubs in schools.

Relationship Between Ongoing and Short-term Open Bible Study Groups

Ongoing and short-term open Bible study groups relate to each other as part of the larger strategy. An ongoing open Bible study group has the goal of starting new ongoing open Bible study groups and developing leaders for those groups. A short-term open Bible study group has the goal of transitioning participants into an ongoing open Bible study group. In this context, the two kinds of groups complement each other and build on each other's strengths.

As a church establishes its goals and defines its purpose, it may choose to use a combination of both ongoing open Bible study groups and short-term open Bible study groups. Ongoing open Bible study groups are best for helping a church achieve its long-range goals. Short-term open Bible study groups are provide the church with flexibility and facilitate access to the church's ongoing open Bible study group ministry.

Other Bible Study Events

Other Bible study events include all-age January Bible Study; all-age Vacation Bible School; and Bible Clubs for preschoolers and children. The Bible study events usually are similar to other short-term groups in that they occur during a set time span, such as a five-day Vacation Bible School.

Some events may be targeted to the spiritually lost as part of the strategic plan to lead people to faith in the Lord Jesus Christ; hence, they are open group Bible study events. Vacation Bible School fits the model of an open group Bible study event because it is intentionally designed as evangelistic Bible study. VBS has been the flagship outreach-evangelism event of the year for many churches in their efforts to reach families for Christ.

Other Bible study events may be targeted toward members as part of the strategic plan to build on-mission Christians. January Bible Study is an example of this kind of Bible study in that it focuses attention on leading members into a deeper study of Scripture during a concentrated time period.

The general actions for planning outlined below will apply to almost every Bible study event. Some events, however, may have additional actions that are unique to the scope and focus of that event. While Bible study events may be handled as independent projects, the greater effectiveness of Sunday School as strategy will be realized when these events are seen as part of the comprehensive plan of the church for doing foundational evangelism and foundational discipleship.

Identify intended participants in the Bible study project.
Consider all evangelistic and discipling possibilities, including those people who are prospects for ongoing open Bible study groups, specific age-group target groups (single adults, senior adults, and so forth), and community target groups (apartment dwellers, mobile home park residents, ethnic groups, business communities, and so forth).

Determine how participants will be grouped.
Depending on the event, participants may be grouped according to age, geography, language, or special needs or interests. Choose the approach that helps you to accomplish your objectives and goals for the event. That grouping may not be the easiest approach; nevertheless, it may be the best.

to make your sunday school work
0123456789101234567

Determine the approach and schedule.
If the event is a Bible teaching event, it may occur on consecutive days in one week or one day per week in consecutive weeks. If the event is a Bible preaching/worship event, then it also may occur on consecutive days in one week or one day per week in consecutive weeks. A retreat event may be one or two days, either at the church or in an off-campus retreat setting. Flexibility is key here. Events involving the different age groups may be conducted using same/different approaches at the same/different times.

Select dates and times
Review the church and community calendars to select dates and times that best meet the needs of intended participants and provide for the best use of church resources, including leadership.

Budget for the event.
Include the event when preparing the comprehensive Sunday School ministry budget. Budget for the following items: (1) planning and promoting the event; (2) leader and study material; (3) compensation for guest leaders, if needed; (4) refreshments, if desired; (5) additional expenses incurred with optional approaches, such as facilities away from the church.

Determine who will lead the study.
Of course, the kind of event, the purpose, and the budget allocation will influence the kind of leaders needed for the event. Basically, the possibilities include (1) the pastor and other church staff ministers; (2) faculty from within the church for any or all age groups; (3) guest leaders for any or all age groups.

Obtain materials.
Get leader and learner resources, teaching aids, and supplies critical to doing the event.

Enlist and train leaders.
Leaders for the event may be enlisted from the pool of leaders in on-going open Bible study groups and from other ministries of the church. Some churches may partner with other churches to share leadership. For example, two churches may schedule January Bible Study at different times and use a

combined faculty from both churches to lead each event. In some cases, a guest preacher, Christian educator, or other competent Bible study leader may be invited to guide the study.

The leaders need to be given specific instructions about expectations and be trained to lead the event. Sometimes, such as with Vacation Bible School, a preparatory training event may be sponsored by the local Baptist association, the state convention, or LifeWay Christian Resources. Follow those training events with local training specific to the setting and situation in which your leaders will be involved.

Promote the emphasis.
People will not come to an event if they do not know about it. Funds should have been set aside to promote the event. Begin the promotion early enough for the target audience to make plans to participate.

Assign space appropriate to each group.
For on-campus events, the space ordinarily used by the age group is the best space to be used for special events. The furnishings, equipment, and supplies already may be available in the area. For off-campus approaches, secure and assign space as appropriate for the age groups and the nature of the event. In some cases, it may be an apartment complex community room. Or, for a Bible Club, it may be beneath a shade tree in a city park.

Complete final details.
Do not assume everybody knows the details or that everything is in place for the event. Be certain. Some final details may include conducting faculty meeting(s), setting up rooms, arranging for breaks or fellowship meals, getting attendance records for study recognition credit, or arranging lodging and transportation for guest faculty.

Conduct the study.
After all the preparation has been made, it is time to enjoy the event. As a leader, you will want to make notes about what could be done differently to make the event stronger next time.

to make your
sunday school work

Conduct follow-up actions.

Within one week, transfer to the prospect files the names of nonmembers who participated. Assign prospects to ongoing Bible study groups—classes or department—for contact. Immediately make contact with them to invite them to attend and enroll in an on-going open Bible study class or department.

In addition, consider the need for other follow-up Bible study events targeted at prospects. For example, a short-term open Bible study group may need to be established off-campus during the week as a way to continue efforts to reach the spiritually lost.

Providing Financial Support

Budget planning is another expression of commitment to the strategy. Budget planning takes on a new perspective when it is related to the annual plan. It becomes more than an independent document of columns of dollars and cents; it represents the financial commitments for carrying out the purposeful actions developed in the annual plan.

Several years ago, one nationally known church consultant identified several functions of a budget beyond being a summary of finances. Here are a few that he mentioned that are appropriate for our purposes.[1]

A Theological Document. The budget identifies what is important to the group for whom the budget was prepared. By examining the amount of dollars allocated to the various elements in the budget, a priority ranking of those elements becomes clear. What does your budget say about your theology?

A Statement of Purpose. A review of the budget and a study of the priorities reflected in dollar allocations reveals the perceived purposes of the group. In truth, a budget ought to be a translation of purpose into financial terms. What does your budget say about your purpose or mission?

A Diagram of Expectations. A budget points to the future. It is a statement of what a group wants and intends to do. It represents a dream and a commitment to accomplishing the group's purpose and living out its theology. What does your budget reveal about expectations?

A Basis for Evaluation. The evaluation does not focus just on receipts and expenditures. The budget can help a group evaluate whether it is doing

ten best practices

what it wanted to do. For example, if dollars were allocated for leader development but at the end of the year no dollars were spent in that area, that may indicate a serious variance between expectation and performance. What can you learn by using your budget as a tool for evaluating your effectiveness in accomplishing last year's plan?

Sunday School is not an entity within itself; it is a strategy of a church. The work you do in budget planning is to be done in conjunction with the policies and procedures used in the church. Budget planning is more than just plugging in dollar amounts. The dollars are to represent the plans that have been developed—plans that maximize the potential of Sunday School to be the foundational strategy in your church for achieving the Great Commission.

Following is a budget planning worksheet that covers several areas of Sunday School ministry. Use the worksheet as a sample, but make adjustments in the headings to reflect more accurately your annual plan.

Budget Planning Worksheet

Literature

Formula for determining cost:

_____ ÷ _____ + _____ = _____

Cost last order / Current enrollment + Anticipated inflation = Cost per person

Enrollment Goal:

_____ x	_____ =	_____
First Quarter	Cost per person	Total cost per quarter
_____ x	_____ =	_____
Second Quarter	Cost per person	Total cost per quarter
_____ x	_____ =	_____
Third Quarter	Cost per person	Total cost per quarter
_____ x	_____ =	_____
Fourth Quarter	Cost per person	Total cost per quarter
		_____
		Cost for year

Funds needed for additional teaching aids_____

Total Literature budget requested $ _____

Supplies *(examples: record forms, paper, art materials, refreshments)*
Consider needs for preschool, children, youth, young adult, adult, special education, and other departments.

Total Supplies budget requested $_____

Furnishings and Equipment *(examples: chalkboards, picture rails, cabinets)*
Consider needs for preschool, children, youth, young adult, adult, special education, and other departments.

Total Equipment budget requested $ _____

Media Resources *(examples: videos, books, maps)*
Consider needs for preschool, children, youth, young adult, adult, special education, and other departments.

Total Media budget requested $ _____

January Bible Study

Resources _____

Refreshments_____

Guest teachers (expenses and gifts) _____

Other JBS expense _____

Total January Bible Study budget requested $ _____

Vacation Bible School

   Curriculum_____

   Supplies _____

   Refreshments _____

   Backyard Bible Clubs/Mission Vacation Bible School _____

   Other VBS expense _____

   Total Vacation Bible School budget requested $_____

Annual Planning

   Lodging, meals _____

   Transportation _____

   Materials _____

   Total Annual Planning budget requested $_____

Launch Event

   Resources_____

   Refreshments/Banquet_____

   Total Launch Event budget requested $_____

Leadership Training

   Resources_____

   Promotion _____

   Guest teachers (expense and gifts) _____

   Registration/Conference fees_____

   Transportation _____

   Lodging, meals _____

   Total Leadership Training budget requested $_____

Outreach-Evangelism Planning

   Outreach-evangelism events and supplies_____

   Promotional materials, postage _____

   Outreach meals, fellowship refreshments _____

   Total Outreach-Evangelism Planning budget requested $_____

Other Needs

   Worker appreciation banquet_____

   Other _____

   Total Other Needs budget requested $_____

GRAND TOTAL BUDGET REQUEST $_____

**to make your
sunday school work**

0123456789101234567

Launching the Plan

Earlier in this chapter, we went through a process for developing annual details for implementing Sunday School as strategy. If you followed those suggestions, you will have set goals and determined actions to accomplish the goals and meet the needs that precipitated the goals.

But consider, what if action ceased? What a waste of time and effort that would have been. So, it is time to launch the plan. That may be done effectively by having a Launch Event in your church.

A Launch Event includes several events designed to prepare individual Sunday School leaders and to mobilize all members for the challenges and opportunities of the new year. Launch becomes a time to celebrate accomplishments, communicate plans, train leaders, commission leaders for service, challenge the church about the potential of Sunday School strategy, and create a sense of excitement and purpose for what lies ahead. In other words, it is the time to go into action.

Some elements of a Launch Event are described below. Use your own creativity in planning and promoting the event. Launch Event resources produced by LifeWay Church Resources also will be useful in planning.

A Sunday School Rally

The rally is for all Sunday School leaders. It may be a Friday evening kickoff event for the weekend. The rally may be held in conjunction with a banquet hosted by the church. Once again, be creative in presenting the information. Make the event one every Sunday School leader will be talking about in anticipation of next year.

Here are a few elements that could be part of the rally:
- Welcome
- Introduction of new leaders; other recognitions
- Dinner
- Celebration of accomplishments
- Presentation of annual theme
- Overview of goals and actions plans
- Music
- Inspirational message
- Closure

ten best practices

Leadership Training Event

Continue the weekend by conducting a leadership training event. This training may be done on Saturday. Promote it as a training spectacular that will equip all Sunday School leaders to function more effectively.

Consider providing a continental breakfast to begin the morning. As part of your planning for the day, determine whether child care needs to be provided as a convenience to participants.

The training may include a general session with all leaders together. During this time, the pastor, Sunday School director, or minister of education may do an overview of the annual plan (unless that was done at the banquet rally the previous evening), review the structure, discuss other training events, preview the annual calendar, and so forth. This general session need not be long, probably less than one hour.

The majority of the time needs to be spent in age-group leadership training. The training should address specific needs that will improve the effectiveness of your Sunday School leaders in doing the work of the Great Commission. Again, annual Launch Event resources produced by LifeWay Church Resources will offer suggestions.

Sunday Morning Worship and a Sunday School Leader Commissioning Service

The excitement and purpose of the weekend continues with Sunday morning worship. If you are the Sunday School director or minister of education, talk with the pastor about planning the worship service. This service is not to be a promotional event but a focus on the work of the church and the calling of God's people to share the good news. Sunday School is highlighted as the foundational strategy for leading people to faith in the Lord Jesus Christ and for building on-mission Christians through Bible study groups.

Commissioning Sunday School leaders as part of the worship service will accomplish several things. First, it will indicate to the leaders the importance of the commitment they are making. Second, it emphasizes to the congregation the value the church places on the ministries conducted through Sunday School and on the people who lead them. Third, it will be a meaningful time of rededication for the entire congregation as everyone is challenged to be part of the effort to do the work of the Great Commission.

The worship service may also include a brief testimony, music, and Scripture reading that support the emphasis of the day and the annual theme.

The pastor's message could place the emphasis in a biblical context. Here are some others suggestion for the service.

Scripture Reading Suggestions

> Deuteronomy 6:4-7
> Deuteronomy 31:12-13
> Matthew 28:16-20
> 2 Timothy 2:15

- Ask individuals of various ages to read the Scripture verses.
- Ask the pastor to use the verses to form the basis for a sermon.
- Combine verses, and read them responsively.

Music Suggestions

> "Take My Life, Lead Me, Lord" (*The Baptist Hymnal, 1991,* 287) or "Share His Love" (*The Baptist Hymnal, 1991,* 567)

- Sing as congregational hymns.
- Enlist the choir or a soloist to sing an arrangement as special music.
- Enlist someone to read the words as a poem.

Testimony Suggestions

- Enlist an experienced leader to give a testimony on what serving through Sunday School has meant to her.
- Enlist a new leader to talk about his sense of call to be a Sunday School leader.
- Enlist a member to describe how involvement in an open Bible study group has changed his life.

Bulletin Insert Suggestions

> Ask various Sunday School members to write brief remarks on the subject "What My Sunday School Teacher Has Meant to Me," "My Favorite Sunday School Teacher," or a similar topic.

Other Suggestions

- Provide all leaders a ribbon to wear that indicates they are leaders in Sunday School. Representatives of each age group should wear a different color.

ten best practices

123456789101234567

- Recognize all leaders during the service by asking them to stand either as a group or by the age group in which they will work.
- Ask all leaders to come to the front of the worship center for commissioning. Use the "Affirmation of Commitment" (see p.56.
- Follow the service with a luncheon for leaders.
- Distribute "My Personal Commitment" sheets (see p.57) during the luncheon. Encourage leaders to complete the sheets and place them in their Bibles.

End Notes
[1]Lyle E. Shaller, *Parish Planning* (Nashville: Abingdon Press, 1971), 38-46.

Affirmation of Commitment

Pastor: Let us all affirm that following the Lord Jesus Christ in obedient service is a joyous privilege and high calling for all who profess His name.

Congregation: We acknowledge that as God's children by faith in Jesus Christ, we are called to be witnesses for Him. We cannot rightfully give away that responsibility to our ministers, Sunday School leaders, or even one another. We are glad to accept the privilege and responsibility of standing for Christ in His power and by His grace.

Pastor: Yet, God does specifically call out some to particular roles of service and leadership. Sunday School leaders, you stand before us today because you have responded to His call and this congregation's confirmation to serve as a leader in our church's efforts to lead people to faith in the Lord Jesus Christ and build on-mission Christians. I challenge you to serve faithfully and by example to show us how to love God, love others, and reach out with the good news to people who are spiritually lost and seeking.

Sunday School Leaders: We affirm that we have answered the call of the Lord. We commit our lives to love and serve Him. We accept the responsibility of leading by example in Christ's power. We will be faithful in sharing the good news that is the power of God to change lives.

Pastor: Members of _____ Church, will you commit to pray for, encourage, and support these who lead us? Moreover, will you join with them in witnessing, ministry, and Bible teaching both in church and family settings?

Congregation: We will.

Pastor: I urge you to keep the commission of Christ foremost in your minds and the love of Christ foremost in your hearts. "May the God who gives endurance and encouragement give you a spirit of unity among yourselves as you follow Christ Jesus, so that with one heart and mouth you may glorify the God and Father of our Lord Jesus Christ" (Rom. 15:5-6).

My Personal Commitment

Because I feel called by God as a Sunday School leader, I am committed to:

The Lord God
- I affirm that I have a personal relationship with God through Jesus Christ that I desire to model before others.
- I will strive to grow in my faith and my devotion to Him through the study of the Bible, His holy Word, and through prayer, the most intimate channel of communication with Him.

The Church
- I will be faithful in gathering with my church family to worship God.
- I will support God's work in the total ministry of my church by giving my time, talents, and money as is expected of a faithful steward.

Those I Lead
- I enjoy (*insert age group*) and desire for them to know of God's love and purpose for their lives.
- I will take the necessary time to prepare to do my work well so that I may lead others to encounter God and continue in a daily life-changing relationship with Him.
- I will care for members and prospects and their families through prayer, witnessing, regular contact, and ministry that affirms the worth of those persons in Christ and helps to assimilate them into the body.

The Leadership Team
- I will participate in scheduled leadership meetings.
- I will communicate regularly with the other leaders on my team.
- I will be faithful in attendance and arrive as early as necessary to prepare for the session and to greet those who attend.
- If I must be absent, I will follow procedure to get a replacement and notify my department or division director.
  - I will participate in at least one leadership development event during the year to improve my leadership skills.

to make your sunday school work

Best Practice Check Up
Commit to the Strategy

__We are intentionally committed to Sunday School as the foundational strategy in our church for leading people to faith in the Lord Jesus Christ and building on-mission Christians.

__We have developed an annual plan that supports the church's thrust in foundational evangelism and foundational discipleship.

__We have established a monthly meeting of the Sunday School Planning Team to provide continuity to planning and to monitor the implementation of the annual plan.

__We have planned for ongoing open Bible study groups that focus on foundational evangelism.

__We have planned for short-term open Bible study groups that focus on foundational evangelism.

__We have planned for at least one Bible study event that focuses on foundational evangelism and at least one other Bible study event that focuses on foundational discipleship.

__We have planned a budget that provides the best possible support for implementing our strategic plans.

__We have prepared to implement our strategic plan through specific monthly and weekly actions.

__We have planned for a Launch Event to focus attention on our plans and to initiate our actions for the new year of ministry.

BEST PRACTICE 2
Organize with Purpose

"Then He (Jesus) directed them to have all the people sit down in groups on the green grass . . . He blessed and broke the loaves. And He kept giving them to His disciples to set before the people. . . . Everyone ate and was filled."

—Mark 5:39,41-42, HCSB

The word *organizing* is about as exciting to most of us as a rubdown with steel wool. It doesn't excite us the way that sharing vision or reaching the lost does. Even so, without organization, the work that we do enjoy—evangelism, assimilation, ministry, Bible teaching—may be weakened if it gets done at all. Simply stated, organization is our mechanism for doing the work and doing it well. Each piece of the organization is to fit together in such a way that enables the whole to operate smoothly and effectively to accomplish the purpose for which it exists. Purpose, then, is a key element. A well-tooled organization may be in place, but it may not be helping to accomplish what is needed. Therefore, purpose needs to influence why and how we develop our organization.

We will organize our Sunday School ministry to accomplish the objectives of leading people to faith in the Lord Jesus Christ and building on-mission Christians by —
  • using the concept of age-graded, open Bible study groups as the

to make your sunday school work

primary organizing principle for Bible study groups;
- *providing groups for all ages and generations, including preschool, children, youth, young adults, and adults;*
- *relying on sound learner-leader ratios proven to be effective for each age group in developing the age-group organizational structures.*

Organizing to Accomplish the Purpose

Sunday School seeks to lead people to faith in the Lord Jesus Christ and to build on-mission Christians through Bible study groups that engage individuals and families in evangelism, discipleship, ministry, fellowship, and worship. The organization that is set in place should be what is needed to fulfill the reason for existence. When the organizational structure ceases to support the strategy, then the structure should be changed. Organization provides the context for attaining the desired results and the most effective behavior out of the people who make up the organization.

Sunday School strategy is implemented by clustering people into groups, primarily on the basis of age. The importance of the organizational unit cannot be overemphasized. These individual units are where the personal touch takes places in Sunday School. They are where people are mobilized to do the work.

An effective Sunday School strategy is one in which a ministry environment exists that encourages unsaved people to come to faith in Christ; encourages believers to be intentional, active soul-winners; facilitates life-changing Bible study; builds fellowship among people; and engages people in pursuing the church's functions—all in an atmosphere of grace, acceptance, love, and support.

The number of participants and prospects for a Sunday School class, department, or other Bible study group; the number of trained and potential leaders identified for service; and available space are important factors that affect organization. Because all of those factors, as well as many others, interact with one another, organizational structures for Sunday School strategy may vary from church to church. Organization is purpose driven but not static. It must be flexible.

In the context of Sunday School strategy, organization helps leaders
- lead members in evangelistic, discipling, ministry, fellowship, and

---

7 Positive Effects of a Good Organizational Strategy

1. Enables a church to fulfill faithfully the Great Commission

2. Serves as a master plan and thus helps avoid costly missteps

3. Enables a church to manage its resources

4. Creates a team spirit

5. Provides for better communication

6. Helps explain the creation of new units

7. Enhances the total ministry of the church

worship actions in the context of open, small-group settings;

- delegate responsibilities to other leaders and potential leaders so that the greatest good can be accomplished;
- meet particular needs of members and prospects with effectiveness;
- effectively manage the time, energy, gifts, and resources available for conducting ministry;
- train and develop new leaders;
- address needs of individuals through Bible study experiences designed to facilitate spiritual transformation;
- communicate with one another in a spirit of understanding and harmony.

When the proper organization is in place, certain desired outcomes can be realized. Leaders will be better able to

- discover, understand, and meet age-group and generational needs;
- provide well-trained, God-called leaders to work in all areas where leaders are needed and provide for appropriate leader-learner ratios for each age group;
- provide a variety of opportunities for new persons to participate in the church's ministry;
- discover, understand, and meet specialized learner needs;
- discover, understand, and meet specific goals and objectives related to evangelism, discipleship, ministry, fellowship, and worship;
- create and implement an effective growth dynamic by starting new units.

Organizational progression describes how many units (classes or Bible study groups, departments, divisions) and leaders are needed to accommodate member enrollment, particularly as enrollment increases. Organizational progression is a dynamic principle a church may use to determine the organization and the progress or movement from one level of organization to the next. See the "Steps to Organizational Progression and Growth" chart on page 76.

Organization and Church Functions

We have established that organization is a means for getting the work done. Organization enables evangelism, discipleship, ministry, fellowship, and

to make your sunday school work

worship to be done well. It is a structure for positioning members in places of service that encourage their growth toward Christian maturity as they do the work of the church, which is ministry in the name of Jesus.

Organization Supports Evangelism

Organization supports evangelism by assigning every member and prospect to an age-appropriate group or class. The leaders and members of that group take actions to give an evangelistic witness to the unsaved and make concerted efforts to lead them to know Jesus Christ as Savior and Lord. The group provides an atmosphere that encourages unsaved people to faith in Christ and encourages believers to lead others to Christ. Leadership structure for the group includes individuals with specific assignments related to evangelism.

Organization Supports Discipleship

Organization supports discipleship (teaching persons that they might grow in maturity in Christ) by providing a context for Bible study that considers the characteristics, needs, and learning styles of the learners assigned to the group. The discipling that takes place through the teaching can be more focused and personal because the teacher, other leaders, and members are able to build quality relationships that nurture one another. The Bible study becomes the focal point for encouraging evangelism, discipleship, ministry, fellowship, and worship. Leadership structure for the group includes individuals with specific assignments related to monitoring the discipleship needs of believers and working with the church's Discipleship ministry to provide opportunities focused to address those needs.

Organization Supports Ministry

Organization supports ministry by placing leaders, members, and prospects in settings to experience direct care and concern for life's needs. People who are members of a small group, such as a Sunday School class, can communicate more openly and clearly to one another about needs and concerns.

Intercessory prayer is a particularly important aspect of effective ministry that is supported by organization. Organization provides also for leaders, members, and prospects to express their concern for others through identifying and implementing ministry and mission projects that utilize the gifts and abilities of the group. Leadership structure for the group includes individuals with specific assignments related to ministry, including responsibilities in missions support and intercessory prayer.

Organization Supports Fellowship

Organization supports fellowship by placing people in groups where they can build relationships with others as together they build upon their relationship with God. Newcomers are easily assimilated into the larger fellowship of the church as they experience the fellowship of the smaller group.

As important and valuable as fellowship is, it is not to become the controlling factor in determining Sunday School groups. Bible study groups that overemphasize fellowship tend to grow stagnant, or crystallize, because members become content and comfortable with one another. The leadership structure for the group usually includes individuals with specific assignments related to building fellowship.

Organization Supports Worship

Organization supports worship by teaching about worship, providing small-group worship experiences that allow for greater participation by members of the group, and encouraging personal worship in home and family settings. The leadership structure for the group includes individuals with specific assignments related to worship.

Building a Case for Age Grading in Sunday School

Few things in Baptist church life in general and Sunday School ministry in particular create as much human anxiety as the concept of organizing according to age. Here is a case in its favor.

Is Age Grading an Adult Thing, Too?

Grading the Preschool through Youth Divisions of a church's Bible study ministry has become fairly standardized, using the secular educational

to make your sunday school work
0123456789101234567

system as a model with some adaptations according to church size. But how about adults—real adults who are independent, married, working, raising families, and so forth. Is age-grading for them, too? Do they need someone to tell them what class to attend?

Many pastors, educators, and lay leaders grimace when you mention grading adults. Even so, some system must be in place for organizing adults or the Bible study ministry will stagnate and become ineffective for either evangelism or assimilation. Using age as the organizing principles has proven to be best—even for adults.

Age Grading Meets the Criteria for an Organizing Principle

The purpose of Sunday School or Bible study ministry ultimately should influence the basis of grading. Thus, your Sunday School should be graded in a manner that best enables you to fulfill your mission statement. In addition, the Bible study ministry needs an organizing principle that is:

- simple enough for members and visitors to understand;
- comprehensive enough to include everyone who presently attends or should be reached by the church;
- flexible enough to grow with the church;
- clear enough to make the reason for creating new units obvious;
- natural enough to allow for the movement of members to counteract introversion and stagnancy;
- practical enough to maximize growth principles.

Age grading passes the test at each point.

Age Grading Is Effective

Grading by age is a natural method that over the years has become the standard practice of Sunday School ministry. Here are some reasons age grading continues to be effective.

- easy to explain to the first-time attender;
- takes advantage of the church growth principles of homogeneity and receptivity;
- counters stagnation by encouraging class members to develop new relationships;
- accepted as a natural system already built into our thinking from preschool through senior adults;

- recognizes that pupils the same age generally have similar spiritual needs;
- easy to organize outreach and call for accountability;
- easy to recognize when the Sunday School is graded;
- makes the Sunday School easier to reorganize.

Age Grading Faces Challenges

Age grading your Sunday School will not necessarily be easy. Everything worthwhile involves both challenges and risks. If you are in a church that has never been age graded or has not recently been age graded, you will hear some objections.

Our officers and teachers don't understand why we need to age grade.
Because a team spirit is important, it is essential that those involved in the task understand both the what and the why. This is where transparency, patience, and communication skills pay great dividends. Explain the value of age grading, and keep the purpose of Sunday School at the forefront.

Our teachers are against age grading because they want to keep their present pupils.
This challenge is couched in the language of "fellowship," but it is more often a reflection of a desire to maintain a comfort zone. Sunday School ministry needs to provide opportunities for fellowship, but age grading will not hurt fellowship. Any organizational plan that enables you to reach more people will require you to move students and create new units.

Our pastor or Sunday School director is afraid of the reaction from members and would rather leave well enough alone.
A great Bible study ministry is rarely found at the end of the road of least resistance.

Annual promotion of adults is just too hard to accomplish.
On a particularly hard day you may find yourself thinking this. Even so, never be deterred from doing the right thing simply because it is difficult.

01234567891011234567
to make your
sunday school work

Finding some way to create new units and to move adults into natural groupings is the right thing to do. Age grading with annual promotion is the best way to achieve that. Make it a big event by promoting the creation of new departments, visiting chronic absentees, and celebrating the beginning of the new Sunday School year.

We don't have enough leaders, or we don't have enough rooms.
If you take seriously either of these excuses, your Bible study ministry will lose its effectiveness no matter how you organize it. If you do not have enough leaders, you must first improve your prayer strategy (Matt. 9:37), then institute a leader training ministry. Provide additional space either off campus or on campus during the "normal" Bible study hour or at another time.

People will leave the church if we force them to advance to another class.
If you are offering quality Bible study and good fellowship, they won't go anywhere. If someone leaves over the commitment of the church to do whatever is necessary to fulfill the Great Commission, you may be better off without them.

Some of our couples have widely varying ages.
The age-grading system must be used with sensitivity to the unique needs of the people involved. To address the age difference issue, many churches allow couples to attend the class that most closely corresponds to the age of the wife.

A Word About Grouping by Study Topic

Of other options that have been used for grouping people, especially adults, perhaps the most popular has been by topical interests or needs. In other words, a person goes to a group that is studying a topic in which he is interested or that addresses a particular need she has in life. This approach has weaknesses that surface for the church that is being driven by the Great Commission mandate, which focuses on leading people to faith in the Lord Jesus Christ. Here are some weaknesses of interest-based groups.

• They tend to become focused on the personality of the teacher as adults gravitate toward the topic group being lead by their favorite teacher;

- The need to change topics regularly requires constant reorganization;
- Finding new and interesting topics becomes more and more difficult as time passes;
- The constant change makes it difficult to build relationships that lead to meaningful ministry opportunities;
- Interest-based groups quickly become "closed groups" because once they are under way it is difficult for newcomers to penetrate the groups;
- As the church grows and the topical options increase, the organization becomes more and more difficult to explain to newcomers.

That being said, some churches have used interest-based groups as entry points into the church's ongoing open Bible study ministry. For example, a single parent may attend a short-term topical group on parenting. Through that encounter, the parent may be enrolled in ongoing Bible study where she may come to profess Jesus Christ as Savior and begin the journey of discipleship.

To use interest-based groups effectively as entry points, the groups need to have a stated termination point. The leaders of the groups need to understand the Great Commission mandate and be committed to leading participants to transition into ongoing Bible study groups at the conclusion of any topical study.

Some Words to First-time Age Graders

If you are age grading for the first time, realize that you are changing well-established patterns and traditions. Move slowly and patiently.

First, communicate positively about age grading and promotion with teachers, department directors, and other leaders. If you can sell the leaders on the concept, they can help make it a positive experience for the members. Develop a team spirit and clearly tie age grading to the mission or purpose statement of the church. When laypeople are treated responsibly and given the why as well as the what, they will respond with enthusiasm.

Nevertheless, *expect some opposition.* A few folk feel called to oppose any new idea. So, how do you handle those who refuse to cooperate? As one

farmer said, "Some stumps simply aren't worth the effort it takes to remove them." In that case, the wise farmer will just plow around them.

Likely, *you may have a few people who want to be the exception.* Let them make the exception rather than you making it. You cannot coerce adults. If you go ahead with most of the people, time will generally deal with the exceptions. Those individuals who remain in a younger class will ultimately feel out of place and move to their appropriate class.

If you must make an exception for an entire class, give it the most natural age classification. Then, start a new class below it and above it when they are needed to reach adults. The new classes will begin to grow. Then, promote persons from below into the stagnant class, requiring the class members to deal with the issue of new relationships.

Grouping by Age Groups

The guidelines that follow are offered as help for grouping people in ways that facilitate transformational Bible study for each age group. At no time is the organizational structure an end unto itself. It exists to enhance the work of the group.

Preschool

The preschool organization is for children birth until the first grade. The age and development of the child provide the priority base for grading preschoolers. The suggested maximum enrollment for a preschool department is 12 younger preschoolers (babies—twos), 16 middle preschoolers (threes—pre-kindergarten [pre-K]), and 20 older preschoolers (kindergartners).

Every preschool class or department needs a minimum of 2 leaders. The recommended leader:learner ratio for babies is 1:2 and for other younger preschoolers is 1:3. For middle preschoolers, the ratio is 1:4, and for kindergartners, the ratio is 1:5.

A new department needs to be organized when the existing department approaches the maximum recommended size or when the room has reached its capacity. The basic leadership structure includes a department director or lead teacher and one or more other leaders.

Grouping Preschoolers		
Age	**Maximum Enrollment**	**Leader:Learner Ratio**
Babies	12	1:2
Ones—Twos	12	1:3
Threes—Pre-K	16	1:4
Kindergarten	20	1:5

Children

The priority basis for organizing children ages 6-11 years is school grades. The recommended maximum enrollment in a children's department is 24, excluding leaders. The leader:learner ratio for all children's departments is 1:6. Every children's class or department needs a minimum of 2 leaders. A new department needs to be organized when the existing department approaches the maximum recommended size or when the room has reached its capacity. The basic leadership structure includes a department director and 1 or more other leaders.

Grouping Children		
Grade	**Maximum Enrollment**	**Leader:Learner Ratio**
Grades 1-2	24	1:6
Grades 3-4	24	1:6
Grades 5-6	24	1:6

Youth

The youth organization in Sunday School is generally based on school grades 7-12. In addition to school grades, age (12-17 years) and gender also may be used to determine youth groupings. The maximum recommended enrollment for youth is 60 for a youth department and 12 for a youth class.

One adult leader is needed for every 12 youth enrolled. Every youth class needs a minimum of 2 adult leaders. A new department needs to be organized when the existing department approaches the maximum recommended size or when the room has reached its capacity. The basic leadership structure includes a teacher, an outreach-evangelism leader, and 1 or more other leaders.

to make your sunday school work

01234567891010123234567

Grouping Youth

Grade	Maximum Enrollment	Leader:Learner Ratio
Grades 7-8	12/class; 60/department	1:12
Grades 9-12	12/class; 60/department	1:12

Young Adults

Young adults, ages 18-24 years, make up one of the most diverse and unreached segments of the North American continent. These 6 years are some of the most volatile in a person's life. These are years in which young adults typically leave the home of parents and establish their own households, determine whether to continue to pursue a formal education, decide whether to marry, choose whether and when to begin a family, and make many other major life decisions.

Too often in the past, one of those decisions is permanent disengagement from God's people. This group needs special attention and focused efforts to lead them to faith in Christ and to build them into on-mission Christians. Organizational patterns must be flexible, but generally follow those of other adult groups. The basic leadership structure includes a teacher, an outreach-evangelism leader, and one or more other leaders.

Grouping Young Adults

Age	Maximum Enrollment	Leader:Learner Ratio
18-24	25/class; 125/department	1:25 (1:4 all leaders)
Collegians	25/class; 125/department	1:25 (1:4 all leaders)
Young Singles	25/class; 125/department	1:25 (1:4 all leaders)
Young Marrieds	25/class; 125/department	1:25 (1:4 all leaders)

Adults

The basis for grouping adults is more complex because the age range is so broad and adults are so diverse. Such factors as the adult's age, generational segmentation, gender, and marital status may be considered when grouping adults. Common age-group patterns for adults are 25-39 years; 40-59 years; 60-74 years; and 75 and older.

Regardless of the basis for grouping, the suggested enrollment ceiling for adults is 125 for an adult department and 25 for an adult class. Yet, some churches increase the class enrollment ceiling to 35-40 for coeducational classes made up primarily of married couples. A new department needs to be organized when the existing department approaches the maximum recommended size or when the room has reached its capacity.

The basic leadership structure includes a teacher, an outreach-evangelism leader, and one or more other leaders.

Grouping Adults

Age	Maximum Enrollment	Leader:Learner Ratio
25-39	25/class; 125/department	1:25 (1:4 total leaders)
40-59	25/class; 125/department	1:25 (1:4 total leaders)
60-74	25/class; 125/department	1:25 (1:4 total leaders)
75 and up	25/class; 125/department	1:25 (1:4 total leaders)

People with Special Needs

Within every age group will be some people with special learning needs that require extra attention when designing the Sunday School organization. Some people may be grouped in a special education unit; others may be mainstreamed into existing departments and classes. The key factor is how their needs may best be met.

Consider these examples: People with hearing impairments may require a special grouping, but they also may be grouped with their peers if they are proficient at lip reading or signing. People with visual impairments can be grouped with their peers, but the teacher and others need to be sensitive to their visual limitations.

Other specific teaching units may need to be provided for the homebound; persons who are living away from their church temporarily, such as college students, military personnel, those on job assignments; or gifted persons. People who speak a language other than that which is dominant in the church may require a group taught in their language. The key is providing that which is essential to meeting the needs of every person so that no one is excluded.

Organizing Special Education Bible Study Groups

Special Education covers a broad field, including mental retardation, visual

impairment, learning disability, gifted, physical disability, multiple disabilities, and other areas like deaf/hearing impairments, behavior disorders, speech impairments, autism, and brain injuries.

An estimated 54 million Americans have disabilities. An estimated 10 to 20 percent of a community's population will include exceptional people. For any 1 person with disabilities, 2 to 4 other family members are affected in some way. Many of them are unchurched and do not know Christ. Yet, more than 90 percent of all churches do not have any type of purposeful ministry in special education. Beginning a special education ministry requires preparation and planning. Here are the steps to take:

1. *Pray.*—This is the Lord's work. It is important to consult Him about it.
2. *Talk to the church ministry staff.*—Share a vision of special education ministry. Obtain their support.
3. *Establish a planning group.*—Don't try to work alone. A group of co-workers can provide support and strengthen the effort.
4. *Survey the building.*—Determine whether the building is accessible to persons with physical disabilities. Assess what modifications will be required.
5. *Survey the membership and the community.*—Church members can help identify prospects Some special-needs persons are in the community waiting for someone to express interest in them.
6. *Contact local agencies.*—Learn what local services are provided for special-needs persons. As the ministry expands beyond Sunday morning Bible study, a church may be able to provide ministry that supplements or complements what is available elsewhere.
7. *Recruit and train leaders.*—Some people in a church will have the interest but lack the skills. Help to alleviate their fears and develop their gifts by providing training.
8. *Remove barriers.*—Possible barriers to be addressed may be physical, psychological, stereotypical, or theological ones.
9. *Promote the ministry.*—People will not know what is available until someone tells them.
10. *Visit prospects.*—Nothing can make an impression like a

ten best practices

personal visit to the person and his family.

11. *Begin the ministry.*—All the preparation and planning will lose its value if the ministry does not have a definite beginning point.

12. *Evaluate.*—Determine what is working and what is not. Make adjustments as needed.

Churches beginning to reach out to persons with special needs may struggle with what approach to take for the most effective response. Two basic approaches are mainstreaming and separation.

Mainstream the person, with an extra leader if necessary to meet particular needs, into existing groups of persons without a handicapping condition. A separate, specialized department should be provided only for those who are mentally retarded with disruptive behavior or extremely low comprehension. Other mentally retarded persons, up through 18 years of age, can be mainstreamed with these prerequisites: a receptive leader who is willing to learn how to work with mentally retarded persons; a sensitized class of peers; and competent co-leaders.

More often than not, preschoolers with mental retardation are more like their regular peers than unlike. It is easiest with this age group to adapt regular preschool curriculum resources to lower functioning levels. More one-on-one attention may be required.

Mainstreaming preschoolers where appropriate is an excellent method for providing modeling for those who have disabilities and for sensitizing the other class members to persons who have disabilities. A helper may be required until there is an adjustment by the other class members to those who have disabilities. In the same way, the special-needs person will need some time to adjust to other members of the class.

Working with children is much like working with preschoolers. In teaching-learning settings, adapting activities to lower functioning levels will help ensure that the children learn biblical truths and apply relevant truths to everyday living. Knowing the individual and his or her interests, strengths, weaknesses, and family will add to the spiritual nurture provided.

Mainstreaming youth with mental retardation can be difficult without a positive and receptive leader, sensitized peers, and an additional helper for the period of adjustment. Youth can appreciate being "different" and can more easily accept differences of abilities in other youth if there is appropriate sensitizing.

Organization Guidelines for Special Education Departments and Classes

- In most cases, the person who is higher functioning should be mainstreamed in the regular department of his or her own age.
- Special departments or classes—versus mainstreaming—are needed for mentally retarded persons in these circumstances: (1) the mentally retarded person has disruptive behavior and needs to have it brought under control; (2) the person's intellectual comprehension is so low that the teaching of biblical truths in his or her regular age-group class would not be appropriate. These departments and classes require qualified leaders and suitable space.
- Special departments may be comprised of a variety of groupings made up of all functioning levels, ages, and causes. Subgroupings should be developed within the department for certain activities.
- Departments for those who are extremely low functioning or who have multiple disabilities should have no more than two members per teacher.

The Value of Annual Advancement Day

Annual Advancement Day recognizes the natural laws of growth and development that occur within people and an organization. Therefore, Advancement Day should be regarded as a necessary factor in the normal growth of Sunday School ministry.

Consider significant benefits of observing Annual Advancement Day in every age group—including adults. Annual Advancement Day —

- keeps the Sunday School structure dynamic;
- provides for normal advancement through the natural stages of life;
- equalizes the enrollment of classes and departments;
- keeps classes from becoming too self-centered and closed to others who need to be reached;
- provides an opportunity for members to change class membership without embarrassment as they move to new teachers and other new class members;
- allows members to experience the wider range of teaching and influence of a larger number of consecrated Sunday School leaders;
- opens the way for new paths of service for more people, when

coupled with beginning new classes and departments;

- brings fresh interest in prospects by reassigning them to new leaders;
- creates greater possibilities for members to develop new relationships;
- gives everyone a fresh start.

When a person moves into a new class, renewed interest is generated for that person's well-being. When members refuse to advance, the profile of the existing class becomes static and the bulk of the enrollment tends to move toward the upper end of the age range of the class. That refusal, in turn, discourages the people in the class below this age group to want to move into it.

Observing an annual Advancement Day can be difficult in those churches where it has not been an ongoing practice. Several objections arise or challenges may come. We should not be deterred from doing the best thing because the practice is difficult or challenged.

Communicate clearly the benefits of observing Annual Advancement Day. Most people, when they understand the reasons for an action, will be cooperative and supportive. Focus attention on the value of Advancement Day for reaching people. Place it in the context of the Great Commission mandate, not rules and regulations from a book or an institution.

Even so, some people still will be uncooperative. Some people—and some classes—will want to be an exception. As stated earlier, let them be exceptions by their own choice. You cannot coerce people into action. In time, as they see the benefits of advancing, they may make the choice themselves.

In the case of a class that does not want to observe Advancement Day, assign it a place in the organizational structure. Continue to begin new classes around it that will intensify your efforts to reach people. This is not to say, ignore the older class; people still need to be moved into it. New members in the class can help others acquire different attitudes toward advancement as a practice.

Annual Advancement Day makes good sense when seen from the perspective of the purpose of Sunday School and the significance of organization for reaching people.

to make your sunday school work

Steps to Organizational Progression and Growth

Sunday School Organization Progression: The principles a church may use in determining its Sunday School organization and the progress or movement from one level of organization to the next. The function of each unit (class, department, division) is the basis for determining organizational structure. Establishing a Sunday School organization based on function may result in a variety of patterns from age group to age group as well as within the general leadership team. Suggested maximum numbers for each unit (class, department) help in determining the need for additional units.

Step 1

General Leadership
Sunday School Director and Secretary

Adults, Young Adults, & Youth: Class
1 class & 1 teacher: 1-25 adult or young adult members

1 class leader for every 6 adult or young adult members

1 class & 1 teacher: 1-12 youth members
1 class leader for every 4 youth members

Children & Preschool: Department
(some churches may call these "classes")

1 department: 1-24 children enrolled
1 leader for every 6 children enrolled

1 department: 1-12 preschoolers enrolled
1 leader for every 3 preschoolers enrolled

A class grows to multiple classes in an age-group department.

Step 2

General Leadership
Sunday School Director, Assistant Sunday School Director, Secretary, and others as needed

All Ages: Department
1 department for 2-6 adult or young adult classes

1-4 leaders for adult or young adult department

1 department for 2-5 youth classes
1-2 leaders for youth department

1 department: 1-24 children enrolled
1 leader for every 6 children enrolled

1 department: 1-16 enrolled in three-year to kindergarten
1 leader for every 4 enrolled in three-year to kindergarten

1 department: 1-12 enrolled in two-year-olds
1 leader for every 3 enrolled in two-year-olds

1 department: 1-9 enrolled in birth to one-year
1 leader for every 3 enrolled in birth to one-year

A department grows to multiple departments in an age-group division.

Step 3

General Leadership
Sunday School Director, Assistant Sunday School Director, Secretary, Outreach-Evangelism Leader, and others as needed in a church's expanded organization

All Ages: Division
2-6 departments for Adult or Young Adult Division

1 worker for Adult or Young Adult Division

2-6 departments for Youth Division
1-2 leaders for Youth Division

2-12 departments for Children's Division
1 leader for Children's Division

2-8 departments for Preschool Division
1 leader for Preschool Division

A division grows to multiple age-group divisions or multiple meeting times.

Sunday School Strategy Growth Worksheet

Age Group	ENROLLMENT				CLASSES				LEADERS			
	1	2	3	4	5	6	7	8	9	10	11	12
	Present Enrollment	Prospects	Total Possible Enrollment (1+2=)	Enrollment Goal	Suggested Maximum Enrollment/Class	No. Classes Currently	Total No. Classes Needed (4/5=)	No. *New* Classes Needed (7-6=)	Suggested Ratio Leaders: Pupils	No. Leaders Currently	Total Leaders Needed (4/9=)	No. *New* Leaders Needed (11-10=)
PRESCHOOL Babies / Ones–Twos / Threes–Pre-K / Kindergarten					12 / 12 / 16 / 20				1:2 / 1:3 / 1:4 / 1:5			
CHILDREN Ages 6-11 years / Grades 1-6					24				1:6			
STUDENT Ages 12-17 years / Grades 7-12					12/Class 60/Dept.				1:12			
YOUNG ADULT Ages 18-24 years					25/Class 125/Dept.				1:25 (teacher) 1:4 (all leaders)			
ADULT Ages 25 years-up					25/Class 125/Dept.				1:25 (teacher) 1:4 (all leaders)			

Best Practice Check Up
Organize with Purpose

___ We have evaluated our organizing principle in light of our Great Commission mandate to lead people to faith in the Lord Jesus Christ and to build on-mission Christians.

___ We have adopted the concept of age-graded, open Bible study as the primary organizing principle for our Bible study groups.

___ We have developed age-group organizations based on the enrollment ceilings and leader:learner ratios recommended for each age group.

___ We have considered the needs and identified specialty groups needed as part of our organization to expand the scope of our ministry to all people.

___ We have placed an annual Advancement Day on our calendar as a target day for making adjustments in our organization.

___ We have used the "Steps to Organizational Progression and Growth Chart " and the "Sunday School Growth Worksheet" to analyze and prepare for the growth of our organization.

BEST PRACTICE 3
Build Kingdom Leaders

"Whoever wants to become great among you must be your servant, and whoever wants to be first must be slave to all. For even the Son of Man did not come to be served, but to serve, and to give His life—a ransom for many."

—Mark 10:43-45, HCSB

In almost every conference about Sunday School ministry, sooner or later the discussion will turn to the need for leaders. One may say, "We are scraping the bottom of the barrel in our search for leaders." Another person says, "We just don't have enough qualified leaders in our church to do what needs to be done." Finally, one leader says about his church, "We have no problem finding leaders. In fact, we have people on a waiting list for opportunities to serve." Most all of us would like to be that person! What is the difference? That is what this chapter is about: a best practice that has as its objective to help you build leaders and a leadership team eager to do kingdom service.

The Holy Spirit has given every Christian at least one spiritual gift to be used for the common good (1 Cor. 12:7). At least one objective of the enlistment process is to help individuals find ways to use that gift in service to Christ, His church, and others. For some, that service may be leadership through holding a particular office in the organizational structure of the ministry.

Let's clarify at the beginning, however, that we are not looking to fill

to make your sunday school work

positions; we are looking to find people. We are not looking for authority figures; we are looking for authentic followers. We are not looking for people who can present good Bible lessons in classrooms; we are looking for leaders to be the lessons lived out in the crucibles of life.

Furthermore, we are talking about more than finding teachers. Teachers are leaders in the teaching dimension of the ministry, but because Sunday School is so much more than teaching and learning in a group session, we will be concerned also with building leaders for evangelism, discipleship, ministry, fellowship, and worship.

Leaders are people who can get followers to focus on a task, get the process going, and then lead the group to achieve its purpose. Leadership is not just having a magnetic personality. What we perceive as a magnetic personality may be nothing more than a glib tongue. Neither is leadership making friends and influencing people; that may be nothing more than manipulative flattery. Leadership is helping people have a greater vision and helping them raise their performance to a higher standard.

Overall, we are looking to identify, enlist, and build people into kingdom leaders. "A kingdom leader can be defined as a person called by God to follow Christ in a life of discipleship, utilizing the leadership gifts given by the Holy Spirit to lead the church in carrying out the Great Commission for the purpose of expanding the kingdom of God."[1]

The effectiveness of Sunday School ministry is highly dependent on the commitment of the leaders. Jesus is to be the model of leadership. His objective was to honor His Father as He addressed the vital needs of all people. His goal for His people is that they, too, honor the Father as they address the needs of those around them.

Jesus desired also that His pupils mature in their faith. That is to be the ongoing goal for Sunday School leaders. Evidences of possessing a mature faith are desire, commitment, and willingness to share the message of Jesus with others.

Choosing the right people to function in leadership roles is a challenge to Sunday School general leaders. Identifying and enlisting people to work in the Sunday School organization is perhaps the most important task of a Sunday School director.

We will build kingdom leaders who are committed to Sunday School strategy as an expression of faithfulness to Christ, His church, and the mission mandate He has given by —

- *praying for God to call out leaders for kingdom service through Sunday School ministry;*
- *implementing a leader enlistment approach that focuses on helping people respond to their personal call from God rather than an approach that is primarily concerned with filling church or organizational positions;*
- *enlisting leaders who themselves are committed to cultivating and multiplying new leaders;*
- *devoting major attention to leadership meetings that focus on the mission, relationships, and Bible study;*
- *providing training that equips leaders for their work and enhances the quality of their leadership;*
- *calling out people who will give their lives to evangelizing the lost and who are willing to participate in ongoing evangelism training and multiplication of evangelism leaders.*

Looking for Kingdom Leaders

Here are some suggestions for discovering people who can be kingdom leaders.

Begin with Prayer

God will guide you to the right people. After all, He has a vested interest in the success of your church. Leader enlistment needs to be both a spiritual and a practical process—and in that order!

In Matthew 9:37-38, Jesus said, "The harvest truly is plentiful but the workers are few. Ask the Lord of the harvest, therefore, to send out workers into his harvest field."

The harvest belongs to God. The workers belong to God, and He is the One who sends them out. That being so, we need to depend on Him when we enlist leaders.

Yet, too often we may have failed to seek the will of God concerning the enlistment of Sunday School leaders. We came to a nominating committee

meeting, someone led in an "opening" prayer, and we immediately started filling slots. We may have had a "closing" prayer before going home. That was the extent of our praying in this matter.

The first step in the process of enlisting leaders needs to be sincere, fervent, seeking prayer. Such praying is designed to discover the person God wants to serve Him in His church. It reflects this question: "God, who do You want to teach this class?" Prayer should never be just an opening or closing ritual or an afterthought. Invest yourself in prayer to discover God's person for each leadership role.

Search the Church Membership Rolls

This is the most natural place to begin, for leaders in Sunday School ministry need to be members of your church. Here are some reasons why that is important:

- Sunday School is the church's foundational strategy; therefore, it needs to be implemented by those who are committed to Christ and His church.
- Church members have already demonstrated that kind of commitment by virtue of having joined the church.
- Sunday School leaders are to be examples of commitment to Christ and His church.

Furthermore, Sunday School leaders need to be adults. While you may be tempted to use some youth in leadership with younger children, remember that youth are still maturing physically, emotionally, socially, and spiritually. They need to experience the ongoing influence of adult leaders who can model for them what it means to follow Christ.

Here are steps for searching the church membership roll:

- Set a time and place to meet.
- Allow sufficient time to do the work.
- Gather what's needed: alphabetized, resident church membership roll, paper, pencils.
- Pray for the guidance of the Holy Spirit.
- Consider each name.

Here are some other places to look for prospective leaders. Remember, even these prospects need to be members of the church.

ten best practices

123456789101 2345678

- Vacation Bible School leaders
- Graduating college students returning home
- Leader training course participants
- Recommendations from adult class teachers
- Persons currently serving in associate positions
- Retirees who have experience and training
- Public and private school teachers
- Former Sunday School leaders not currently working
- Persons who respond to interest surveys

Ask the Right Questions

When reviewing lists of prospective leaders, ask these questions about each name being considered:

Is this person already a Sunday School leader?

If no, then continue asking the evaluative questions below. If yes, then some other questions need to be asked that would confirm whether the person needs to be reenlisted in the same role or another role? Some questions may be: *Is the person working effectively in the current role? Is the person needed in another area where someone else is not qualified to serve?*

Is this person a child or youth?

Children should not be considered for a leadership role and, as noted earlier, generally neither should youth.

Could this person serve if he would?

Don't ask "Will this person serve?" That is a question only that person can answer. We may not place a person on a list of potential leaders because we assume the person is not willing to serve. Perhaps he was asked to serve last year and turned down the opportunity. Maybe she got mad at the preacher a few years ago and resigned all her responsibilities. Or, two years ago he quit in the middle of the year with little explanation. So, this year we decided not to ask.

Even so, we don't know that the person may have made a significant recommitment. He may quietly have rededicated his life to the Lord a few Sunday nights ago. Perhaps she said: "I am ready to go to work for the Lord. The next time I am asked to serve, I'm going to accept."

to make your sunday school work

Don't say no for God's people. If a person is capable and acceptable to the church, put him on the list of potential workers and include him in the prayer process.

Would this person be acceptable to the church according to the standards of the church?

Don't get bogged down at this point. If a serious question exists, then move on to the next name. Avoid engaging in extended or unnecessary talk about the person. If the answer is affirmative, then record that person's name, address, and phone number on an information card.

Identify Positions to Be Filled

Start with the most critical positions and work downward. Be careful, however, not to fill a position just because it's important and vacant. Filling a position does not always guarantee that the work will be done.

Identify Spiritual Gifts

Several good resources are available to help leaders to discover and analyze spiritual giftedness. (See S.E.R.V.E. in Appendix C for one suggestion.)

Identify Leader Relationships

Leaders should be interviewed and enlisted by the person to whom she will be responsible. In other words, whomever the new leader would call if he were unable to be present the next Sunday is the person who should make the enlistment visit.

Decide on One Person

Decide on one person to be contacted about the service opportunity—the one person God is leading you to contact. Avoid developing a backup list in case the person turns down the opportunity. If you have sought the will of God and believed that God wanted you to ask a certain person to serve in a certain position, is a backup list needed?

"What if God told me to ask someone, but that person wasn't listening to God when He told them to accept the position?" you may ask. If that happens, you would pray again specifically to determine the next person God would have you approach, not just go to the next name on a list.

ten best practices

Make an Enlistment Visit

Leaders have been enlisted in a variety of settings. Perhaps one too common is the hallway enlistment contact. Enlisting leaders in the hallway at church may communicate something unintended. The message may be: "This position is not important! In fact, I didn't even take the time to make an appointment with you." Another reason for not doing leader enlistment in the hallway is that the person you are enlisting may have something to say or ask in privacy. Trying to talk privately in a public setting can be awkward and may prove to be embarrassing.

Therefore, make an appointment! This is important work. Communicate that importance by enlisting Sunday School teachers in their homes. If enlistment at the prospective leader's home is inappropriate, make an appointment to talk privately at the church.

Making a Leader Enlistment Visit

Properly enlisting a person is the first step toward good leadership. Someone has said, "We enlist our problems." Many problems with ineffective leaders may be eliminated if a thorough enlistment visit is part of the enlistment process. Here are some guidelines for conducting the enlistment visit:

- *Pray for God to lead you during the visit, and ask God to move in the person's heart to provide clarity of direction.*

- *Explain again why you wanted to visit.* Let the person know you feel that God is leading you in a particular direction and that you want to discuss it with him.

- *Provide the prospective leader with a written list of duties for the position you are asking her to consider.* Make sure the list includes all expectations, such as participation in visitation, leadership team meetings, and witness training.

- *Inform the prospective leader of the term of service intended.* In most cases, except when someone is enlisted to fill a vacancy during the year, the term of service would be one year. Indicate also that service for this year is no guarantee of being in that position next year. Explain that

to make your
sunday school work

your goal is to give every person an opportunity to serve God in a position that makes best use of his or her talents and spiritual gifts.

• *Provide the prospective leader copies of essential materials that will help in doing the work.* Leader and learner Bible study materials, resource kits, maps, and information about other available resources should be provided. If the prospective leader declines to serve in this position, ask him to return the materials.

• *Give the person adequate time to discuss with you what is expected of leaders serving in this position.* Explain what support systems are available and who will be working in similar capacities. Encourage the prospective leader to ask questions now, but provide your telephone number for contact later when other questions arise. Be honest. The prospective leader has the right to know as much as possible about the responsibilities.

• *Ask the prospective leader to pray about the position, and promise to do the same.* Live up to that promise. Your objective is for the person and you to discern God's direction for the situation.

• *Set a time (usually a week later) when you can contact the person for a decision.* Setting a time to call back takes pressure off the person of feeling that a decision must be given immediately.

• *Accept the person's answer.* Do not try to force the person to accept responsibilities he or she really does not want to accept. If the person accepts the position, provide additional details about planning, worker enlistment, and training. If this new leader is responsible for enlisting others, train him to use the same techniques in enlisting others that you modeled in his enlistment.

A Model Leader Enlistment Visit

Cathy Contact is a member of the leadership enlistment team for her church. She has come to visit with *Patsy Prospect* about a leadership role in Sunday School ministry. Look over Cathy's shoulder, and see how she handles this leadership enlistment visit.

Cathy: Hi, Patsy. I'm Cathy. I called about coming by to
talk to you about being a leader in our Sunday School ministry.
Patsy: Hello, Cathy. Of course, come in. I've been expecting you.
Cathy: What a lovely home, Patsy.
Patsy: Thank you, we enjoy it.
Cathy: Patsy, as you know, I am on the church's Sunday School ministry leadership team. We have a leadership role in Sunday School that we think you would enjoy.
Patsy: Why me? I have never worked in Sunday School.
Cathy: As a team, we developed a list of persons who seem to have the qualifications for leadership. You were included on that list.
Patsy: I'm flattered the group felt that way, but . . .
Cathy: Let me tell you more about the leadership role we have in mind . (At this point Cathy describes the leadership position and the age group, identifies other people with whom Patsy would work, discusses expectations, reviews curriculum materials, and so forth. She allows Patsy to ask questions for additional information or clarification.).
Patsy: That sounds exciting and challenging! But as I said, I have no experience, and I have had no training in this area.
Cathy: We recognize that this is a new step for you. That is why you will be working with some experienced leaders. You can learn from them as you develop your own competencies. Furthermore, a Sunday School leader training event is planned in a few weeks. In addition, we will have our annual Launch Event where some planning for next year will take place and other training related to your work will be provided. At other times during the year, we participate in Sunday School leader training in our local association, state convention, and even some national training. Our commitment is to help you do the best job you can do.
Patsy: Well, this is a serious matter for me. May I talk it over with my

husband? We are in the same department in Adult Sunday School. I don't know how he would feel about me leaving to work in another area. And of course, I want to pray about a decision.

Cathy: Sure, Patsy. We don't want to rush you into a decision about something so important. We want you and your husband to have a sense of peace about your decision that comes from your recognition that this is God's call for your life at this point in time. I would like us to agree on a time I can call you to talk about your decision. Would that be OK?

Patsy: Oh, yes! That would be great. How about next Saturday morning? I will do my best to reach my decision by then.

Cathy: Great! Let's pray together now about your decision.

Patsy: I would like that.

Cathy: (Leads in prayer, asking for the Holy Spirit to give clarity to Patsy in deciding about this opportunity for service.)

Cathy: It has been nice visiting with you, Patsy. Here is my phone number if you think of other questions later.

Patsy: Thanks, Cathy. You have been helpful to me, and I feel that you are interested that I do what God is leading me to do. I appreciate that. I look forward to talking with you Saturday.

Cathy called back on Saturday. Patsy was excited. She had a deep trust that God wanted her to serve in this way. Her husband had affirmed her decision. She was eager to learn. Patsy proved to be a valuable leader.

The Sunday School Leadership Team: Who They Are and What They Do

The Sunday School leadership team is made up of every person who has been enlisted as a Sunday School leader in any age group. Everyone is a member of the team working to implement the Sunday School strategy.

All persons deserve the benefit of knowing the expectations and responsibilities of their role. Furthermore, a clear statement of basic roles and major responsibilities can be a tremendous encouragement to those who are considering accepting a position of leadership. When leaders understand what they are supposed to do and can see that they are not alone, but are

ten best practices

working as a part of a team, they are more likely to respond positively to the call to lead and serve. They are more likely to be effective and satisfied in their role.

The Sunday School Planning Team
Basic Role
The Sunday School Planning Team is comprised of the leaders with responsibility for the general oversight of a church's Sunday School ministry and leaders who provide administrative leadership for a particular age-group division or major affinity group, such as a Special Education Division. As a team, these leaders are responsible for the overall direction, planning, and operation of the church's Sunday School strategy. This team includes the pastor; other church ministers with responsibilities related to Sunday School; Sunday School director; the general outreach-evangelism director (or FAITH director); Sunday School secretary; division directors for each age-group division, and the Discipleship director, or mission ministries directors.

Major Responsibilities
- Set goals that lead Sunday School toward fulfilling the church's strategic objectives.
- Develop action plans for accomplishing the goals.
- Set calendar dates for special events that support the ongoing objectives of Sunday School ministry and contribute significantly to achieving its goals.
- Communicate the overall mission (objective) and message of Sunday School strategy to other leaders and the entire church.
- Provide direction for, and coordinate the work of, age groups, including leader enlistment and leader training, toward the overall objective of Sunday School.
- Evaluate the effectiveness of the Sunday School strategy as implemented.
- Set a positive example for others by living as an authentic witness of Christ and by being thoroughly involved in the life and ministry of the church.

The Pastor and Other Ministers
Basic Role

The pastor is the primary leader for a church's Sunday School strategy. Rarely will a Sunday School stay on its purpose without the visible, vital leadership of its pastor. The pastor and other ministers on the church staff are responsible for the overall direction of all of the church's ministries, including Sunday School.

The pastor works with the Sunday School Planning Team to set goals and evaluate the Sunday School's effectiveness in engaging people in evangelism, discipleship, ministry, fellowship, and worship through Bible study groups.

Major Responsibilities

- Provide overall leadership to the Sunday School Planning Team.
- Lead the team in keeping Sunday School ministry focused on its objective.
- Give vital and visible support to Sunday School and its leaders.
- Communicate the overall mission (objective) and message of Sunday School to the entire church.
- Guide team members toward spiritual maturity and assist them in developing skills that enhance their ability to fulfill their responsibilities.
- Set a positive example for others by living as an authentic witness of Christ and by being thoroughly involved in the life and ministry of the church.

The Sunday School Director
Basic Role

The Sunday School director serves as the general administrative leader of a church's Sunday School ministry. This person is responsible for coordinating the work of all Sunday School classes, departments, and other Bible study groups toward the overarching objective of Sunday School. He leads the Sunday School Planning Team in planning, organizing, enlisting and equipping leaders and in mobilizing members to achieve goals toward the stated objectives.

As your Sunday School ministry expands in size and scope, additional leaders may be needed or desired to deal with specific responsibilities that are assigned to the Sunday School director. For example, a church may need an assistant Sunday School director or a Bible projects director (such as VBS director or January Bible Study director). These persons may become members of the Sunday School Planning Team and be responsible to the Sunday School director.

Major Responsibilities

- Meet regularly with the Sunday School Planning Team.
- Communicate goals and actions to leaders and participants and evaluate progress.
- Lead in developing an effective organization that facilitates spiritual transformation.
- Lead in efforts to call participants into service and in enlisting and developing new leaders.
- Lead in evaluating needs related to space, budget, Bible study curriculum, supplies, and other resources; recommend needed actions.
- Set a positive example for others by living as an authentic witness of Christ and through full involvement in the life and ministry of the church.

The Outreach-Evangelism Director (FAITH Director)
Basic Role
The outreach-evangelism director provides overall direction and leadership toward involving unreached people in Sunday School classes and departments. This person gives essential leadership to keeping the focus on evangelism. The Sunday School director assumes this role in churches without an outreach-evangelism director.

In churches using FAITH, the FAITH Director should fill this position.

Major Responsibilities

- Meet regularly with the Sunday School Planning Team.
- Assist in discovering, enlisting, and training age-group division outreach-evangelism directors and outreach-evangelism leaders for youth and adult departments and classes.

- Promote outreach and evangelism objectives with other leaders and members.
- Guide all actions for outreach and evangelism through Sunday School ministry, and coordinate those efforts with other church outreach and evangelism efforts.
- Lead in keeping the focus on evangelism.
- Ensure that accurate records are kept so that contacts with visitors and prospects can be effectively maintained and Sunday School classes and departments can effectively work to meet needs.
- Lead in evaluating outreach and evangelism efforts made through Sunday School ministry.
- Set a positive example for others by living as an authentic witness of Christ and by being thoroughly involved in the life and ministry of the church.

The Sunday School Secretary
Basic Role

The Sunday School secretary assists the Sunday School Planning Team by providing vital support related to record keeping, reports, and other communications; securing Bible study curriculum, supplies, and other resources; and coordinating the distribution of resources. The Sunday School director or outreach-evangelism director assumes this role in churches without a Sunday School secretary.

Major Responsibilities

- Meet regularly with the Sunday School Planning Team.
- Process and maintain general records for Sunday School and compile reports, including prospect information.
- Coordinate ordering and distribution of Bible study curriculum materials, supplies, and other resources.
- Set a positive example for others by living as an authentic witness of Christ and by being thoroughly involved in the life and ministry of the church.

The Age-Group Leaders

Basic Role

By far, the majority of leaders in Sunday School ministry relate to specific age groups. These leaders relate to one of the following basic roles:

- division directors, department directors, and others who provide administrative leadership for the work of an age group;
- teachers, coordinators, apprentices, and class team leaders who guide participants in Bible study and in doing the functions of evangelism, discipleship, ministry, fellowship, and worship.

Major Responsibilities of Division Directors

Division directors are responsible to the Sunday School director for the total ministry of their age-group division, including planning, organizing, enlisting leaders, and evaluating the work in light of the objectives of Sunday School. Division directors also serve on the Sunday School Planning Team. They must work closely with other members of that team as well as with their age-group division and department leaders. `

Their primary responsibilities are to

- meet regularly with the Sunday School Planning Team;
- coordinate the work of the division and determine organizational needs;
- discover, enlist, and train new leaders;
- evaluate, encourage, affirm, and direct age-group leaders in their ministry;
- meet regularly with department leaders for planning and evaluation;
- evaluate all needs related to space, budget, Bible study curriculum, supplies, and other resources; recommend actions related to needs;
- set a positive example for others by living as an authentic witness of Christ and by being thoroughly involved in the life and ministry of the church.

Major Responsibilities of Division Outreach-Evangelism Directors

Division outreach-evangelism directors work with the division directors for their age groups and the general outreach-evangelism director to lead their divisions in outreach and evangelism. They work closely with department leaders.

In churches using FAITH Sunday School Evangelism Strategy, these persons should be FAITH Group Leaders or Team Leaders.

Their primary responsibilities are to

- coordinate all evangelism and outreach activities of the division;
- coordinate prospect-discovery efforts of the division;
- assist in training division and department leaders and members in evangelism and outreach;
- evaluate, encourage, affirm, and direct age-group leaders in their evangelism and outreach efforts;
- promote outreach and evangelism objectives with other leaders and members;
- maintain active division and department prospect records;
- greet visitors and guide them to the meeting place of their Bible study group;
- set a positive example for others by living as an authentic witness of Christ and by being thoroughly involved in the life and ministry of the church.

Major Responsibilities of Division Secretaries

Division secretaries assist the division directors by providing vital support related to record keeping, reports, and other communications; securing Bible study curriculum, supplies, and other resources; and coordinating the distribution of resources.

Their primary responsibilities are to

- meet regularly with the division leadership team;
- process and maintain general records for the division and compile reports as requested, including prospect information;
- coordinate ordering and distribution of Bible study curriculum, supplies, and other resources;
- set a positive example for others by living as an authentic witness of Christ and by being thoroughly involved in the life and ministry of the church.

Major Responsibilities of Department Directors

Department directors are responsible to the division director of their age group for the total ministry of their department. Department directors work closely with teachers, encouraging them and assisting them in fulfilling their responsibilities.

Their primary responsibilities are to

- lead in planning and administering the total work of the department;
- meet regularly with teachers for prayer, planning, and making assignments related to evangelism and outreach, ministry, fellowship, and Bible teaching;
- serve as a greeter / host for the department;
- serve as the lead teacher for the department, directing the overall teaching-learning experience and teaching during parts of the session that involve all participants and teachers together;
- evaluate all needs related to space, budget, Bible study curriculum, supplies, and other resources; recommend actions related to needs;
- maintain attendance records and other participant information that strengthens the groups' pursuit of the overall objectives of Sunday School;
- set a positive example for others by living as an authentic witness of Christ and by being thoroughly involved in the life and ministry of the church.

Other department leaders, such as a department outreach-evangelism director or department secretary, may be enlisted as needed or desired to assist the department director with administering evangelism and record-keeping tasks.

Major Responsibilities of Department Outreach-Evangelism Directors

Department outreach-evangelism directors work with the department directors for their age groups, the division outreach-evangelism director, and the general outreach-evangelism director to lead their departments in outreach and evangelism. They work closely with class outreach-evangelism leaders.

In churches using FAITH Sunday School Evangelism Strategy, these persons should be FAITH Group Leaders or Team Leaders.

Their primary responsibilities are to

- coordinate all evangelism and outreach activities of the department;
- coordinate prospect-discovery efforts for the department;

- assist in training department and class leaders and members in evangelism and outreach;
- evaluate, encourage, affirm, and direct age-group leaders in their evangelism and outreach efforts;
- promote outreach and evangelism objectives with other leaders and members;
- maintain active department prospect records;
- greet visitors and guide them to the meeting place for their Bible study group;
- set a positive example for others by living as an authentic witness of Christ and by being thoroughly involved in the life and ministry of the church.

Major Responsibilities of Department Secretaries

Department secretaries assist the department directors by providing vital support related to record keeping, reports, and other communications; securing Bible study curriculum, supplies, and other resources; and coordinating the distribution of resources.

Their primary responsibilities are to

- meet regularly with the department leadership team;
- process and maintain general records for the department and compile reports as requested, including prospect information;
- coordinate ordering and distribution of Bible study curriculum, supplies, and other resources;
- set a positive example for others by living as an authentic witness of Christ and by being thoroughly involved in the life and ministry of the church.

Major Responsibilities of Teachers

Teachers are responsible for leading people toward faith in the Lord Jesus Christ and for guiding them to serve Him through evangelism, discipleship, ministry, fellowship, and worship. In pursuing that mission, teachers understand that teaching moves beyond the Bible study session into the daily living of participants. Teachers look for opportunities to mentor participants before and after Bible study sessions. They help to ensure that a positive ministry environment is provided during the session, one that facilitates the work of the Holy Spirit. They invest themselves in building positive relationships with participants, and they involve learners in meaningful Bible study.

Their primary responsibilities are to
- lead a small group in meaningful Bible study;
- build positive relationships with participants and prospects and ensure that they are contacted regularly in order to meet needs;
- maintain attendance records and other participant information that strengthens the group's pursuit of the overall objectives of Sunday School;
- lead participants toward faith in the Lord Jesus Christ and to become on-mission Christians. In youth and adult groups, organize the class to support effectively those objectives;
- in adult groups—enlist other class leaders to assist with major responsibilities (See class leader position descriptions below.);
- set a positive example for others by living as an authentic witness of Christ and by being thoroughly involved in the life and ministry of the church.

Major Responsibilities of Class Outreach-Evangelism Leaders
Class outreach-evangelism leaders work with the department outreach-evangelism director to lead the class in outreach and evangelism. In churches using the FAITH Sunday School Evangelism Strategy, these persons work with the department outreach-evangelism leader to administer classes' involvement in FAITH.

Their primary responsibilities are
- coordinate all evangelism and outreach activities of the class;
- coordinate prospect-discovery and prospect enlistment efforts of the class;
- lead class members to create an atmosphere that encourages unsaved people to place their faith in Christ and encourages believers to lead others to Christ;
- maintain class prospect records;
- set a positive example for others by living as an authentic witness of Christ and by being thoroughly involved in the life and ministry of the church.

to make your
sunday school work

Major Responsibilities of Class Coordinators

Class coordinators are adults who may be enlisted for adult or youth Bible study classes to direct the overall work of the class, relieving the teacher of administrative responsibilities. The class coordinator works closely with both the teacher and class team leaders to ensure that all functions are addressed appropriately and that the class is properly organized and mobilized for its mission of leading people to faith in the Lord Jesus Christ and building on-mission Christians.

Major Responsibilities of Apprentices

Apprentices are enlisted from adult classes to assist a teacher in his major responsibilities. The apprentice serves as a substitute for the teacher when the teacher must be absent. The apprentice is a class leader and needs to be enlisted according to the same procedure used in the church to enlist other class leaders. One long-term objective of enlisting apprentices is that of helping to prepare leaders for new Bible study units that will be created. When an apprentice is enlisted as the teacher for a new Bible study group, however, he should be enlisted according to the same procedure used to enlist other teachers.

Major Responsibilities of Class Secretaries

Class secretaries assist class teachers by providing vital support related to record keeping, reports, and other communications; obtaining Bible study curriculum, supplies, and other resources; and coordinating the distribution of resources.

Their primary responsibilities are to

- meet regularly with the class leadership team;
- process and maintain general records for the class and compile reports as requested, including prospect information;
- coordinate ordering and distribution of Bible study curriculum, supplies, and other resources;
- set a positive example for others by living as an authentic witness of Christ and by being thoroughly involved in the life and ministry of the church.

ten best practices

Major Responsibilities of Other Class Leaders

Class leaders are enlisted by the teacher of an adult or youth Bible study class to assist with the total work of the group. Class leaders work in one or more of the five function areas in either a leader-based approach or a team-based approach. Generally, the class outreach-evangelism leader heads efforts that address the evangelism function.

- *Evangelism.*—Create an atmosphere that encourages unsaved people to place their faith in Christ and encourages believers to lead others to Christ. In churches using the FAITH Sunday School Evangelism Strategy, members of this team should be on a FAITH Team.
- *Discipleship.*—Create an atmosphere that encourages believers to grow in maturity in Christ; monitor the discipleship needs of believers and work with the church's Discipleship director to provide learning opportunities focused to address those needs.
- *Ministry.*—Create an atmosphere in which members and prospects can experience direct care and concern for life's needs and avenues through which they may identify and implement ministry and mission projects that utilize the gifts and abilities of class members; lead out in intercessory prayer as a integral ministry and missionary efforts of the class.
- *Fellowship.*—Create an atmosphere conducive to members building relationships with one another as together they build upon their relationship with God; lead actions that help new members be assimilated into the fellowship of the class and the team or group to which they are assigned.
- *Worship.*—Create a worshipful atmosphere, encourage participation in the church's corporate worship events, lead small-group worship experiences, and encourage personal worship in home and family settings.

The Participants
Basic Role

The people who attend Sunday School classes, departments, and other Bible study groups are not merely the intended recipients of Sunday School's ministry. They are the grassroots ministers.

Sunday School is concerned with building on-mission Christians. All of the class leaders, teachers, directors, ministers, and pastoral leaders needed for now and in the future may be found on the membership or prospect lists of Sunday School classes. Every participant should receive an opportunity to serve according to the leadership of the Holy Spirit. Such opportunities may be provided through their participation in Sunday School.

Major Responsibilities

- Participate in personal and group Bible study regularly, giving attention to the leadership of the Holy Spirit.
- Be receptive to God's efforts to draw people to faith in Christ through His Word, His Spirit, and His people.
- Actively participate in efforts to lead others toward faith in the Lord Jesus Christ.
- Participate individually and with the class to serve Christ through evangelism, discipleship, ministry, fellowship, and ministry.
- Follow God's leadership in responding to opportunities to grow spiritually and to serve God's people in leadership roles.

Building Kingdom Leaders Through Weekly Leadership Meetings

The weekly leadership meeting is to help all Sunday School leaders to be more effective in all aspects of Sunday School ministry. The meeting provides a regular time for Sunday School leaders to focus on the mission of the church; on relationships with people, both members and prospects who are related to the Sunday School; and on life-changing Bible study that is critical to effective Sunday School ministry.

123456789101012345678
ten best practices

Benefits of Weekly Leadership Meetings

Here are some reasons a weekly Sunday School leadership meeting can be beneficial:

- *Encourages and strengthens leaders.*—Sunday School leaders have high accountability to God and to their church. The content of leadership meetings needs to be designed to encourage leaders to live out their calling from God, strengthen their own character as they model what it means to be a people of faith, and improve their competency as leaders in ministry.

- *Strengthens outreach and evangelism.*—Weekly leadership meetings provide a wonderful opportunity for leaders to discuss outreach and evangelism efforts. Reviewing the names and needs of prospects, discussing ways to involve members in outreach, determining how to enroll and win to Christ the spiritually lost, and praying for prospects lead to greater effectiveness.

- *Focuses on evangelism, outreach, ministry, and efforts to build fellowship.*—Many churches depend only on the promotion of a visitation night for the involvement of their people in witnessing, reaching, and ministry. Built into leadership meetings is time to discuss witnessing to the lost, reaching prospects, ministry to Sunday School members, and making plans for assimilation actions that involve members and prospects in loving and caring relationships.

- *Improves administration in the department and class.*—Sunday morning is not the time to deal with administrative concerns that may arise, such as determining the process for receiving and completing records, addressing space problems, adjusting Sunday schedules, determining starting and stopping times, previewing resources, and ordering materials. Those concerns can be better dealt with as a team during a weekly leadership meeting.

- *Promotes stronger team spirit.*—Establishing common goals, developing plans, hearing and understanding the same information, dreaming together, sharing burdens and concerns, understanding what other people in the department or the other age-group departments are trying to accomplish, and praying together contribute to a team spirit.

- *Includes evaluation, leading to better work.*—Leadership meetings allow leaders to evaluate continually their work and the work being done in their classes and departments. Ongoing evaluation allows for continual improvement.
- *Improves coordination and communication.*—Weekly leadership meetings provide a time to coordinate aspects of the work and to communicate information pertinent to other leaders.
- *Improves teaching as leaders prepare for Bible study.*—Preparing for Bible study on Sunday includes more than each teacher studying the lesson and making individual plans. The Sunday morning session is to be the culmination of the joint effort of all the leaders in a class or department to prepare to accomplish the goal that has been determined for the session. An effective weekly leadership meeting brings together all the elements of a Sunday morning session and moves them toward a common purpose.
- *Increases involvement of members and prospects in Sunday Bible study sessions.*—Leadership meetings not only focus on the content of the Bible study, but provide leaders a time to determine how the Bible will be taught. Methods can be discussed and a plan built for maximizing the involvement of members and prospects in Bible study that changes lives.
- *Makes better use of space and equipment.*—The weekly leadership meeting will help leaders to determine the best way to use the space and equipment to create the best environment on Sunday.
- *Calls attention to enrollment and attendance goals and reports.*—A leadership meeting is a time to make leaders more conscious of the progress being made in the department or class in attaining enrollment and attendance goals. Records can be studied and appropriate actions determined.
- *Leads to greater involvement of departments and classes in the work of the church.*—Leadership meetings provide opportunities for departments and classes to determine ways they will support events, emphases, projects, and other concerns of the church, such as missions offerings and revivals.
- *Provides for ongoing training.*—The ongoing evaluation, planning, and preparation included in weekly Sunday School leadership

meetings provide an opportunity for ongoing training. As leaders evaluate teaching sessions, they can discuss how the session could have been improved. Planning for future sessions involves discussions of the best procedure for teaching the session.

Some churches may find it impossible to schedule weekly leadership meetings. Even so, every church needs to allocate some time for meeting. Monthly leadership meetings may be a viable alternative. All the items that are included in the weekly leadership meeting schedule need to be covered during a monthly meeting. Note.—This monthly leadership meeting for all Sunday School leaders is different from, and in addition to, the monthly meeting of the Sunday School Planning Team.

Content of a Weekly Sunday School Leadership Meeting

Regardless of the frequency of the meeting, the leadership meeting has some basic content. A brief general promotion period with all leaders together may be desired. Following that segment, age-group department leadership meetings are conducted by the respective department directors to focus on the church's mission, relationships with members and prospects, and life-changing Bible study. In churches without departments, the focus areas become the object of class planning. Class leaders gather with the class teacher to discuss focus areas.

General Period (15 min.).—This period is a brief gathering of all Sunday School leaders led by the Sunday School director, pastor, or minister of education. The purpose of the general period is to motivate and inform leaders in areas of concern to all age groups. Help for leading this period is found in monthly issues of *The Sunday School Leader.*

Department/Class Leadership Meeting.—This period is the primary focus of the weekly leadership meeting. Generally, the department directors or class teacher leads it. Each segment is to contribute to the achievement of the objectives of Sunday School. Instead of a segmented prayer period in which prayer tends to become generic, prayer is to permeate the discussion in each area of work. This will allow for more specific and focused praying about issues and people.

Focus on the Mission (10 min.).—This portion of the meeting is an opportunity to relate the work of the Sunday School departments and classes to the mission and the ministry of the church. Information is shared

concerning the church's ministry. Leaders are made aware of churchwide emphases, needs, and concerns.

Focus on Relationships (25 min.).— During this time, relationships with members and prospects are discussed, individual needs are assessed, and, as appropriate, plans are made to involve members in responding to them. Approaches are determined for being involved with members and prospects beyond the Sunday morning session, especially ways to involve members in evangelism. Specific plans are made for following up on ministry needs of members and prospects. Plans are made for fellowship activities and various assimilation actions to involve members and prospects in caring relationships. Visitation assignments and reports can be shared.

Churches using the FAITH Sunday School Evangelism Strategy will use this time to review assignments, give reports, and make follow-up assignments. Occasionally during this time, a study and review of witnessing approaches may be conducted.

Focus on Bible Study (25 min.).—Teaching for spiritual transformation is facilitated when leaders work together to plan the best way to bring members into a life-changing encounter with the Bible message. Bible study is not seen as an independent task but is the focal point around which people are reached for Christ and becomes the foundation for leading people to evangelism, discipleship, ministry, fellowship, and worship. During this time, previous Bible study sessions may be evaluated and assignments made for subsequent studies, in particular plans deciding how the Bible content for subsequent Sundays will be taught.

Sample Meeting Schedules

Following are three model schedules for weekly leadership meetings. Model 1 is for smaller churches or churches that choose to have all leaders meet together for most of the meeting. Models 2 and 3 are for churches that choose to have age-group departments meet separately after a brief general session. Model 3 adds a department directors' meeting to the schedule preceding both the general session and the department meetings.

**Model 1: For Smaller Churches or Churches with All Leaders
         Meeting Together**

Minimum: 60 minutes

- Sunday School General Period (5 minutes)
- *Focus on the Mission* (5 minutes)
- *Focus on Relationships* (25 minutes)
- *Focus on Bible Study* (25 minutes)

Model 2

Minimum: 75 minutes

- Sunday School General Period (all workers together, 15 minutes)
- Department Planning Period (by departments)
  Focus on the Mission (10 minutes)
  Focus on Relationships (25 minutes)
  Focus on Bible Study (25 minutes)

Model 3

Minimum 75 minutes

- Department Directors' Meeting (in separate room)
- Sunday School General Period (all workers together, 15 minutes)
- Department Planning Period (by departments)
  Focus on the Mission (10 minutes)
  Focus on Relationships (25 minutes)
  Focus on Bible Study (25 minutes)

Beginning a Successful Weekly Sunday School Leadership Meeting

Taking several actions in advance can ensure a successful weekly leadership meeting.

Discuss thoroughly with the Sunday School Planning Team the advantages of a weekly Sunday School leadership meeting. The Sunday School director may choose to review the benefits of the meetings and the positive effect they can have on the work of the church.

Secure the commitment of the pastor and staff. The pastor, other church staff, Sunday School director, and the Sunday School Planning Team need to demonstrate strong initial support for weekly leadership meetings. Their

support will be useful in leading the church to establish this meeting as a priority and in strengthening the concept that attendance is required as part of the leader's responsibility.

Choose a Time.—The best meeting time is that which fits the needs of the church and the people who are to participate. The meeting time chosen needs to be coordinated with other church leaders. Generally, a minimum of one hour needs to be available for the meeting.

Establish an appropriate schedule.—See sample schedules above.

Make provisions for children.—Child care needs to be age-graded, ongoing, and self-sustaining, which means materials and leaders do not have to be secured week-after-week. Such ongoing organizations as children's music and missions are ideal ways of providing for children during weekly leadership meetings.

Work through regular church processes to bring a proposal to the church.—While church approval may not be required, taking this action demonstrates the value and support the church places on the meeting.

Train department directors to conduct leadership meetings.—The department director is a key person to the meeting's success. Don't assume he or she knows how to lead the meeting.

Become familiar with resources.—Resources can help leaders better understand their roles and the kind of activities that need to be taking place in the age-group meetings.

Publicize the value of the meeting.—The value of the leadership meeting needs to be clearly communicated before securing commitments from leaders to attend them. Describe the meeting's purpose, agenda, and benefits.

Prepare the people.—When beginning a leadership meeting or seeking renewed commitment to the meeting, allow sufficient time to prepare people for the change. Don't announce one Sunday that meetings will begin on Wednesday. Lay a foundation by helping leaders to understand the value of the meeting and by training those persons who will conduct them.

Enlist workers with a commitment to attend.—When enlisting department directors, clearly outline the director's role in leading a leadership meeting and the priority of the meeting to the work. Information about leadership meetings needs to be available to those who will be enlisting other leaders as well.

Establish a reporting (record) system.—A simple reporting system that records those present and absent is sufficient. Such a reporting system will establish accountability for attendance and enable general officers to be aware of struggling departments.

Recognize those who effectively conduct leadership meetings.—Share success stories from departments that have effective leadership meetings. Tell about ways the meetings are strengthening the work of the departments. Describe what the directors are doing to keep the leadership team meetings alive and productive.

Give help to struggling departments.—Giving attention to a department with a struggling leadership meeting is easier than reviving a failed meeting later.

How to Keep a Weekly Sunday School Leadership Meeting Strong

Some churches are careful in their effort to start a weekly leadership meeting; even so, once the meeting has begun, the church and its leaders may turn their energies to new projects. That results in struggling, ineffective meetings that eventually fail. Even churches with ongoing leadership meetings do not derive full benefits if they do not continue those actions that were used in beginning the meeting. The following actions will help the meetings stay strong.

Provide the necessary resources.—Leaders need curriculum materials and access to member and prospect records. Remember that these meetings are about improving the work as it relates to the Great Commission with its focus on people.

Check with department directors about weekly leadership meeting needs or problems.—Ask department directors how they feel about their leadership meetings. Listen for the good things happening in the meetings, and share them with others. Be sensitive to weaknesses or needs, and assist the director in overcoming them.

Clearly communicate church and Sunday School plans.—Clear communication enables departments to plan support actions for emphases that involve the entire church.

Continue to train leaders.—Never assume that training is complete. Veteran leaders need to be updated on changes; new leaders need the support of continual training.

The Pastor's Role in Weekly Sunday School Leadership Meetings

The pastor is the leader of Sunday School. Here are some ways he can be involved in weekly leadership meetings.

By his presence at leadership meetings, the pastor shows his leadership and commitment to them. By his participation, the pastor can encourage the highest quality Bible study.

The pastor needs to be heard as well as seen at the meeting. He does not have to be on the meeting agenda every week, but from time-to-time he needs to speak to all of the Sunday School leaders in attendance. During this time, the pastor can

- support the concept of Sunday School being the foundational strategy leading people to faith in the Lord Jesus Christ and building on-mission Christians;
- encourage the leaders;
- highlight the progress being made through Sunday School;
- update leaders on progress being made on annual goals: new members, total attendance, contacts;
- emphasize special events, such as revivals, and churchwide emphases;
- share his heart for evangelism, discipleship, ministry, fellowship, and worship.

The Sunday School Director's Role in Weekly Sunday School Leadership Meetings

The weekly leadership meeting must be a high priority for the Sunday School director. Here are some specific areas in which that high priority can be expressed.

Understand what should take place.—The Sunday School director is the leader of the weekly leadership meetings. Therefore, he must clearly understand the concept and purpose of the meeting if he is to communicate with others and influence them to be faithful participants.

Provide resources.—The director needs to see that the department directors have the resources they need to plan and conduct an effective meeting.

ten best practices

Communicate with the church's total ministry leadership team.—The director needs to discuss with the pastor and other staff members (minister of music, minister of education, and so forth) the value of weekly leadership meetings for the effectiveness of Sunday School ministry. In that context, he will talk about ways that Sunday School ministry is supportive of the other ministries of the church.

Training Kingdom Leaders

Finding and enlisting kingdom leaders is a vital task of the general Sunday School leader. When the task is over, you may heave a deep sigh of relief. Don't! Rather, catch a big breath because in many ways the work is just beginning. Those individuals enlisted need some basic training. Even experienced leaders need additional training. Even previous to those kinds of training events, some people in the church are potential leaders who need a training experience that helps them to discern their personal leadership potential, assess their areas of interest, and explore the counsel of God in seeking leadership opportunities.

Sunday School leaders want to do their work well, and they can when they are trained. Of course, training has to be offered. Assessing training needs and planning training events are major responsibilities of the general Sunday School leader that must not be overlooked or taken lightly.

Potential Leader Training

Potential Sunday School leader training includes a basic orientation to the ministry of Sunday School, transformational Bible teaching, and age-group work, including observation of age-group sessions. Potential leader training includes also a Bible survey, helps for developing a personal devotional life, a foundation in servant leadership, an introduction to outreach and evangelism techniques, an overview of effective planning skills, and an understanding of purposeful leadership team meetings. Potential leaders can even do practice teaching.

The training is to help discern the leadership of God concerning an area of service that is best suited for them. Participants are exposed to ministry techniques appropriate to each age group through a mentoring/modeling process. The participants receive technical as well as practical training,

including practice on the job. The goal is to develop a readiness and sensitivity to a particular age-group area in hope that the participant will discover a place of service.

The *Christian Growth Study Plan Catalog* lists leadership skills and personal growth diploma study plans that can be used in designing a potential Sunday School leader training course for your church. Other undated resources can be incorporated into a plan to address specific needs that you identify.

Ongoing Training for Sunday School Leaders

Sunday School leaders need opportunities to improve their work through training, which will sharpen their skills, improve their understanding of methods, and expose them to new insights. That is the purpose for ongoing Sunday School leadership training. A church needs to create a climate that encourages training or leaders are not likely to see its importance. Training becomes part of the church's expectation for its leaders and a way in which leaders are held accountable.

Training is to address felt needs among the leaders. Moreover, a continuous focus on mission, vision, and action statements can help to perpetuate the desire for additional training. Some ways of discovering training needs are through observing leaders at work, conversing with leaders, discussing training needs during Sunday School Planning Team meetings, using evaluation instruments, and reviewing Sunday School leaders' progress toward their own individual training goals. Because all the training needs cannot be met in one year, strive to provide training that meets priorities and that contributes to greatest improvement in performance.

Of course, budget is a key factor in developing an ongoing training plan. Funds are to be allocated for resources and leaders of training events conducted at the church. Training fees and travel expenses may need to be included in the budget for leaders attending state events or national conference centers.

Leader training is not always dependent on assembling a training group. Individualized study using books, study modules, audio, video, or other electronic means is a valid and convenient means for leaders to develop skills needed for their job assignment. In fact, more persons may be willing to do individualized training than may commit themselves to a series of group training sessions.

ten best practices

The *Christian Growth Study Plan Catalog* suggests leadership skills and personal growth diploma study options.

Perhaps one of the most overlooked opportunities for ongoing training is to make full use of dated curriculum resources for Bible study leaders, especially the age-group leader guides. Each leader guide includes a section for leader and ministry development, providing help throughout the year to develop leaders into more effective practitioners of Sunday School strategy. Other resources, such as *The Sunday School Leader* monthly magazine, supplement ongoing training for all Sunday School leaders.

Ongoing training needs to address the relationship of church functions to Sunday School strategy, curriculum understanding, age-group characteristics, learning styles, tools and techniques for transformational teaching, spiritual growth and development, the concept of servant leadership, evangelism and outreach techniques and tools, fellowship, relationship-building skills, ministry ideas, and helps for class members.

Assessment of Training Needs

Any number of approaches can be used to identify training needs. Here are a few to consider in addition to those currently used by your planning team.

- *Make training a regular topic of discussion in Sunday School Planning Team meetings.* This type of discussion may occur naturally as the planning team considers its work in evangelism, discipleship, ministry, fellowship, and worship; and its progress toward goals. In case it does not simply surface periodically, keep training needs as an agenda item.
- *Listen to leaders.* Times of informal conversation can reveal valuable information. You can learn a lot by "listening" to situations as well as to words. Does leader turnover in a certain area tell you something? Are leaders frustrated? Are once-happy members becoming chronic absentees? Talk with age-group division/department directors about needs they observe. These leaders are the closest to their area of work. Rely on their impressions, and follow up on their input.
- *Periodically survey all leaders.* In addition to times of informal listening, provide formal times in which you ask workers to identify their training needs.

- *Evaluate training events, and use the information comments or insights to shape future training.* Responses will help bring to completion a training event. Such evaluation can indicate other areas in which training is needed.
- *Observe how leaders are doing in Christian Growth Study Plan activities.* Look at records for what they indicate about training progress. Encourage those who are involved to continue, and provide the assistance they need. Help other leaders see how the Christian Growth Study Plan can help them to achieve training goals. Provide the resources all leaders need to participate fully.
- *Look at job descriptions.* Changes in job responsibilities indicate potential training needs.
- *Observe in classes and departments.* Seeing firsthand what goes on in a class or department may reveal areas in which training is needed.

A Sunday School Leadership Training Plan

Follow these six simple steps to provide effective, flexible training opportunities for your workers:

1. *Enroll leaders in a Christian Growth Study Plan.*— The Christian Growth Study Plan assists churches in providing a systematic approach to leadership and skill development and Christian growth. Two categories of diploma plans are available: (1) Leadership and Skill Development; (2) Christian Growth.

Leadership and Skill Development Diplomas are available to help train leaders in various ministries. The same course titles are given for leaders of a specific audience.

For example, the course "Administration of Preschool Ministries" is one course for all preschool leaders. Preschool Sunday School leaders can choose either to read *Preschool Sunday School for a New Century* or attend a preschool leadership conference at LifeWay Glorieta® Conference Center or LifeWay Ridgecrest® Conference Center. Courses in addition to "Administration" include "Understanding Preschoolers and Their Families," "Teaching Preschoolers," and "The Preschool Leaders' Role in Ministry,

10

1234567891012345678 **ten best practices**

Witnessing, and Reaching People." Similar choices exist within each course and among other diplomas.

Diploma plans are available for the other age groups, special education, and general leaders. A "Reaching People Through Bible Study Projects and Groups" Diploma Plan allows trainees to focus on off-site Bible studies, Vacation Bible School training, and other special projects.

Information about the Christian Growth Study Plan can be obtained from state Sunday School offices. Ask for the current *Christian Growth Study Plan Catalog*. You may also get information about the Christian Growth Study Plan, including your church's member list/summary, by accessing the Web site at: *http://www.lifeway.com/cgsp*.

2. *Make a list of available training opportunities.*—Include events sponsored by your association and your state convention. List events sponsored by LifeWay Glorieta® Conference Center and LifeWay Ridgecrest® Conference Center.

3. *Determine which courses should be offered in your local church.*— Some of your leaders will not see the need to travel to another city or even another church for training. For those leaders you probably need to offer some training at your local church.

4. *Calendar at least one training event at your church.*—Consider offering at least one training event each year. Set aside some choice calendar time for the event. Plan well. Promote with genuine excitement.

As a Sunday School leader, you may be the best person to lead the training in your local church. You may choose to encourage some leaders to study a book and to take the lead in guiding others in a study of that resource. Your association probably has a group of trained Sunday School leaders who may be available to assist you in a training event at your church. Another option is to call on Sunday School leaders from neighboring churches to help you with training events.

5. *Encourage your leaders to use individual and group study to continue work toward their diplomas.*—Some approaches which may work in your church follow:

to make your sunday school work

- *Training blitz.*—This approach is usually a one-day event in which one or more of the books needed for a leadership diploma are studied. This could be done on a Sunday afternoon. Leaders could have lunch at the church and participate in the training in the afternoon.

- *Weekend conferences.*—These events are usually conducted on Friday night and Saturday morning. Your people may enjoy a retreat setting, or this training can be held at the church.

- *Write-up sessions.*—In this approach, leaders in an age group agree to read a book by a given date. On that date, leaders meet together and take one or two hours to do the personal learning activities required in the book.

- *Directed reading.*—Leaders agree to read specific books during a set period of time. For example, leaders may agree to read one book a quarter. If all the leaders in an age group read the same books, you can schedule opportunities for brief, purposeful discussions of the material they are reading.

- *Wednesday nights.*—A portion of the midweek service may be used for training. Choose a study that would interest all church members.

- *One-day training extravaganzas.*—Many churches are finding that adults will give a Friday evening or a Saturday morning, even a Saturday afternoon, to training. One approach, called "Midnight Madness," begins with a banquet, followed by a training event, and ends with prayer at midnight.

- *Quarterly training.*—Choose a yearly theme, and then develop a detailed, age-graded training plan for each quarter. Each event can include dinner followed by a short training event. Potential leaders are included in this event to introduce them to the nature and scope of Sunday School ministry.

- *Semiannual preparation.*—The events are tightly focused on such needs areas as caring skills, evaluating and using records properly, team building, or creative teaching methods.

- *Ongoing weekly leadership meetings.*—Often overlooked as training opportunities, the weekly leadership meeting provides a natural time to train leaders in specific areas of effective Sunday School ministry. Training in how to use the lecture method properly, how to

ten best practices

be a good listener, how to witness, or how to plan an effective fellowship can be covered in 15 to 20 minutes with all leaders together. Age-group leaders then gather in age-group meetings to debrief and dialogue how the material applies to their work.

- *"Home-Grown" training packets.*—Many church members have video cameras and audiocassette tape recorders. Leaders can create their own training resources by staging a training session or recording parts of a planned training event. Additional copies of these audio and video clips could be made with written activities or assignments included with the clips. These could be packaged and checked out through the church office media library.

- *On-the- job training.*—Few training experiences are as effective as on-the-job training. Don't confuse this with "trial by fire" training. The latter is sending an unsuspecting novice into a class and telling the novice to learn the hard way. On-the-job training is giving prospective age-group leaders opportunities to serve as apprentices under effective experienced leaders.

6. *Publicly recognize leaders who have earned leadership diplomas.*— Some of your leaders will invest quality time in training for ministry. Recognize that effort. Some churches recognize leaders by presenting diplomas during a Sunday morning worship service. Others plan a banquet to thank leaders and recognize those who have earned diplomas.

7. *Conduct a Sunday School Launch Event.*—See Launch Event resources produced by LifeWay Church Resources for help in planning and conducting this event.

8. *Visit online resources.*—Web surfers around the world can access information about LifeWay Church Resources products and services that are designed to strengthen Sunday School ministry and equip leaders. For example, teachers can access EXTRA!, weekly online updates of lesson-related current events, illustrations, teaching approaches, and other timely tips for users of Youth, Adult, Children's, and Preschool Sunday School materials. This and other information may be secured by visiting *www.lifeway.com* and clicking on Sunday School from the menu.

01234567891010234567
**to make your
sunday school work**

Security Issues in Leader Enlistment

The current social climate has created special concerns that need to be raised when enlisting persons to work with preschoolers, children, and youth. To protect young children and youth and the church, the church needs to develop screening procedures that provide background information on anyone who would work with any of these age groups.

Consider these tips from *Reducing the Risk of Child Sexual Abuse in Your Church*[2]. These tips apply to enlisting or hiring any persons who may encounter young children or youth, such as Sunday School leaders, staff members, childcare workers, custodians, and the like.

- *Confirm identity.* If an applicant is unknown to the church leaders, look for ways to confirm the person's identity.
- *Screen all workers.* The screening procedure should apply to new members as well as current staff members.
- *Lower the risk.* Think of the screening procedure in terms of risk reduction. Consider other actions that need to be taken to reduce risks.
- *Use professional help.* The services of a local attorney should be solicited in drafting an appropriate screening form to ensure compliance with state law.
- *Use well-prepared forms to get appropriate and acceptable information.*
- *Fulfill legal requirements.* Be aware of any additional legal requirements that apply in your state.
- *Maintain confidentiality.* Churches are required to treat applications, records of contact with churches, and references as strictly confidential information.

End Notes

[1]Michael D. Miller, *Kingdom Leadership,* (Nashville Convention Press, 1996), p. 72.
[2]Richard R. Hammar, Steven W. Klipowicz, and James F. Cobble, *Reducing the Risk of Child Sexual Abuse in Your Church,* (Matthews, NC: Christian Ministry Resources, 1993), 34.

ten best practices

Volunteer Leader Screening Form

This application is to be completed by all applicants for any position involving the supervision or custody of minors. It will help our church family to provide a safe and secure environment for all preschoolers, children, and youth who participate in our ministries and use our facilities.

Personal

Name _____ Date _____

Present Address _____ Social Security # _____

City _____ State_____ Zip _____

Day Phone (_____)_____ Evening Phone (_____)_____

Occupation _____ Marital Status _____

On what date would you be available to begin?_____

What is your minimum length of commitment?_____

Do you have a current driver's license? ___Yes ___No

Please list your driver's license number:_____

Have you ever been charged with, indicted for, or pled guilty to an offense involving a minor?
_____ Yes _____ No

If yes, please describe all convictions for the past five years: _____

Were you a victim of abuse or molestation while a minor? ____ Yes ____ No

(If you prefer, you may refuse to answer this question. Or, you may discuss your answer in confidence with one of the ministers rather than answering it on this from. Answering yes or leaving the question unanswered will not automatically disqualify you.)

Church Activity

When did you make your profession of faith in Christ? _____

When were you baptized?_____ Are you a member of our church? _____ Yes ____ No

If no, where are you a member? _____

List (name and address) other churches you have attended regularly during the past five years:

_____

_____

_____

_____

List all previous church work involving preschoolers, children, or youth:

Church Name _____ Address _____

Type of Work Performed _____ Dates _____

_____

_____

List all previous nonchurch work involving preschoolers, children, or youth:

Organization_____Address _____

Telephone No(s). _____

_____

_____

List any gifts, calling, training, education, or other factors that have prepared you for teaching preschoolers, children, or youth:

_____

_____

Personal Reference (not former employers or relatives)

Organization_____ Address_____

Telephone No. _____

Organization_____ Address_____

Telephone No. _____

Organization_____ Address_____

Telephone No. _____

Applicant's Statement

The information contained in this application is correct to the best of my knowledge. I authorize references or churches listed in this application to provide information (including opinions) they may have regarding my character and fitness for working with preschoolers, children, or youth. I release all such references from any liability for furnishing such evaluations, provided they do so in good faith and without malice. I waive any right I may have to inspect references provided on my behalf. Should my application be accepted, I agree to be bound by the bylaws and policies of this church and to refrain from unscriptural conduct in the performance of my services on behalf of the church. I further state that **I have carefully read the foregoing release and know the content thereof and I sign this release as my own free act.** This is a legally binding agreement that I have read and understand.

Signature _____

(**Disclaimer:** This form is solely for illustrative purposes. State and local laws may vary. It is recommended that each church solicit the advice of an independent and qualified attorney. LifeWay Christian Resources and the Southern Baptist Convention assume no liability for reliance on this form.)

ten best practices

Something to Think About

Think about the leaders in your Sunday School, and respond to the questions below. Include preschool, children's, youth, and adult teachers.

Do they have an evangelistic mindset? What evidences do you see?

Do they understand the fundamental responsibility of being a preschool, children's, youth, or adult Sunday School leader? Why do you think so?

Write here some things you will do to help make sure your leaders understand their commission.

What if your Sunday School leaders were asked these questions about you? How do you think they would answer? How do you answer them about yourself?

to make your
sunday school work
0123456789101234567

Best Practice Check Up
Build Kingdom Leaders

___ We have implemented an intentional approach to praying for God to call out kingdom leaders for service through our Sunday School ministry.

___ We are using an enlistment approach that focuses on people over positions by conducting enlistment visits to help prospective leaders see the opportunity for service in light of God's call to them to be a kingdom leader.

___ We have developed descriptions for each position for which someone is to be enlisted.

___ We have established a regular Sunday School leadership meeting to focus on the mission, the relationships, and the Bible study that are at the heart of implementing our annual plan.

___ We have established a goal that at least 75% of our leadership team will be present in each leadership team meeting.

___ We have assessed the training needs of our leadership team and have planned a training calendar that begins to address those needs.

___ We have established a goal to have every leader involved in at least one training event during the year.

___ We have implemented appropriate security measures for enlisting volunteers who lead Preschool, Children, or Youth Sunday School classes, departments, or Bible study groups.

BEST PRACTICE 4
Develop Soul-Winners

"You then, my son, be strong in the grace that is in Christ Jesus. And the things you have heard me say in the presence of many witnesses entrust to reliable men who will also be qualified to teach others."
$\qquad$ –2 Timothy 2:1-2

We are reminded when we read the morning newspaper or watch the evening news just how much our world is in desperate need of hope. The oppressed hope for relief; the suppressed hope for release, and the depressed hope for recovery. The deprived hope for provision; the depraved hope for forgiveness; and the despised hope for love.

The good news is that Jesus Christ offers hope to those who feel hopeless. He has a clearly developed blueprint for how the message of hope is to be shared. He has given His followers a clear mandate to go and tell the good news to people who need to hear about Him and His saving power. His plan is in place; it just needs to be followed.

If present trends continue, the vast majority of 21st-century North Americans will live their lives as if God does not exist. Believers in Christ will have to respond even more to a society that is becoming more and more secular. We will have to break the traditional thought pattern that thinks of North America as a Christian continent and the rest of the world as pagan. The truth is, even the communities surrounding our churches are part of a vast mission field in the western world.

to make your
sunday school work

0123456789101234567

Annually, thousands of Southern Baptist churches report no baptisms. On the average among Southern Baptists, it still takes 42 believers to lead one person to Christ. We praise God for those who are being won for Christ, but "look at the fields! They are ripe for harvest" (John 4:35). "Ask the Lord of the harvest, therefore, to send out workers into his harvest field" (Matt. 9:38).

In the face of growing secularization and a decline in the evangelistic thrust of many churches, how will we respond? We could throw our hands up in despair. But, such a response would be an ignoring of the Great Commission, a disregard of the priority purpose of the church, and a denial of the potential of an evangelistic Sunday School ministry. Rather than retreat, we must advance. We must commit ourselves to developing more soul-winners.

We will lead leaders and members to become soul-winners and witnesses for Christ in all life settings, including the home, by —
- *teaching members to view being a practicing soul-winner as the role of every believer;*
- *challenging members continually to be aware of the spiritually lost people they encounter daily;*
- *focusing attention on the responsibility of Sunday School leaders and members to lead people to faith in the Lord Jesus Christ;*
- *training leaders and members how to share the gospel through an intentional, ongoing strategy;*
- *providing regular opportunities for leaders and members to share the gospel as part of personal home visits.*

Without Christ, People Are Spiritually Lost

Southern Baptists are strongly identified with their conviction and commitment to the Bible as God's Word and an equally strong conviction and commitment to evangelism. Those convictions are inextricably bound together: Scripture is a testimony to Christ who is the focus of divine revelation. There is no salvation apart from personal faith in Jesus Christ. Hence, we preach and teach the Bible so that those who are spiritually lost can be saved from their sin.

ten best practices

Our effectiveness as evangelists requires that we know the message to be shared and that we know people with whom it needs to be shared. More will be said about teaching and learning the message in chapter 8, "Teach to Transform." For the moment, let's focus attention on challenging ourselves and others to be aware of the spiritually lost people around us.

Who Are the Spiritually Lost?

The spiritually lost are people alienated from God because of rebellion against Him. Rebellion against God is sin. Rebellion and sin are matters of choice; they are not imposed on a person. Alienation, rebellion, and sin against God do not always express themselves in violent or despicable actions. Therefore, a lost person can appear as a good person by personal or societal standards. In the sight of God, however, all have sinned and have fallen short of His glorious purpose. That includes the most moral, upright person in the land. We must not confuse personal goodness with salvation. A good person can be spiritually lost.

The sinner cannot bridge the gap between himself and God nor escape the condemnation of sin by his own effort or on his own merit. Jesus alone bridges the gap; Jesus alone justifies us before God. He made that possible by His sacrificial, redemptive death on the cross to take away our sin, pay the price for our sin, and face the judgment for our sin. By His victorious resurrection, He makes possible a new life of victory to all who accept Him. Nevertheless, unless the message is heard, Christ is received, and His gift of eternal life accepted—unless Jesus Christ truly becomes a person's Savior and Lord—there is no salvation and the person is lost without hope.

Jesus said, "I am the way, the truth, and the life. No one comes to the Father except through me" (John 14:6, HCSB). He alone is the way to salvation. Thus, a person can be religious and even be a church member and still be lost. Therefore, we must not be deterred from sharing the gospel because a person professes a religion or attends a church. Christ is the difference between being spiritually lost and being saved.

Where Are the Spiritually Lost?

The spiritually lost are all around us. We can encounter lost people on the job, at the mall, at the service club, and in our homes. We may tend to see them only as co-workers, shoppers and clerks, club members, and family

0123456789101234567
to make your
sunday school work

members, not as the spiritually lost individuals they are.

The Great Commission is a call to a global thrust with the gospel of Christ. The potential for going global is greater than at any time in history. In one sense, the world continues to become smaller and smaller as travel becomes more and more accessible and as communication outlets become more and more extensive. We are able to know more than ever about worldwide missions needs. Through information disseminated by the International Mission Board, we are aware of the large numbers of people groups around the world who do not know about Christ. Through the IMB, state conventions, and local churches, we have multiple opportunities to be part of mission teams that carry the gospel to the spiritually lost who live at the farthest points of the globe.

Nationally, we are not exempt from masses of people who are spiritually lost. We have almost with a sense of pride thought of ourselves as a "Christian nation," though in reality that has never been so. For example, over two-thirds of the U.S. population is spiritually lost. The great metropolitan areas in themselves are massive mission field filled with people who do not know Jesus Christ. Moreover, we may be surprised at the number who have not heard of Jesus except as a name used in derision or in cursing.

The spiritually lost are close to us. While we need to respond to the need to share the gospel across the land and across the seas, we also need to go and tell those across the street, across the fence, across the hall, or across the room in our own households. Wherever you live is likely teeming with people who are spiritually lost. Those people need the touch that can come from the concerted effort of your church's Sunday School ministry—leaders and members—as they share the gospel.

How Can We Discover the Spiritually Lost?

We see, then, that evangelistic and unchurched prospects are everywhere. Next, we need to identify who they are. See chapter 5, "Win the Lost," for suggestions for identifying lost people and developing a prospect file system for tracking information on contacts with spiritually lost people.

Who Is Responsible for Reaching the Spiritually Lost?

One unifying theme that permeates Scripture is God's initiative to redeem sinful humanity. His unchanging desire is that everyone be saved. His loving purpose reached its zenith in sending Jesus Christ, His Son, as the sacrifice for the sin of the world.

Following His resurrection, as the Lord ascended to heaven, He commissioned His followers to bear witness to what God had made possible in Christ. That commission is not history; it is contemporary. It was not given to those few; it is given to all who profess Christ as Savior and Lord. It cannot be altered; it is constant. It is not an option; it is a commission with the authority of heaven behind it.

Hence, we are steadfastly bound to this Great Commission to carry the gospel to all peoples. The Great Commission is our mission statement; it says why we exist: to make disciples. It is our vision statement; it tells what we are to become: "disciple-makers." It is Christ's instructions to us; it tells what we are to do: go, proclaim, assimilate, disciple.

Who else can reach the spiritually lost with the good news of Christ except those who know Him personally and have experienced the efficacy of the message? The role of discipleship is clear and the work inescapable. We are to make disciples.

Some Reasons for Doing Ongoing Evangelism Through Sunday School

Sunday School is the best strategy for enabling a church to achieve its evangelistic mission. As churches properly utilize Sunday School, the potential for doing the Great Commission is unlimited. Sunday School is a powerful force for evangelistic witness, nurture, and ministry. Here are some reasons why this is true.

- Sunday School open Bible study groups are already prepared to reach, teach, witness, and disciple through class outreach-evangelism leaders and group leaders. No new ministry, organization, or systems are needed.
- Sunday School ministry is structured into small groups where individual caring and reaching can take place.
- Witnessing is identified as a clear responsibility of Sunday School leaders and members.
- Sunday School ministry functions fifty-two weeks a year and is ready to do its work. It is a stable, reliable, and dependable ministry

to make your
sunday school work

designed to witness about Jesus and to teach God's Word.

- Sunday School ministry has the largest number of leaders (approximately one million leaders in Southern Baptist churches) and participants of any ministry in the church. The potential impact on a lost world of such a group of people is staggering.

Training for Evangelism

Many Sunday School leaders and members will never effectively share the gospel if they are not trained to do so. If we fail to give people a systematic approach for sharing their faith, most will feel uncomfortable and probably avoid witnessing situations.

Some churches use a variety of training approaches of varying lengths ranging from one-day seminars to multiple session training coupled with practical visitation experience. Each church will have to determine what will work in its context. Here is a word of caution. The tendency is to look for the easiest way. Don't fall into the trap of thinking that the easiest way is the most effective way.

We need to catch a fresh vision of our mission, then renew our commitment to that mission. That commitment should express itself in subscribing to the most effective approach to evangelism training and practice.

Consider FAITH Sunday School Evangelism Strategy described below. Hundreds of churches and thousands of Sunday School leaders and members can testify to its effectiveness in changing lives—both the lives of those who have been touched by the powerful gospel message and the lives of those who have stepped out to share it.

FAITH Sunday School Evangelism Strategy

FAITH is an evangelism process and training system linked directly to Sunday School. FAITH provides a church with multiple opportunities and incentives to strengthen its ongoing Bible teaching and reaching ministries. By implementing FAITH, a church can mobilize its army of Sunday School leaders and members to share the gospel, give unsaved persons an opportunity to accept Christ, and enable believers to grow through its ministries.

ten best practices

The Philosophy of FAITH

Second Timothy 2:1-2 is the key to understanding the strategy and success of FAITH. Others are to be taught so they can teach more people to share the gospel. FAITH is an intentional multiplying approach of evangelism training through Sunday School. It also supports Sunday School ministry by providing opportunities to keep in touch with members and meet their special needs; through worship and discipleship functions, by providing opportunities to grow in Christlikeness; and in fellowship, by uniting the church in a common goal and in celebration of results.

FAITH is not a program, but a process and a means for growing on-mission Christians. The FAITH Sunday School Evangelism Strategy is built around important ingredients designed to help a person investigate, understand, apply, and pass on the gospel message. On-mission Christians are not made overnight; the process takes time. A person easily can learn the gospel presentation that is part of FAITH, but more is involved.

In one sense, FAITH calls for a high level of commitment from leaders and members. At the same time, it takes people where they are— willing to obey—and helps build their commitment as on-mission Christians. FAITH does not require persons to start off knowing everything—only that God will cause them to grow in grace as they practice those things Scripture teaches.

The Primary Components of FAITH

An awareness of the key components of FAITH provides some important background and context.

• *The Sunday School class.* FAITH focuses on the work assigned to the class of each age division. Therefore, a worthy goal is to have at least one three-person FAITH Team enlisted from each Sunday School class or department. The Team is assigned visits to prospects and members of its class or department. FAITH Team members should serve as outreach-evangelism or other ministry leaders in their classes.

Giving Sunday School ministry high visibility, some FAITH visits are to members who need care or maintenance; others are to members who have short- or long-term crises or concerns; and some are to members who may have dropped out of ongoing participation or involvement in Sunday School.

Other visits are to people targeted for the class, people who do not know the Lord or may not be participating in any ongoing Bible study.

Who better to try to reach them than persons of similar age, needs, and life situations?

• *Sunday School leadership meetings.* Sunday School leaders regularly to deal with people issues as they are impacted by God's Word and the ministry of caring believers. As prospects are discovered and people are visited, follow-up actions are planned and implemented. Those actions affect both members and prospects. This ongoing meeting focuses on a Sunday School class accomplishing all of its functions.

• *Coordination meetings.* Those persons who relate to multiple FAITH Teams and Team Leaders are called FAITH Group Leaders. They should serve as department or division outreach-evangelism directors. They meet regularly to coordinate assignments and follow-up. The leaders build accountability and motivation into the FAITH ministry. They are also among FAITH's strongest and best promoters.

• *Evangelism training.* Integral to FAITH is an intentional process and plan to train persons to share their faith using a simple visitation sequence and easy-to-remember gospel presentation. FAITH as an acronym is used in making the presentation. Training includes classwork, home study, and on-the-job training by individuals who already have been trained and are mentoring others in the process.

Sixteen sessions of training, visitation, and home study provide enough information, practice, and modeling for learners to put into practice a recommended sequence for visits and to learn the specific FAITH gospel presentation. During this time of equipping, trainees experience opportunities to learn the gospel and to share it personally as they visit Sunday School members and prospects.

• *Public profession of faith and assimilation into the church.* There is a big difference between leading a person to make a personal commitment to Christ and that person's making a public profession of faith. FAITH intentionally links persons through the nurturing ministry and ongoing fellowship of Sunday School classes and helps them to come to the point of making a public declaration of faith.

One reason many converts do not follow up on their profession of faith is because church leaders have not helped them relate to the church and other Christians. When we connect new converts to Sunday School classes, we increase the possibility of their being baptized and discipled. The second semester, FAITH Advanced, gives strong emphasis to assimilation, follow-up, and baptism as a next step of obedience.

• *Discipleship of those being trained.* One of the intentional distinctives of the training materials and process is to help participants in their personal journey of Christian faith. Learners and Team Leaders model the process that helps them to see personally how God is at work in their lives and in the lives of those who are being visited.

Strategic Assumptions About FAITH Training

1. The FAITH Sunday School Evangelism Strategy is, first and foremost, a Sunday School strategy. FAITH is done in, and through, Sunday School. If FAITH becomes another program, it will die within five years. To position FAITH for maximum effectiveness, it must be implemented through Sunday School ministry.

2. FAITH is also a churchwide evangelism training strategy that is implemented through a church's Sunday School to equip participants to become soul-winners.

3. FAITH training centers around 16 consecutive sessions of training in evangelism scheduled one session each week and conducted during a fall or a spring semester.

4. All participants in all age groups are required to complete the first 16-week basic course of study (FAITH Basic) before advancing to additional semester courses of study (FAITH Advanced followed by FAITH Discipleship).

5. A semester of training requires a commitment by FAITH Learners to participate in classroom study, on-the-job training, and home study. It also encourages faithfulness in Sunday School.

6. Participants include (1) Team Leaders who have been trained and are equipped to lead a Team in a FAITH home visit and (2) Team Learners who have committed to receive training. The only persons who can teach FAITH in the local church are (1) persons who have participated in a

FAITH Training Clinic at a host church certified to teach FAITH and (2) persons trained in the local church under the leadership of the pastor who was certified in a clinic. Even these trainers are encouraged to attend a clinic to gain a wider scope and understanding of the FAITH strategy.

7. Each FAITH Team is comprised of a Team Leader and two Learners (in some cases, a Team member may be an Assistant Team Leader). Ideally, the Team Leader and Learners are members of the same Sunday School class or department visiting prospects assigned to the class or department in order to integrate evangelism through Sunday School. Some visits will be class ministry contacts or visits to take a neighborhood opinion poll.

8. Each Team should have both male and female representation. A man and a woman not married to one another should not visit together. The three-member makeup of each Team each week is essential to protecting the integrity of the ministry as well as the safety of the person(s) visiting and being visited.

9. Team Leaders are responsible for leading their Team Learners to put into practice the parts of the FAITH Visit Outline for which they have received training. Team Leaders are responsible for leading Team Time, when Learners recite memorization from home study and previous sessions.

Team Leaders and Learners have separate Teaching Time sessions in different rooms. Team Leaders gather with their Teams immediately after Teaching Time for home visits during Visitation Time, a sequence that maximizes learning. Teams return to the church for reports during Celebration Time.

Team Leaders are expected to participate as appropriate in two essential weekly meetings: FAITH Group Leader meetings (if a Group Leader) and weekly Sunday School leadership team meetings (if elected Sunday School workers).

10. Team Learners are responsible for memorizing the entire FAITH Visit Outline, including a gospel presentation built around the word FAITH. The entire presentation requires approximately 30 minutes to present. Learners participate in the home visits, expanding their role each week to practice presentation elements studied in the classroom and at home. The Team Leader assesses his or her Learners' readiness and encourages them to take part in the visit, while being ready to help as needed.

11. By the conclusion of the second 16 weeks of foundational FAITH training (FAITH Advanced), Team Learners should be equipped to be soul-winners—acceptable and confident in conducting a FAITH visit, in presenting the gospel of Jesus Christ, and in sharing their faith in any life-witness opportunity.

To learn more about FAITH and to identify the locations of FAITH Traininig Clinics that may be conducted in your area, call 1-877-324-8498 or visit the FAITH Web site at *www.lifeway.com/sundayschool/faith.*

to make your
sunday school work

Best Practice Check Up
Develop Soul-Winners

___ We regularly remind Sunday School leaders and members to be sensitive to the presence of people around them who are spiritually lost.

___ We regularly challenge all leaders and members to be faithful to the commission of Christ by making efforts to lead people to faith in Him.

___ We regularly emphasize the evangelistic potential and objective of Sunday School ministry.

___ We have in place an evangelism training process for all Sunday School leaders and members.

___ We have in place an evangelism process that provides regular opportunities for leaders and members to share the gospel through visits in the homes of prospects.

___ We have in place an evangelistic visitation process and training system that in linked directly to our Sunday School ministry.

___ We have specific plans for the pastor and others to participate in a FAITH Training Clinic or National FAITH Institute.

___ We will be implementing or continuing FAITH Sunday School Evangelism Strategy.

___ If FAITH has been our evangelism and training process, we have as a goal to have at least one FAITH Team from every class.

Best Practice 5
Win the Lost

"'Everyone who calls on the name of the Lord will be saved.' How, then, can they call on the one they have not believed in? And how can they believe in the one of whom they have not heard? And how can they hear without someone preaching to them?"

—Romans 10:13-14

In God's wisdom and providence, He has chosen to use redeemed sinners to tell unredeemed sinners about salvation in Jesus Christ. Many people who are drowning in sin will be saved only when some believers care enough to go personally to share the means of salvation.

When witnessing visits are made, some hear the Word and in faith believe it. Even if no one is saved during the visit, the gospel has been shared. Salvation may come at a later time. God's Word does not return void but accomplishes His purpose (Isa. 55:11). The labor of the faithful servant is not in vain (1 Cor. 15:58). Every visit is successful as it is made in the power of the Holy Spirit.

The Lord commissioned His followers to witness (Acts 1:8) and to make disciples (Matt. 28:19). In bearing witness of Christ, we make it possible for the hearer to learn of Christ. As the person determines what he will do with what he knows and what he will allow God to do in him, that person can be saved.

Salvation is God's work of grace in response to the faith of the individual (Eph. 2:8-9). That being true, we do not actually "win" a person to Christ, but we can engage in actions wherein the good news is declared and people are brought into a life-changing encounter with God in Christ. That is what we are about in Sunday School ministry.

We will engage in evangelistic actions that result in winning the lost to Christ, as well in as other actions that target the unchurched and reclaim the spiritually indifferent, by —

- *involving members in discovering individual and family prospects;*
- *maintaining up-to-date master and working prospect files and implementing an ongoing approach for making evangelistic prospect visitation assignments to members;*
- *providing regular, specific times for evangelistic, outreach, and ministry visitation;*
- *committing ourselves to witness for Christ in all life settings, including the home;*
- *teaching evangelistically, including foundational teaching, especially with preschoolers and children, that becomes the basis for a later conversion as the Holy Spirit brings conviction of sin;*
- *challenging unchurched or spiritually indifferent individuals and families to commit to living as followers of Jesus Christ.*

Advantages of Organizing Evangelistic, Outreach, and Ministry Visitation Through Sunday School

The age-graded Sunday School ministry provides the best organizational structure for organizing a church's evangelistic, outreach, and ministry visitation effort. FAITH Sunday School Evangelism Strategy is a detailed process for doing the work (see chapter 4). Here are some advantages of using Sunday School rather than creating another structure or organization.

 • *Organizing through Sunday School takes maximum advantage of the twin principles of homogeneity and receptivity.* According to the homogenous principle, people seek a small group where they share some characteristics and feel they belong. This principle recognizes that the gospel tends to travel with greater receptivity through relationships that are kindled through small groups.

The receptivity principle states that a church should invest most of its energies and resources where they will return the best evangelistic harvest. Small groups for Bible study usually open a door of opportunity to create and foster growing receptivity for evangelistic results.

• *Organizing through Sunday School creates a multi-targeting approach to evangelism.* In an age-graded Sunday School, all ages are targeted for ministry based on an understanding of each age group's level of spiritual need and ability to learn and respond to Bible truth.

• *Organizing through Sunday School provides a simple, flexible, and workable plan for reaching out to others.* The plan is simple. Each newcomer or prospect is to be visited by a team from a small group, the team being made up of people of the same age group.

• *Organizing through Sunday School takes advantage of the power of enrollment.* Attendance grows in proportion to the increase in enrollment. About one-half of those enrolled who are unbelievers will attend. About one-half of those unbelievers who attend will be saved. Of course, this assumes that the church has a focus on evangelism in Bible teaching.

• *Organizing through Sunday School combats the tendency of the organization to stagnate.* Small groups tend to become introverted and to crystallize. That tendency is combated by continuing to focus on the evangelistic mission that is at the heart of the Sunday School Bible study group.

• *Organizing through Sunday School provides a sufficient reservoir of people to keep evangelistic and ministry visitation functioning.* Rather than relying on open volunteers to be participants in evangelistic and ministry visitation, the Sunday School small group becomes the focused source for recruiting volunteers who can be given specific assignments that relate to the group of which they are part.

The Sunday School organization can be used to organize evangelistic and ministry visitation with every age group. Leaders in Preschool Sunday School visit preschool age children to help cultivate relationships with the child and increase the teaching opportunity. In visiting the child, however, the Preschool leader may also have the opportunity to witness and minister to unsaved parents and other family members. The same may be true of visits made to younger children.

Older children should be visited by Children's Sunday School leaders even if the family receives a visit from a team from an adult class. If the child attended Sunday School alone, obtain the permission of the child's parents or guardian before making the visit. Children's leaders need to be equipped to share the gospel with the older child but should be prepared to talk with an unsaved parent or relative who may be in the home.

Youth may have another specific time for participating in evangelistic and ministry visitation with other youth. In most cases, the youth need to have been trained in giving an evangelistic witness and be accompanied by Youth leaders who also are trained in sharing the gospel.

As noted earlier, adult evangelistic and ministry visits need to be carried out by teams from the Bible teaching group that are part of the Adult Sunday School organization. A worthy goal is to have a team from every group present on the ongoing visitation night. Teams may visit at other times as well. Each Adult class or group needs to have a class outreach-evangelism leader to coordinate the evangelistic and ministry visitation efforts. A brief description of the responsibilities of this class leader was given in chapter 3.

Identifying Prospects for Your Church

An evangelistic prospect is any unsaved or unchurched person who is in such proximity as to be reached by a church. For most churches, this definition means that their neighborhoods, communities, towns, and cities are filled with prospects.

More specifically, however, an evangelistic prospect is any unsaved or unchurched person who is in such proximity as to be reached and cared for by a church and for whom the church has a name, address, and other pertinent information that enables that person to be assigned to an appropriate class for a visit. By receiving assignments to visit specific unsaved or unchurched people, each class has opportunity to encounter them personally so they can hear and respond to the gospel.

Many churches are not calling the people they are seeking to reach, *prospects.* Many churches are beginning to refer to prospects as *V.I.P.'s* guests, or some other friendly term that communicates that prospects are extremely important to them and to the Lord.

That importance is communicated in other simple yet subtle ways: by staffing a welcome center with friendly, knowledgeable members who escort guests to the rooms where the Bible study group meets; by greeting guests in the parking lot; by wording prospect information cards in user-friendly ways (for example, asking guests to indicate the most convenient time for someone to call); and by how guests are welcomed in classes and worship services. Consider how your church views prospects. Make any adjustments needed.

Sources for Evangelistic Prospects

As we observed earlier, evangelistic and unchurched prospects are everywhere. Reaching them is a matter of identifying who they are and how to contact them. In many cases, people already have had some contact or relationship with your church. Do not overlook them.

- Church members not enrolled in Bible study
- Visitors in worship services
- People who attend special-emphasis events, revivals, or seasonal presentations at, or sponsored by, the church
- Parents and siblings of preschoolers, children, and youth enrolled in Sunday School classes or departments
- Parents and siblings of preschoolers, children, and youth enrolled in Vacation Bible School and Bible Clubs
- Extended family members, friends, neighbors, and associates of people who are members of your church or are enrolled in Sunday School classes or departments
- Unsaved members of Sunday School classes or departments

Prospect-Discovery Actions

Conduct prospect-discovery events through the church. While prospect discovery is an ongoing action, periodic emphasis needs to be given to this important work. At least once each quarter, Sunday School leaders and members should conduct a prospect-discovery event that will provide information about people who have not been reached through the ministries targeted by your (or any other) church.

Some of the events described may be community-wide. Others may

focus on a geographical area of the community or a particular target group, such as single adults, senior adults, homebound adults, parents of preschoolers, and so forth.

- *Gather names of people who attend special events and ministries through the church.*—They include but are not limited to worship services, Vacation Bible School, special concerts, bus ministry, recreation, and socials.
- *Conduct a direct-mail opinion survey* with a return card providing the name and address of the responder.
- *Conduct a telephone survey.*
- *Obtain information from a newcomer welcoming organization* and other agencies that will release information on individuals or families who have recently moved into the community.
- *Designate a Sunday in which all members are asked to complete a card providing information on people they know.*—Ask members to list the name, address, and phone number of a family member, neighbor, work associate, and others who are evangelistic, enrollment, or ministry action prospects. Give the day a theme or special name (for example, Friends Day).
- *Organize a "Prospect Watch"* in member neighborhoods, encouraging members to look for persons and families moving into the area.
- *Conduct community or neighborhood Scripture distribution visitation* during which members are on the lookout for prospects.
- *Invite the community to seminars and workshops addressing community issues, family concerns, or personal needs.*—Follow up on registrants and participants who are prospects.
- *Locate demographic data* available through computer online people-search engines.
- *Develop a corps of members to survey the newspaper for potential prospects.*—This process may include reviewing birth records, hospital lists, death notices, new-home purchases, announcements about new professional and businesspersons who have moved into the community, marriage announcements, and other such public information. Determine appropriate ways to learn more about such people and their life needs.

ten best practices

• *Conduct community surveys to make contact with, and get information from, people who have had no contact with the church.*—A community survey can be a nonthreatening way to discover new names and to assess community interest in ministries sponsored by the church. Taking opinion polls is an important action associated with FAITH Sunday School Evangelism Strategy.

Developing and Maintaining Prospect Files

Develop and maintain a prospect file and membership file as part of the system for recording, distributing, and receiving information about people. The prospect file will help you to determine the growth potential of your church. The number of prospects on file needs to be equal to the total enrollment of your Sunday School ministry.

Your church may choose one of several options: card files and preprinted assignment forms, a pocket-and-card system, or electronic files and electronically generated assignment forms. Whichever you choose, here are some elements that need to be part of your file system.

The Master File

The master file is a permanent file in which all information about each prospect or member is logged and tracked. The file should include such information as name, address, phone number, class or department to which assigned, spiritual condition, and other information you determine to be helpful. This file may be arranged alphabetically by family units or by individual names.

Other options for arranging the file include geographical areas and age groups. You may choose to use more than one approach for master files. For example, you may have a family master file and an age-group master file. Remember, these are master files, not working files for making assignments.

Keep a separate file for prospects and for members. Make sure the member file can be accessed by Sunday School division, department, and class leaders.

to make your sunday school work

Working Files

These are the files from which assignments are made and on which members make notes about visits attempted or made. New or corrected information about the prospect needs to be recorded so both the working file and the master file can be updated. No information needs to "sit in a file" but ought to be used regularly and updated for visitation and follow-up. Each Sunday School class and department must have access to information regarding people who would relate to it.

Maintenance of master and working files needs to be assigned through the church office to someone who can receive and update information each week, distribute up-to-date outreach information in time for weekly leadership meetings, prepare visitation assignment cards based on updated information, and assign prospects to the appropriate class or department. See the visual on page 141 for a possible "flow" of information.

A Basic Assignment Process

Every prospect discovered should be assigned to a Sunday School class or department for follow-up. In the case of family prospects, assignments can be made to adult classes and classes of preschoolers, children, or youth. Leaders in all age groups related to the family can coordinate visits and contacts and may make some visits together. Here are some other suggestions related to assignments.

- Enter information about the prospect into the master prospect file.
- Complete an age-group prospect assignment record; forward it to the outreach-evangelism leader for the class or department working file.
- Assign a member of the class or department to make the contact. Give a date by which the visit should be made, with instructions to return the assignment material to the person making the assignment.
- Following the contact, receive the member's report on the outcome. Forward information on the outcome of the visit to the Sunday School outreach-evangelism director for updating the master prospect file.
- Make other contacts based on the initial results and the needs of the person.

EVANGELISM VISITS

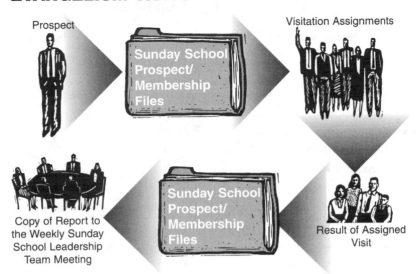

Prospect

Sunday School Prospect/ Membership Files

Visitation Assignments

Result of Assigned Visit

Sunday School Prospect/ Membership Files

Copy of Report to the Weekly Sunday School Leadership Team Meeting

This visual shows a possible flow of information between a prospect visit and the different church or Sunday School groups who need or can share updated information. Similar information is provided for Sunday School ministry visits.

MINISTRY VISITS

Information About Sunday School Member/ Need

Weekly Sunday School Leadership Team Meeting

Sunday School (FAITH) Secretary or Outreach-Evangelism (FAITH) Director

Visitation Assignments to Appropriate Sunday School Class/ Department

Results to Secretary or Director

Copy of Report to the Weekly Sunday School Leadership Team Meeting

to make your sunday school work

Providing a Regular, Specific Time for Evangelistic, Outreach, and Ministry Visitation

Anything that is done on a regular basis over a relatively short period of time tends to stay current, fresh, and interesting. The likelihood of losing interest in something is lessened when it is done regularly.

Moreover, some things seem to work better when they are used regularly. Just think how sore your back muscles get when you engage in digging in the yard after a long layoff over the winter months. Or, how about your heart? Are you comfortable with it beating irregularly? Likely not. That isn't in the best interest of your health.

So it is with visitation ministry. A vital and relevant church needs the regular exercise of ongoing visitation. Visitation cannot be done with a sense of competency and earnestness unless it becomes part of a church's weekly regimen. Most people need the structure and accountability that comes from knowing of a specified time for visiting others.

The time your church selects for regular, ongoing visitation needs to be the time that will attract the greatest number of participants and the time during which people in the community are most likely to be accessible.

Evangelistic Bible Teaching

The Bible is the written record of God's redemptive work in history that climaxed in the incarnation of Jesus Christ to be the Savior of the world. Comprehensive Bible teaching must include the Bible's greatest truth, the gospel, the good news that Jesus Christ is the only way to God. Chapter 8, "Teach to Transform," will provide more information about the place of teaching in Sunday School ministry. The emphasis here is on the specific relationship of Bible teaching to evangelism.

Evangelistic Bible Teaching in the New Testament

New Testament evangelism occurred through preaching, witnessing, and teaching. Jesus is our biblical model for evangelistic teaching. We read in Matthew 4:23 that "Jesus went throughout Galilee, teaching in their synagogues, preaching the good news of the kingdom." Teaching was Jesus' primary activity. His teaching had an evangelistic urgency. He was confrontive but not offensive. He imparted the necessary and appropriate information so that the people He was teaching could make a decision. He invited His hearers to act decisively in response to the truths He shared. Notice, too, that Jesus did most of His teaching outside the classroom. He went to where people were; He responded to people wherever He encountered them.

Many Scripture passages show us the evangelistic teaching style of Jesus. He taught the woman at the well in Samaria, telling her about God and helping her to acknowledge her sins (John 4:16). He spoke at length to Nicodemus, telling him, "No one can see the kingdom of God unless he is born again" (John 3:3). After dealing with the question of the rich young ruler, Jesus clearly called for him to make a decision when He said, "If you want to be perfect, go, sell your possessions and give to the poor and you will have treasure in heaven. Then come, follow me" (Matt. 19:21).

After Jesus returned to heaven, His disciples followed His command to tell the world about Him and began to preach and teach in the same manner Jesus Himself had taught——evangelistically. Their desire was to lead their learners to make a life-changing decision by accepting Jesus Christ as Savior. The civil and religious leaders of that day were not happy when the disciples "were teaching the people and proclaiming in Jesus the resurrection of the dead" (Acts 4:2).

Scripture reveals that teaching was the most prominent evangelistic strategy in the Jerusalem church. In fact, the apostles were commanded by the Jewish religious authorities "not to speak or teach at all in the name of Jesus" (Acts 4:18). The spread of the gospel continued and spread beyond Jerusalem through the evangelistic teaching of those followers who obeyed Jesus' command. Can we, His followers today, do less?

The Holy Spirit in Evangelistic Bible Teaching

Evangelistic teaching is a spirit-led endeavor. Authentic Bible teaching occurs when Bible truths intersect human need under the guidance of a Spirit-led teacher. The Holy Spirit is the powerful living presence of the resurrected Christ. The Holy Spirit convicts of sin and draws the sinner to Jesus.

to make your sunday school work

In evangelistic Bible teaching, the Holy Spirit makes His presence known in at least three ways. *First, the Spirit speaks through the Bible we teach.* Many people have found Christ by reading the Bible without the help of anyone but the Holy Spirit. That does not discount either the teacher or the witness. Rather, it reminds us that the Bible is a powerful evangelistic tool because God, in the person of the Holy Spirit, speaks through its pages.

A second way the Spirit makes His presence known in evangelistic teaching is to, and through, the teacher. Notice the role of the Holy Spirit in Philip's encounter with the Ethiopian eunuch when the Spirit said to Philip, "Go to that chariot and stay near it" (Acts 8:29). After the conversion and baptism of the eunuch, "the Spirit of the Lord suddenly took Philip away" (8:39). Philip was under the leadership of the Holy Spirit before, during, and after the evangelization of the eunuch. The Bible teacher who prays to be used to lead class members to be converted can expect that kind of leadership from the Holy Spirit.

A third way the Holy Spirit works in evangelism is in the heart of the lost person. The Spirit's leadership is prominent in the Book of Acts. One example of His work was in the life of Cornelius, the Roman centurion who was led to send to Joppa for Peter, who would tell him how to be saved (Acts 10). When Peter responded to the guidance of the Holy Spirit, he discovered a house full of people ready to respond to the gospel. The Spirit led the church at Antioch to separate Barnabas and Saul to begin their evangelistic mission (13:2). On their journey, they witnessed the work of the Spirit opening the heart of Lydia (16:14) and leading the trembling jailer in Philippi to say, "Sirs, what must I do to be saved?" (16:30).

Guidelines for Evangelistic Bible Teaching in the Sunday School

People, while they can fit in many different categories, fundamentally are spiritual beings. Who we are, what is real, what we will become, how we live, what we believe to be absolute truth, what we value, and where we will spend eternity identify the very essence of people.

All the people in a Sunday School class—whether male or female, rich or poor, black or white, single or married, young or old, educated or illiterate, live in the South or in the West, have a passive or an aggressive personality—all have one thing in common. They have a spiritual nature.

God is more concerned about a person's spiritual condition—that people have a right relationship with Him—than He is about any other issue that people face.

The Scriptures teach repeatedly that salvation is not only a life-changing experience at a specific point in time but also a process that begins at conversion and continues throughout a believer's life. Through salvation, the Holy Spirit transforms the unbeliever with a secular worldview into a believer with a Christian worldview. The goal of spiritual growth is Christlikeness (Rom. 8:29).

Paul encouraged the early Christians to move beyond the initial step of faith. Citing his own example, he urged them to run the Christian race. "I press on to take hold of that for which Christ Jesus took hold of me. . . . I press on toward the goal to win the prize for which God has called me heavenward in Christ Jesus" (Phil. 3:12-15).

A church assists people in growing and developing as believers by helping them to:

- develop biblical knowledge, concepts, and attitudes that lay the foundation for conversion and Christian growth.
- seek and to know God as revealed in Scripture and also in Jesus Christ;
- respond to Jesus in a personal commitment of repentance and faith.
- strive to follow Christ in the full meaning of discipleship;
- relate effectively to Christ's church and its mission in the world;
- obey God by being holy, set apart for service by the guidance and power of the Holy Spirit;
- grow toward spiritual maturity in Christlike values, beliefs, attitudes, and actions.

A proper understanding of the spiritual needs of members provides a valuable tool for Sunday School teachers to map and design teaching-learning objectives and ministry approaches to guide members on their spiritual journey. Teaching the Bible to believers and unbelievers provides the foundation for making disciples. Teaching the Bible provides also those evangelistic Bible study opportunities that result in knowledge and application of the Bible to life. Whether at the church on Sunday morning or through small-group Bible studies at other times and places, the key is teaching God's Word.

to make your sunday school work

As teachers prepare to teach, they must keep in mind that all the members and prospects may be at different spiritual levels. While that may seem like an insurmountable task, God's Holy Spirit surely is in the preparation and teaching of God's Word and is the One who can take the prepared material and make it real in everyone's life.

Here are some general points of which a teacher must be aware.

- Each person has a spiritual nature or life in the pre-conversion state. Strictly speaking, spiritual "growth" begins with conversion.
- The Holy Spirit is at work before conversion, convicting each lost person of his or her need for Jesus. Spiritual growth is the result of God's Spirit at work throughout the post-conversion process.
- A person does not grow into being a Christian. Rather, a person becomes a Christian—experiences a personal conversion—as the result of a personal act of repentance and faith to follow Christ.
- Teaching of foundational biblical concepts prepares people for more advanced understandings and responses.
- Although all conversions result from repenting of sin and trusting Christ as personal Savior, the circumstances, emotions, and memories of conversions vary from person to person.
- All true conversions lead to spiritual growth in Christ.
- The rate of spiritual growth is directly influenced by a person's level of maturation, including mental, emotional, and social development, and certainly church and family influence.
- God gives gifts to His people through the Holy Spirit for service in the church to enable them to witness, teach, and train people in their spiritual journey.
- While people receive eternal life at conversion, believers may experience periods of rapid growth, periods when they have plateaued, and even periods of moving back to a previous level of growth—but not to a pre-conversion state.
- The individual must understand the need to grow in Christ and make an effort and commitment to do so.

Foundational Bible Teaching and Evangelism

Conversion and a changed way of life is the goal of Bible teaching. Foundational teaching is the teaching that precedes the learner's Christian

ten best practices

conversion and baptismal experience. Learners come to understand about God, about Jesus, about self, and about the Bible. Such understanding will lead them to make a life-changing commitment to Christ under the conviction of the Holy Spirit. This foundational role of Bible teaching is expressed in the first part of Jesus' commission to His followers to "make disciples of all nations, baptizing them in the name of the Father and of the Son and of the Holy Spirit" (Matt. 28:19). Disciples are learners. Learning follows teaching. In this case, the implication is more than learning or being taught facts. It is teaching and learning that results in completely identifying oneself with God in all His fullness and power.

Teaching continues following the conversion of the learner. The role of Bible teaching at that point is to nurture converts to become faithful followers of Christ. That involves learning the truths Jesus taught and applying them through holy living and faithful service. This fulfills the second part of Jesus' command, "teaching them to obey everything I have commanded you" (Matt. 28:20). At least one goal of teaching that nurtures is to lead people to express their own obedience to the Great Commission by becoming witnesses of salvation in Jesus Christ.

Foundational Bible teaching applies to people of all ages—preschoolers, children, youth, and adults. In the case of preschoolers, children, and younger youth, the stage of foundational teaching lasts much longer, and the material and presentation are significantly simpler and more basic than a foundational presentation to older youth and adults.

Guidelines for Foundational Bible Teaching with Preschoolers and Children

Teaching preschoolers and children in Sunday School is influenced to a large degree on how you would answer the following questions.

When Does a Child Become Accountable to God?

The ultimate goal of the work with preschoolers and children is that they may someday accept Christ as Savior and live an effective Christian life.

First, the question of when a child becomes accountable must be resolved. The spiritual condition of young children should concern Christian adults. Church leaders need to know the answer to the question of

accountability so that teaching and evangelistic approaches in the church can be structured appropriately for the children.

There is no easy answer to this question, however, we have not been given a specific "age of accountability." A child becomes accountable when the Holy Spirit convicts him that he is "lost" from God—is a deliberate sinner.

Scripture indicates the following as necessary for conversion with no exception made for children:

- Conviction of personal sin against God;
- Believing God's plan to save us from sin through the death and resurrection of Jesus;
- Personal repentance of sin;
- Receiving Jesus as Savior through faith.

Only one gospel exists, and it is for adults and children alike. A person must have enough maturity to understand the basic concepts of the gospel, and the Holy Spirit must initiate and complete the process before conversion is possible.

What Spiritual Goals Do We Have for Children?

If you could determine what would happen to a newborn until he is a teenager in your church, what ideas and feelings and, what knowledge and skills, would you want him to bring to his teen years?

The years birth through age 12 should be considered years for building strong foundations for faith. They are critical years in the life of a child when she learns to trust; to make decisions; and learns biblical knowledge, skills, and principles for making right choices.

Through the teaching and personal concern of teachers and parents, children should arrive at the teen years with good foundations for following Christ as their Savior. Some will already have made their decision to trust Christ during their childhood years; others will not yet have made that decision.

The importance of childhood years for laying foundations cannot be overstated. Young children can and do learn about God from His creation and from significant people in their lives. It is critically important that parents and teachers know what to teach children and what specific ideas are appropriate for them.

What Are Some Foundations of Faith for Preschoolers and Children?

The following statements are summary, not detailed, statements of goals for preschoolers and children at church. Curriculum for preschoolers and children published by LifeWay Church Resources focuses on these goal areas. For clarity and convenience in reference, these foundation areas are separated into age groups.

Preschool Foundations—Birth-Kindergarten

God—We want preschoolers to have positive feelings about people and things associated with God. We want them to associate the created world with God.

Jesus—We want preschoolers to sense that Jesus was born, grew, belonged to a family, and was a special person. We want them to know that Jesus loves them.

Creation—We want to teach preschoolers that God made the world good and beautiful and that "Thank you, God" is an appropriate response to Him.

Bible—We want to help preschoolers think of the Bible as a special book that tells about God and Jesus.

Self—We want each preschoolers to know that God made him and to think of himself as a person of worth.

Community and World—We want to help preschoolers become increasingly aware that others are important, too. With proper guidance, preschoolers should begin to act and respond to others in appropriate ways.

Family—We want to help preschoolers become increasingly aware that God planned for families. We want them to learn some ways in which families are special to them.

Church—We want preschoolers to have good experiences at church and to have positive feeling about church.

Children's Foundations—Grades One through Six

Christian Conversion—We want to lay foundations for a genuine conversion experience on the part of each child as led by the Holy Spirit.

Church Membership—We want to lay foundations for understanding what it means to be a church member.

Christian Worship—We want to help each child know God; develop the ability to participate actively and intelligently in worship; and to find satisfaction in worship.

Christian Knowledge and Conviction—We want to help each child gain such knowledge of the Bible and Christian faith that can be related to his daily life.

Christian Attitudes and Appreciations—We want to guide each child in the continuing development of attitudes and appreciation that will encourage personal growth.

Christian Living—We want to guide each child to develop and use in everyday life habits and skills that will help her grow spiritually.

Christian Service—We want to guide each child to use his talents and skills in ways that will help others and serve God's purpose.

Evangelistic Objectives in the Sunday School

Balanced evangelistic Bible teaching seeks to lay a foundation for the learner's conversion, follow the Holy Spirit's guidance to lead the learner to be converted, and nurture converted learners to be effective disciples of Christ. The specific objectives, however, may vary somewhat between the age divisions according to the maturity level and awareness of the learners.

Evangelistic Objectives with Adults

The evangelistic objective of the adult Sunday School teacher is to lead the class in evangelizing other adults, including both unsaved class members and prospects. The fast-growing population of adults in America presents the Sunday School with its greatest evangelistic challenge and opportunity. Jesus focused His ministry on adult evangelism. The Sunday School that follows His example will place priority on evangelizing adults. Certainly, both children and youth can be saved and need to be saved, but a church cannot be a genuine church when it writes off the adult generation because adults are more difficult to reach.

The responsibility for evangelizing adults is actually shared by all age-

ten best practices

group Sunday School leaders. They must join together in an aggressive effort to lead unsaved parents and all other family members to Christ.

Evangelistic Objectives with Youth

The evangelistic objective for Youth Sunday School leaders is to guide youth to experience the saving grace of God through Jesus Christ and to make a commitment of their lives to Jesus as Lord. The need for repentance is a vital element of this salvation experience. A further evangelistic objective with youth is to lead them to become evangelists themselves by sharing their faith with other youth.

Because developmental changes come fast and furious in the youth years, youth will be excited to know that the good news of Christ's salvation affects every area of life. Following Christ helps youth to know God's abundant life now and after death. Youth need help to cope with, and be responsible for, their sexually developing bodies. They need help to cope with the emotions involved in moving them from family reliance to self-reliance. They need help in thinking through their faith so that it becomes their own. They need help in the development of moral values based upon the right personal beliefs. And they need help in choosing vocations compatible with God's will for their lives.

Sometimes youth who have made a decision for Christ as young children may begin to question their relationship to God as they move through their adolescent years. The leader of youth has the special challenge to counsel with such youth to help them determine whether their earlier conversion experience was valid. The leader may discover that some youth need to recommit themselves to a new understanding of their Christian faith.

Evangelistic Objectives with Children

The evangelistic objective with children is to prepare each boy and girl for a conversion experience. There is no uniform age that applies to every child at which they may have that experience.

As a child develops, he learns to act out adult roles to gain acceptance by his peers or by adults. Children like to please. Such childhood characteristics should prompt Sunday School leaders to take great care to eliminate any pressures either from the teacher or from other children that may cause the child to make a premature profession of faith.

to make your
sunday school work

01234567891010234567

Leaders and parents need to be sensitive to discern when the Holy Spirit is dealing with the child. Eugene Chamberlain suggested the following possible signs by which the child may give "hints" that the Holy Spirit is at work in his life:

- begins asking questions related to becoming a Christian;
- demonstrates a shift in the usual level of activity;
- exaggerates fears about things once accepted as normal;
- has more lively interest in Bible study;
- initiates conversations about spiritual matters.[1]

Evangelistic Objectives with Preschoolers

The evangelistic objective with preschoolers is to help establish a strong foundation during the preschool years that will be the basis for a later conversion. The preschool curriculum focuses upon eight major subject areas selected to develop and cultivate the preschooler's total personhood. The subject areas are God, Jesus, Bible, Church, Self, Others, Family, and the Natural World. Meaningful learning experiences in those eight areas under the guidance of a Spirit-led teacher help preschoolers to develop a sense of self-worth and trust in others that looks forward to the time when they will come to trust Christ as Savior.

Characteristics of an Evangelistic Teacher

First, an evangelistic teacher must know Jesus as Savior and Lord. You cannot introduce someone whom you do not know. Knowing Christ as personal Savior is the basic prerequisite for an evangelistic teacher. A Bible teacher should be able to remember what his life was like before he accepted Christ, how and when he accepted Christ, what Christ has meant to him since that time, and what Christ means to him today. Because many adult Christians accepted Christ as children, conscientious thought needs to go into remembering the experience and the events surrounding it.

Next, an evangelistic teacher must follow Christ's example. The way Christians live has a great bearing on their usefulness as an evangelist. This fact is particularly true among the younger age groups where children and preschoolers, and even youth, are looking to grownups for a model of Christlikeness. Lost persons have a perception of how Christians should live.

Personal integrity is a vital factor in evangelism. To lose it in the eyes of an unsaved learner is to lose the opportunity to lead him or her to Christ.

An evangelistic teacher must know and understand the people to be taught. Having that knowledge means the teacher can help learners apply Bible truths in appropriate ways. Studying books and being trained in age-group characteristics contributes to that understanding. But nothing takes the place of time spent with the learner in the Bible study hour, visiting in the home, and sharing in fellowship and other activities.

Being aware of the spiritual condition of learners also is necessary. Are your learners Christians? Are they church members? What about their family members? Such knowledge is especially significant for learners in the younger age groups. Getting to know the learner, his or her family, and the learner's circle of friends may open up a whole new world of evangelistic opportunities.

Finally, an evangelistic teacher must know the biblical plan of salvation and how to share it. Every Sunday School quarterly and leadership piece produced by the LifeWay Church Resources contains the plan of salvation to encourage unsaved learners to accept Christ and to lead learners and teachers to share Christ with the lost. The plan includes an explanation of the plan of salvation as well as appropriate Scriptures. Several passages of Scripture are appropriate when talking about salvation. You may want to choose your favorite verses, memorize them, and mark them in your Bible The important thing is to be aware of the lost learner and to be able to lead the person through the steps of repentance, confession, and trust that are required to experience new birth.

End Notes

[1]Eugene Chamberlain, *When Can a Child Believe?* (Nashville: Broadman Press, 1984), p. 12.

to make your sunday school work

Best Practice Check Up
Win the Lost

__ We give regular encouragement and provide opportunities for leaders and members to discover and contribute names of evangelistic and outreach prospects.

__ We engage in prospect-discovery actions at least one time each quarter.

__ We have a prospect file that includes both a master file and working files for each class or department in our Sunday School ministry.

__ The number of prospects in our prospect file is at least equal to the number of people enrolled in our Sunday School ministry.

__ We use our Sunday School classes and departments as the basic structure for making our evangelistic, outreach, and ministry visitation assignments.

__ We have a regular and specific time set aside for evangelistic, outreach, and ministry visitation.

__ We have a visitation assignment process in place for making assignments on visitation night as well as on Sunday morning in Sunday School classes and departments.

__ Our Sunday School leaders are trained to teach evangelistically as is appropriate for the age group they teach.

__ Our Sunday School leaders are enlisted to serve with the expectation that they will be part of the church's ongoing evangelistic ministry.

BEST PRACTICE 6
Assimilate People

"The body is a unit, though it is made up of many parts; and though all its parts are many, they form one body. So it is with Christ. For we were all baptized by one Spirit into one body—whether Jews or Greeks, slave or free—and we were all given the one Spirit to drink. Now the body is not made up of one part but many."

—1 Corinthians 12:12-14

Every church with a heart for evangelism must be concerned about assimilation. If a church has no intention or plan to care for the newborn Christian, it will not be able to sustain the excitement of evangelism. The failure to assimilate new believers into the life of the church gives a false perception that the church is growing. Evangelistic results do not automatically translate into church growth. Some churches report a large number of conversions but show little increase in Bible study attendance, giving, or other measurements of healthy growth. This suggests that those who are being won to Christ are not being assimilated into the body.

Assimilation is more than becoming a member of a group. In fact, a person may be a member but never be assimilated into the body. The goal is to help people feel that they are wanted, that they belong, and that they are needed. Just as every piece in a jigsaw puzzle is important if the picture is to be complete, every person who becomes part of a church is important and

needs to feel a sense of identity. Assimilation is helping members know where they fit in to complete the picture.

Assimilation cannot be accomplished without some small-group process in place. A church may do well at attracting people through dynamic worship, but if people are to feel wanted and needed, they need the relationships that are developed in the context of a small group. The Sunday School ministry with its open, small Bible study groups provides the most comprehensive system for ensuring that everyone of every age has the possibility of a small-group experience.

We will assimilate individuals and families into the life of the church and facilitate their growth as disciples of Christ by —
- *encouraging new believers to identify with Christ and His church through baptism and church membership;*
- *emphasizing regular participation in systematic Bible study as the foundational step of discipleship;*
- *enrolling people anytime, anywhere in ongoing Bible study and other short-term Bible study groups;*
- *providing an atmosphere for building relationships with one another in an environment of grace, acceptance, support, and encouragement;*
- *encouraging all believers to strengthen their walk with Christ by participating in various discipleship opportunities;*
- *developing a system for tracking individual and family participation in ongoing Bible study and in discipleship groups;*
- *developing a system for tracking actions that serve as indicators of spiritual growth and personal spiritual vitality;*
- *providing opportunities for new Christians and church members and their families to discover how they fit into the life and ministry of the church;*
- *planning opportunities for individuals and families to pray together and to work together toward fulfilling the Great Commission;*
- *promoting systematic biblical giving and the stewardship of life as the norm for believers.*

ten best practices

New Member Orientation and the Sunday School

New Member Orientation provides a basic orientation for all new Sunday School members and church members. Through it, they become familiar with the buildings, schedules, and ministries of their new church. By learning about the church's ministries to children, parents can find relief for their own anxieties and better address concerns of their preschoolers, children, and even youth. Moreover, such orientation is an opportunity to introduce the relationship of Bible study to personal spiritual growth.

Orientation for new members needs to be conducted by current members and workers—the teacher, youth class leader, care leaders, outreach-evangelism leader, and members who are sensitive to welcoming new members. It is best conducted, within the available organization, when one person is assigned to coordinate the assimilation efforts. Persons who do orientation need training, resources, and opportunities to access information channels and opportunities to plan and network their ideas with others.

Orientation is to be a weekly event. Contact should be made with new Bible study participants in the church. In-church contacts include: building relationships; inviting the new participant to sit with members during worship; introducing the new participant to other members of the Bible study unit; and answering questions regarding curriculum and other particularly "Baptist" processes.

While the primary place for orientation is the Sunday School class, orientation and assimilation may take place in other settings as well. For example, new members may need help finding their way around the church building or need assistance in using the hymnal, bulletin, or Bible in worship. Some encounters with new members may be intentional contacts away from the building or spontaneous meetings in the community.

Other out-of-church contacts could include phone calls, personal visits, and written cards and letters, each expressing concern that the new member have their questions answered and their needs met.

to make your sunday school work

Age Grading Aids Assimilation

Here is another word in favor of the age-graded Sunday School ministry and why it has proven to be not only an effective tool for evangelism but also for assimilation of new members. First, age-grading, dealt with in Chapter 2, creates both homogeneity and receptivity. Second, age-grading keeps the small groups from becoming stagnant and crystallized. The longer a particular group stays together, the harder it is for a new member to penetrate the group. Most small groups reach that point within the first twelve to eighteen months. Age grading and regular advancement of all classes, including adults, will counteract the tendency to crystallize. Until people feel that they have been accepted, not enough has been done to assimilate them.

Assimilate by Enrolling People in Ongoing Bible Study

In some churches, especially smaller congregations, knowing who is present and who is not present may be as easy as looking around the worship center to see if people are in their "regular" seats, that place where they tend to sit Sunday after Sunday. As the congregation grows larger, keeping track of people by sight becomes increasingly more difficult. By the time a person is missed, the situation that led to his inactivity may have escalated to the point of severity where reclamation may be nearly impossible.

One way to keep track of every member is to have every member, including current church members, enrolled in an ongoing Bible study group—a Sunday School class or department. Some churches automatically enroll new members at the time they join the church. The small group to which a person is assigned becomes a direct link for assimilation, Bible study, and discipleship.

The Power of Personal Invitation

Various research has concluded that over three-fourths of the people who join a particular church do so because of the invitation of a friend or family member. That reminds us of the power of the personal invitation. If we want people to become part of an ongoing Bible study group, the chances of that will increase dramatically if we invite them.

ten best practices

That being true, part of our strategy ought to be an intentional plan to invite prospects, guests, and new church members to attend a Bible study class or group. Someone should be given that assignment in every class. This person would call new members who joined the church one Sunday to invite them to Bible study the next Sunday. The receptivity will be enhanced if the person extending the invitation is a member of the group to which the new member is being invited. The person calling can offer to meet the person at a particular place to accompany him to the classroom and introduce him to other members. The natural person, at least in the adult class organization, to make these calls would be the class fellowship leader or a member of the class fellowship team.

Inviting people to become members of classes or departments is a way of saying we want them to be part of us. It becomes an expression of interest and concern.

Enroll Anytime, Anywhere

Because our mandate is to reach all people, there is a need for openness in the enrollment process. Rather than making it difficult to become a member of a Sunday School class, we need to make it easy. The basic requirement for a person to enroll is a desire to do so. Therefore, a person or family may be enrolled anytime, not just on Sunday, and anywhere they are encountered. No attendance requirements are necessary.

Enrollment is not to be perceived as a list of people who have proved their worth. Enrolling people is not the end of assimilation. In essence, it is the beginning. A class roll is a ministry list, not a list of dedicated Christians. The class roll ought to include persons who need to study the Bible and receive ministry and grow in the Lord. Adult and Youth Sunday School classes should include even people who have not professed Christ and who may not be regular attenders.

The general secretary in one small church noted as she completed the records for the day: "We have several 100 percent classes today. That may not be good. It may mean that we have not reached out to others but have become dependent on the 'regulars' to be here Sunday after Sunday." She understood the concept of the enrollment being a ministry list, though she may have never talked about it in those terms.

Hints for Enrolling Current Church Members

As you know, some people are members of your church but are not members of a Sunday School Bible study group. Even so, they also need to be enrolled in appropriate small groups that can be attentive to their needs and help them be assimilated into the life of the congregation beyond attendance at worship.

You may be concerned that some people would get upset and perhaps leave the church if assigned to a Sunday School small group without their being asked. While that could occur, the positive benefits of enrolling people outweighs the negative possibilities.

Implement the enrollment policy with minimal conflict by clearly communicating the need and the plan. Connect the policy with the Great Commission, which you have already acknowledged as the driving force for what you are doing through Sunday School as strategy. Explain that while attendance at small group Bible study cannot be forced, the need to enroll everyone is based on the church's desire and commitment to care for everyone. Of course, that means every small group will need to be engaged in providing the care that is essential to assimilation.

Here are a few thoughts on enrolling church members who are not currently involved in an ongoing small Bible study group.

- Obtain an endorsement for the plan from the deacons, and ask the congregation to give its approval.
- Notify all members about the plan, its intent, and how assignments will be made.
- Have ministry teams from each class or group visit all those persons assigned to them to extend an invitation to attend and to explain the value of the enrollment effort.

Hints for Enrolling New Church Members

Enrolling some new members, on the other hand, may not be difficult because they generally are not as tied to tradition or some previous practice.

- Many new members already will be enrolled and assimilated in a Sunday School Bible study group before they join the church.
- Enroll others during new member counseling or new member orientation sessions.

ten best practices

- Inform the teacher and other class leaders, especially the ministry leader or ministry team, of persons who have been assigned to their class.
- Make an assimilation visit within the week.
- Maintain regular contact and ministry through the ongoing ministry efforts of the group.

Once Enrolled, Always Enrolled

It ought to be easy to join; on the other hand, it ought to be difficult to be dropped as a class member. Sometimes leaders have the tendency to drop persons in an effort to "clean out" the roll. Dropping names is a sure way to lose contact with nonattending members and evangelistic prospects. Purging the roll seems to indicate more concern for records than for people.

Remember, records are about people. Sunday School is about people. Church is about people. We do not want to do anything that results in lost contact with people.

Some churches still are influenced by the desire to have 100 percent attendance to enrollment. That is a worthy goal, but we have learned the easiest way to achieve it is to delete the names of those who do not attend. Those people usually are the lost, the uncommitted, the spiritually immature—the people we are trying to reach.

So, what do we do with the records of those people? Here are some things not to do.

- Don't move their enrollment cards to the back of the record book or their names to the bottom of the list, as if to hide them.
- Don't write inactive across the card as if providing a warning sign to any who would be looking at the records.
- Don't move their cards to the prospect file, for usually the newest prospects get all the attention.

Instead, take some positive actions aimed at encouraging and reclaiming the inactive. Here are some suggestions.

- Keep the individual's records intact in a place where they can be seen.
- Assign FAITH teams or other class representatives to visit the individuals.
- Pray for members regularly.

to make your
sunday school work

- Organize class members to communicate with one another.
- As a leader, communicate regularly with members.
- Involve people in caring for one another.
- Provide relationship-building fellowship opportunities.
- Make it easy for absentees to come back without calling unreasonable attention before others to their presence or to their extended absences.
- Conduct projects designed to involve absentees.

Three valid reasons exist for dropping people from class membership:

    (1) the person died;

    (2) the person joined another church;

    (3) the person moved out of the ministry reach of the church.

Aside from those reasons, a person continues to be the responsibility of the class to which he or she is assigned.

Actions a Bible Study Group Can Take to Assimilate People

Assimilation is a process for enabling members to express their interest in a new member and for the new member to experience that interest on the part of others. The goal is to lead the person to that point where he or she begins to assimilate other new members into the life of the Sunday School class and church.

People who come to a Bible study group or class may be turned away by the feeling that no one is interested in them. The interest of another person, particularly someone who has the gift of influence with other people, can make a tremendous difference to a new member. Here are some ways that Sunday School classes in particular can create opportunities for expressing interest and concern for others and can build personal relationships with new members.

- *Class Greeters.*—Every class or group should have someone at the door to greet guests. Some guests will find their own way to a classroom; others may be brought to the classroom by someone from the church's welcome center. No matter how they got there, it can be intimidating to walk into a room of strangers, even if they are smiling and talking to one another. A greeter at the door can begin to help the guests feel welcome, and by introducing them to others, help them to ease into the group.

ten best practices

• *Name tags.*—No one wants to be addressed by, "Hey, You!" But failing to call people by name is not much better. Knowing people's names indicates that you have enough interest to remember who they are. Being addressed personally says that someone considers you to be significant; it is a way of saying, "You are special, so I have made an effort to remember your name." Name tags can help everyone get to know one another and help leaders in calling everyone by name in every class session.

• *Get-acquainted activities.*—Occasional get-acquainted activities can stimulate relationships. In the case of adults and youth, groups of three or four members (or couples) can be formed for informal get-togethers during a given quarter. These get-togethers can be anytime other than on Sunday mornings. Participants can use such open-ended comments as, "I came to Sunday School the first time because . . ." and complete the statement with personal information. Participants can share favorite experiences, hymns, holiday stories, childhood memories, and so forth.

• *Sunday morning Bible study.*—Sunday mornings provide an opportunity for members and guests to enjoy typical Christian fellowship. They may visit informally before and after the session. During the session, participation in Bible study becomes a common bond that can draw people together.

• *Words of encouragement and affirmation.*—This is a simple but impressive way to let people know that they are appreciated. Affirm good answers to difficult questions. Let newcomers know that their contributions are appreciated. Affirmations can be given outside class as well. Make a phone call during the week to express appreciation to a newcomer for attending a class.

• *Celebration of special occasions.*—Birthdays are something all people have, wanted or not. When the birthday of everyone in a class is celebrated in simple ways, everyone is affirmed. Monthly birthday activities build fellowship.

• *Social events.*—Do not overlook the obvious. Every newcomer and guest should be invited to every social event. Social events allow relationships to grow and barriers to disappear. When newcomers are included in fellowship events, everyone's "comfort zone" grows. Make sure that prospects are not ignored during the events. Enlist someone to "adopt" newcomers during social events. Encourage this person to introduce the newcomers to others and involve them in different aspects of the event.

• *Newsletters and printed information.*—Regardless of whether newcomers enroll immediately, including them on class mailing lists will let them know someone considers them part of the group already. Add newcomers and prospects to the list for at least six months. After this "trial period," ask prospects whether they want to continue receiving the newsletter.

• *One-on-one mentoring.*—In adult and youth classes, a spiritually mature member of the class may be assigned as a mentor to a new member to encourage spiritual growth and development. The mentor and new member may meet together regularly for prayer and additional study periods.

Record Keeping as an Assimilation Tool

A record-keeping system is a valuable tool for assimilating people into the life of the church and facilitating their growth in discipleship. Therefore, select a system (manual or computerized) that fits your church's needs and provides for recording pertinent personal, family, spiritual development, and church participation information for every individual. Train all leaders with responsibility for record keeping in effective use of the system. Provide appropriate forms to participants, and provide all necessary forms for those with record-keeping responsibilities in classes, departments, and other Bible study groups. Some record-keeping systems are available from LifeWay Church Resources. See copyright page for ordering information.

Keep Records to Minister to People

You can't provide excellence in ministry if you don't keep good records. Jesus' parable of the shepherd and his sheep in Luke 15 is a model for Sunday School class leaders in seeing the value of keeping good records. The shepherd knew that he had a sheep missing when he compared the number he was supposed to have with the actual number he had in the fold. Because he knew one was missing, he went into action to find the sheep, rescue it, and reclaim it.

A record-keeping system should be based on the purpose of Sunday School ministry: to lead people to faith in the Lord Jesus Christ and build on-mission Christians. Whether you purchase a record system from a publisher, used a computerized system, or develop your own, use records to help you to respond to people, not just for the sake of gathering a total number of participants. Keep records only on the information that can be used and will help accomplish the purpose. Asking for and recording information that no one uses creates needless work and may raise questions about the relevancy of the whole process.

Records are more than numbers. Written records or electronic printouts report on the involvement and growth of people. When used properly, records reflect the life and health of classes and departments by revealing information about members and prospects. Individual records should be compiled by each Sunday School class, department, or other Bible study group. The total record of smaller units, such as classes, within an age group make up the records for larger units, such as departments or divisions, of the age group. The total record of those larger units should be summarized on a churchwide basis by the Sunday School secretary or other designated leader. Every individual associated with a Sunday School class, department, or other Bible study group should be represented by a record in the general, churchwide record system.

A good record system begins in an up-to-date member roll and an up-to-date prospect file. Every name in the member file and the prospect file represents a person who needs a regular systematic encounter with God and the ministry of a concerned, compassionate teacher and group of Sunday School class members. The member and prospect data tell who people are, where they live, what their spiritual condition is, and to which group they have been assigned. Weekly individual member and class records tell who is and who is not present.

A record-keeping system is a tool that helps to identify people and their needs, track their participation, and give some indication of spiritual growth. The system takes the efforts of Sunday School out of the realm of generalization and personalizes it. Record keeping becomes a way in which leaders have accountability for members and members become accountable for the commitments they have made to their class, their church, and God.

If we have only records that constitute a head count, we will know how many attended Sunday School on a given Sunday, but we won't know who attended, and perhaps more importantly, who did not come. Over an extended period we may know how many came on an average Sunday, but we won't know how often any one person attended during that time.

In a class, for example, 11 people may have been present each Sunday

for Bible study, but were they the same 11 or a different 11? Were visitors included? Of those visitors, were any of them prospects who needed follow-up? With only an attendance count, those questions can't be answered.

Therefore, complete records should be kept on every member and prospect every week. Records should be taken and compiled whenever and wherever Sunday School classes, departments, or other Bible study groups meet.

Records should also identify guests on any given Sunday or meeting time. The names of guests should be given to the evangelism-outreach leader for a follow-up contact. The attendance of guests would be tracked until a connection is made with the group and ultimately a decision is made for Christ. The number and frequency of in-town visitors is important to track. This information tells how effective a class has been at inviting the unsaved.

If the church members give offerings during the Bible study group time, records can be maintained to evaluate growth in stewardship. Any other data that helps to track the spiritual growth of believers and the ministry of the group to others should be kept and reviewed periodically as part of an evaluation of the effectiveness of the group.

Records of ministry and evangelistic visits are important. Here again, the interest is not so much in the numbers as such, but in the ministry results. Records of ministry and evangelistic efforts can be reported out to the group from time to time so the class can share in the results and be aware of specific prayer needs. Let it be said, however, that information that is shared needs to be treated with sensitivity. Confidences should not be broken even as information for prayer.

A class or Bible study group will be less successful in achieving its goals if it does not take seriously the matter of record keeping. Every group needs someone who sees this task as his calling and who is gifted as a helper. See the position descriptions in chapter 3 for division, department, and class secretaries.

Use Records to Strengthen the Ministry

Leaders with responsibilities related to record keeping in a class, department, or other Bible study group should use records to build up people and strengthen the work of the church through Sunday School. Keeping accurate records is more than busy work; that is, unless the records are never put to any practical use. Use records with people in mind. Here are some ways:

ten best practices

To Evaluate

By analyzing class, department, and school records over a period of time, leaders can note areas of advancement or decline. Records can indicate spiritual decline or indifference on the part of members. Thorough records can help leaders answer questions about the effectiveness of the Sunday School as a strategy for helping a church do the work of the Great Commission. Here are some examples:

- What has happened to the total Sunday School class and department enrollment this year? Are unsaved persons being added to classes? Such questions speak to the evangelism, discipleship, ministry, fellowship, and worship functions of the church.
- What has happened to total attendance this year? This question also speaks to the evangelism, discipleship, ministry, fellowship, and worship functions of the church.
- How many members participate also in Sunday worship? Are members reading their Bibles and praying daily? Such questions speak to the worship function of the church.

Notice that the use of records helps to answer questions about people. When leaders use records in this way, they can see where people's needs exist, plan actions that address those needs, and work to bring about improvement where it is most needed.

Accurate records provide leaders with direction in planning. Having the facts at hand adds credibility to the concerns and efforts of leaders as they lead Sunday School to accomplish its objectives. Records give leaders the information needed to set priorities and goals with authority and confidence.

To Motivate

Records can be motivational tools for members. As they record their own achievements in whatever areas information is requested, they may be inwardly convinced of the need to improve a certain spiritual discipline.

As leaders review records, they may identify areas where improvement is needed. They may be areas in which the leaders themselves need to make improvements or disciplines in which the leaders need to challenge members to make improvements.

Following are a few areas of spiritual discipline that can be monitored and where encouragement can be offered, especially to individuals who are

new believers. As individuals grow in these disciplines and others, they will become more and more a part of the life and ministry of the church. They will move from talking about the church as "they" to talking about the church as "us."

Participation in systematic Bible study.—Knowing God through Jesus is the first step of discipleship. Bible study is a foundational step of discipleship for involving people in knowing more of what it means to be in the kingdom of God and how they can do kingdom ministry through the church. Members of a Sunday School class are to help one another to be accountable at this point of being faithful in attendance at Bible study time.

Involvement in corporate and personal worship.—All else that we do as a church stems from our worship of Jesus Christ as Redeemer and Lord. Until a believer comes before Christ in humble recognition of who He is, the person cannot respond in sincerity to what the Lord calls him to do and be. The Sunday School class will include times of worship, but more than that, it will encourage members to be involved in corporate worship and to engage in personal and family worship.

Commitment to biblical stewardship.—The call to follow Christ includes the submission of all we are and all we have to His lordship. We talk about giving not because we need money but because systematic giving—the tithe and the offering— is a message of Scripture and an expression of one's worship and commitment to Christ. Biblical stewardship doesn't stop with money. The stewardship of life, including our time, skills, talents, spiritual gifts, and so forth, is part of living in, and for, the kingdom. The person who is right on the matter of stewardship is usually right in almost all other spiritual responsibilities. The Sunday School leader has a prime opportunity to teach biblical stewardship and to model, not flaunt it, it before others.

Investment in ministry.—A great need among many Sunday School members is the need to move beyond thinking everything in the class is to be for their personal benefit. A significant part of spiritual growth is coming to the point of becoming aware of others and focusing attention on their needs. Opportunities need to be provided for class members to know of ministry needs and to engage in ministry action. Ministry may be such simple actions as taking a casserole as part of a meal being provided a member family, participating in a major class project to assist another member or prospect or, joining a mission team on a journey to another part of the nation or the world.

Actually, each of those disciplines have been part of many record systems in the past, where people were asked to record Bible study attendance, worship participation, Bible reading, giving, and visits made or ministries performed. In more recent years, churches generally have stopped asking for or recording such information. Perhaps it was because once the information was received it was not used in a profitable way. Such information can be useful to show where emphasis needs to be given and to help members identify areas of weakness.

Recording Enrollment and Attendance

Leaders occasionally ask if and when Bible study events beyond Sunday morning can be counted in Sunday School ministry enrollment and attendance records. Actually, the decision is a local church decision, but the suggestions below offers some suggestions that may help you to decide.

You may want to differentiate between how many persons are participating each week in ongoing Sunday School classes and departments and how many persons are participating each week in the total Bible teaching ministry at any level. Remember, ongoing small-group Bible study may meet at times other than Sunday morning. A "Sunday School" can meet on a day other than Sunday. A Sunday School class is defined by its reason for existing, not by its meeting time or designation as a small group, class, department, cell group, or other name. The question to ask is, Is this group focused on leading people to faith in Christ and building on-mission Christians? If so, it is likely a "Sunday School" class.

to make your
sunday school work

Best Practice Check Up
Assimilate People

— We encourage new believers to identify with Christ and His church through baptism and church membership.

— We have an intentional plan in place to enroll all church members in ongoing Bible study groups, using age as the primary criterion for assigning them to groups.

— We emphasize the expectation that members participate in ongoing, systematic Bible study as the foundational step of discipleship.

— We have in place a discipleship ministry that provides additional opportunities for believers to grow and mature as on-mission Christians.

— We have a record system in place that tracks individual and family participation in ongoing Bible study and discipleship groups.

— We have a record system in place that allows us to track indicators of personal spiritual growth and vitality and, in addition, a process for using the information to plan actions that address areas where spiritual deficiencies are evident.

— We provide new member orientation that helps individuals and families discover how they fit into the life and ministry of the church.

— We encourage Sunday School classes and departments to plan opportunities for individuals and families to pray together and work together toward fulfilling the Great Commission through local, national, and international mission projects.

— We promote systematic biblical giving and the stewardship of life as the norm for believers.

BEST PRACTICE 7
Partner with Families

"We will tell the next generation the praiseworthy deeds of the Lord, his power, and the wonders he has done. . . . So the next generation would know them, even the children yet to be born, and they in turn would tell their children."

—Psalm 78:4,6

The present is a link in time that joins together the past and the future. In the introduction, we briefly described how this generation of Sunday School ministry is linked to the past. While we want to help churches to have an appreciation for the past, our primary focus is on the future. The future of Sunday School ministry is dependent on churches strengthening the effectiveness of their Sunday School ministries. Someday, we want others to look back on our day with appreciation as well for being strong links in the chain of Sunday School history.

One of the strategic principles of Sunday School for a New Century is the Principle of Family Responsibility. It is through the implementation of this principle that Sunday School ministry is linked or becomes partners with God's first institution and the basic unit of all society—the family. A strong partnership between Sunday School and family will strengthen both.

How can the partnership between Sunday School ministry and family be carried out in the life of a church? That is what this chapter is about. Some

of the suggestions will be familiar because the linkage to families has been present, especially in preschool and children's departments. We will, however, consider the need for this partnership and ways that it can be made stronger and become a more intentional element in Sunday School strategy.

We will partner with parents and families to build the home as the center of biblical guidance by —

- *providing an appropriate open Bible study group for every member of the family, including family members with special needs;*
- *providing training and resources to help parents fulfill their responsibility as the primary Bible teachers and disciplers of their children;*
- *developing family-oriented evangelistic and ministry strategies that help families reach other families for Christ and the church and minister to their needs;*
- *building a leadership team that believes in and models the essential partnership of home and church in Bible teaching;*
- *providing Bible study and devotional materials that encourage and support family worship and Bible study in the home;*
- *exploring the possibilities for intergenerational ministries that enable the different generations to interact with each other rather than being isolated from one another.*

Whose Is Responsible for Bible Study Anyway?

Personal Bible study is a responsibility for every believer. Engaging in ongoing, systematic, life-changing Bible study both as a member of a group and in personal devotional time is one of the disciplines of living as a believer in Jesus Christ.

The church has a responsibility to provide Bible study opportunities. Teaching God's Word, even before it was in written form as the Bible, has been an assignment of God to His people. Jesus' ministry was characterized by teaching. The early church was a teaching church. Today's church

ten best practices

continues this emphasis on the ministry of teaching. Many churches add staff ministers with specific responsibilities in that area. We, Southern Baptists, have come to expect that our churches will engage in Bible teaching through the Sunday School ministry.

Where does the family fit in? Certainly, the family benefits from the Bible study of its individual family members. If individuals are being transformed by encounters with God through His Word, then their influence will be felt by those to whom they relate. For most, those people to whom they have the closest relationship, either in physical proximity or emotional quality, are their family members. Therefore, a family can be strengthened by a family member or members who engage in individual Bible study.

How about Bible study as a family unit? Who is responsible for family Bible study? Foremost are parents. It is to be regarded as a sacred obligation and a continuous process. Deuteronomy 4:6-9 states: "These commandments that I give to you today are to be upon your hearts. Impress them on your children. Talk about them when you sit at home and when you walk along the road, when you lie down and when you get up. Tie them as symbols on your hands and bind them on your foreheads. Write them on the door frames of your houses and on your gates."

Parents are charged to quote God's Word, read it aloud, explain it, discuss it, symbolize it, write it down, and so incorporate it into the fiber of their lives so their children will see the value of it to godly living. In short, parents are to assume the responsibility of being the primary Bible teachers and disciplers of their children.

The home is the most basic unit for biblical instruction. The home as a teaching unit becomes a microcosm of the church. The parents as leaders are to teach their children evangelistic foundational truths that lead to conversion and then to discipleship, ministry, fellowship, and worship. Neither the home nor the church can replace one another, but their success in numerical growth, spiritual growth, ministry, and worship are intertwined. The church should seek to build on, and support the work of, the home and family.

How Can a Church Be a Faithful Partner with Families in Bible Teaching and Ministry?

The church with Sunday School as its strategy will be committed to providing appropriate age-group Bible study and intent on equipping parents to fulfill their role as the spiritual teachers of their children.

Create Age-specific or Need-specific Bible Study Groups

This takes us back to examining the organizational structure in place. Organization is not just an administrative process. It facilitates outreach, evangelism, teaching, and ministry. It enables a church to employ Sunday School as strategy with a specific purpose in mind.

As part of the Sunday School ministry, every church needs to provide a designated Bible study group for every family member. This Bible study group is to be so designed as to provide an environment that is customized to the spiritual needs and development of each individual in that age group.

Earlier, we identified some Bible study groups may be needed to deal with special-needs individuals. Additional units may be needed to provide Bible teaching and ministry to the homebound, adults living away temporarily, those people with language needs, and so forth. Sunday School ministry needs to be considered a family ministry. There is a place for everyone no matter their age, need, or situation.

Provide Resources for Every Family Member

The Bible is the primary resource, the basic textbook, for Bible study through Sunday School. It should be so in the home and family setting as well. As is described in more detail in chapter 8, supplemental Bible study resources are beneficial in providing a plan for Bible study and in giving assistance in understanding how Bible truth affects life. The published learners guides and supplementary devotional resources available for each age group enhances individual, group, and family Bible study experiences.

Lead By Example

Almost everyone looks for or needs models when trying to develop new behaviors. Preschoolers, children, and youth need positive role models of

Bible truth. As stated previously, the primary role models ought to be their parents. Even so, their Sunday School leaders are responsible to be exemplary in discipleship as well. Some preschoolers, children, and youth will not have the benefit of strong parental spiritual role models. For them, it becomes even more essential that their Sunday School leaders model the powerful effects of God's Word in life.

Parents and other adults need leadership examples, too. Leaders who model family Bible experiences establish greater credibility when they talk about the need for parents to be the spiritual leaders in their homes and with family members.

Help Families To Reach Other Families

Encourage families to look for opportunities to reach other families. We frequently talk about reaching individuals, and so we should. Families sometimes come under the influence of a church's ministry and into right relationship with the Lord because one member of that family was reached. That happy circumstance does not prevent a believing family from focusing attention on a spiritually lost or unchurched family with the objective of leading the members of that family to know Christ as Savior.

Here are some actions for families to reach families:

- Identify family units who are prospects. Family unit prospects can be discovered the same way as other prospects are discovered. Rather than focus on individuals, look at the family.
- Provide training to families on how to reach other families. The purposeful training may deal with Bible study on God's will for families; on characteristics of strong, spiritually healthy families; on tips for cultivating relationships with others; on creating an accepting, caring environment within the church family; on discovering needs of prospect families; and on ministering to families with special needs.
- Include family visitation as part of the ongoing visitation ministry of the church.
- Develop a plan for enlisting church families to host Bible Clubs or other Bible study groups in their homes as a way to discover and cultivate relationships with spiritually lost and unchurched families.

to make your sunday school work
0123456789101234567

- Conduct family-oriented special events, and ask each family to invite another prospect family unit to attend as their guest. Following the event, the host family may want to invite the guest family to their home for refreshments and conversation.

Expand Your Definition of Family

Perhaps in a former time it was true that a family consisted of only a mother, father, and children. That typical family is becoming atypical in today's climate. The family picture has changed. Whether we like the change is another issue. What we are faced with is how we can respond to dysfunctional or fragmented families in our communities.

Furthermore, our focus on families needs not ignore or overlook single-parent families, single adults who have never been married, adults single because of divorce, widows and widowers, children who live in group homes or are in foster families, and senior adults who either live alone or are in assisted-living centers.

Partner with Parents of Preschoolers and Children

Preschool and Children's Sunday School department leaders can provide tools and resources for parents to use in teaching preschoolers and children the Bible at home. Leaders can build relationships with parents and communicate to parents what happens at church.

Preschool and Children's leaders and parents can link together to support and reinforce Bible teachings so the children can obtain strong spiritual foundations for conversion later in life. Parents may need help in understanding what foundational Bible truths the child has encountered in the Sunday School department and how the parent can continue that teaching at home during the week. Parents can be made aware of suggestions included in take-home resources distributed through the Preschool and Children's Sunday School departments, and other such help available through computer online channels.

In addition, your preschool and children's divisions in Sunday School provide parenting conferences, seminars, and support groups. A time may be set aside each quarter to meet with parents to build relationships and offer suggestions for continuing Bible study in the home, guiding behavior, dealing with difficult questions, reading to a child, and other topics of interest to parents of preschoolers and children.

Partner with Parents of Youth

Youth obviously are more independent than preschoolers and children. It is not uncommon for youth to be participants in Youth Sunday School even when no other family members are involved or may be only nominally involved in the church. This situation may make partnering with families a challenge to implement in Youth Sunday School. How do you partner with people who are not there? How do you partner with parents who indicate little interest in the spiritual development of their youth or themselves?

In situations where youth are the only members of their families who attend a Bible study group, here again we see the critical need for leaders to be the lesson, to be people who are real-live models of a Christian disciple. Sunday School leaders must do what they can to contribute to the spiritual development and growth of teens.

Even so, parents of youth still have the ultimate responsibility for their spiritual nurture. They obviously cannot provide that kind of nurture if they have not been born into the kingdom themselves. Youth leaders can join with the appropriate adult class or department in efforts to reach the parents of youth.

Youth Sunday School leaders will have opportunity to partner with parents of youth who are concerned about the spiritual development of their teens and who eagerly want the support Sunday School leaders can provide. Leaders need to make intentional efforts to get to know parents through in-home visits, inviting youth parents to family forums or parent-youth dialogues, and asking parents to participate in areas of youth ministry. Together, leaders, parents, and other family members can become co-workers with God to change the way that youth think, feel, and act.

Be a Partner to Adults

In the discussion about Sunday School ministry partnering with families, a heavy weight is placed on adults. Adults are the parents; the parents are to be the primary Bible teachers and disciplers of their children. While they are being attentive to that responsibility, they need also to be growing as

disciples themselves. As they grow, they are better equipped to fulfill their parental responsibility.

Adults need someone to be a partner to them. Leaders in Adult Sunday School can help to fill that need. Therefore, helping adult leaders know how they can support adult members becomes critical to the whole practice of partnership. Consider these suggestions to help you and Adult Sunday School leaders develop and strengthen the partnership between Sunday School ministry and families.

Affirm your commitment to being a partner.—The family is a powerful influence in building, or possibly destroying, personal faith. Many of us can point to ways that family members helped to shape our faith and influence who we are as Christians. Some can point to the failures and inconsistencies of family members that hindered their spiritual growth and development. Lead Adult Sunday School leaders to acknowledge the powerful influence of the family and to commit to developing the kind of partnership with families that will result in family members accepting Christ.

Collect information about the families.—This may be as simple as a collection of notes or as detailed as a computerized database. Include such information as names of family members, birth dates, anniversaries, interests, accomplishments, and so forth. Some of this information can be gathered by asking. After all, the families need to know that the collection is being done. It is not a secret. Other information can be garnered by listening to conversations, seeing news stories, and getting to know people. The body of information becomes a way to gain insight into families and open the door for ministry to them.

Meet and get acquainted with family members.—This may be accomplished by going to dinner together, attending family events, and participating in various church functions where families are involved. You can increase the effectiveness of your ministry to adults when they know you are aware of the children who are in their household. The behavior, attitudes, and feelings displayed by adults sometimes can be traced to an occurrence in the home involving their children.

Pray for the families.—Pray about specific needs of which you are aware. Ask adults to identify things affecting their families for which they want you to pray.

Encourage adults to have a regular family Bible study time.—This in-home study will be enriching not only to the adults but to the family as a unit. Adults who live alone can develop or strengthen family-style relationships by having a regular study time with neighbors or other class members who live alone.

to make your
sunday school work
0123456789101234567

Best Practice Check Up
Partner With Families

__ We provide an appropriate open Bible study group for every member of the family, including family members with special needs.

__ We provide age-appropriate Bible study resources, including devotional resources that enable families to have a regular family Bible time.

__ We build a leadership team that believes in and models the essential partnership of home and church in Bible teaching.

— We help Sunday School leaders know how to relate to the families represented by the learners in their class or department.

— We include as part of our ongoing Bible study with adults help for parents to fulfill their responsibility as the primary Bible teachers and disciplers of their children.

__ We provide information to families who are looking for other families to whom they can minister.

__ We plan some events that allow families to participate together at church rather than being in separate activities.

__ We design our ministry to be inclusive of senior adults, single adults, single parents, and children in settings other than the traditional family.

BEST PRACTICE 8
Teach to Transform

"Whatever you have learned or received or heard from me, or seen in me—
put it into practice. And the God of peace will be with you"

—Philippians 4:9

The goal of the Bible study and biblical instruction that take place in Sunday School ministry is transformed lives that exhibit love for God and others. Such lives glorify God as they are shaped by God's Word and molded by the Holy Spirit into Christlikeness, much as a potter shapes and molds clay into a useful vessel that brings to fulfillment the image he had in mind from the beginning.

The Sunday School teacher—and all other Sunday School leaders—must model the truth that God transforms lives day-by-day. The leaders must move beyond being content with transferring biblical information and calling for discussions about application to walking with their learners in obedient, Christ-centered living.

Exposing God's Word to the hearts and minds of people, both lost and saved, so that they may be transformed in Christ is what Sunday School is about! The teaching that takes place in Sunday School must do more than deal with "felt needs," where people make mental assent to biblical relevance for a "hot topic" or pressing issue. The ultimate teaching goal is that all learners—and all leaders—integrate intimately into their minds and hearts the biblical truth that sets the course for living.

to make your
sunday school work

That goal is to teach for spiritual transformation. Spiritual transformation is defined as God's work of changing a believer into the likeness of Jesus by creating a new identity in Christ and empowering a lifelong relationship of love, trust, and obedience to glorify God. Spiritual transformation begins when a spiritually lost person repents and places personal faith in Christ. It continues as the believer lives out his new identity in Christ in obedience to the Word of God.

We will engage individuals and families in the biblical model of instruction that leads to spiritual transformation by —
- *preparing faithfully for the open-group Bible teaching session, including personal spiritual preparation and participation in leadership meetings;*
- *encountering God's Word in a Bible study group guiding learners toward spiritual transformation;*
- *continuing to guide learners toward spiritual transformation in daily living and family relationships;*
- *centering the transformational teaching-learning process around these Bible teaching elements: acknowledge authority, search the truth, discover the truth, personalize the truth, struggle with the truth, believe the truth, and obey the truth;*
- *preparing open-group lesson plans to teach in a variety of ways including relational, musical, logical, physical, reflective, visual, and verbal approaches;*
- *looking for opportunities in other settings to both teach and model the message of the Bible;*
- *equipping parents to be the primary Bible teachers in their homes;*
- *choosing open-group Bible study curriculum materials that lead learners to explore the entire counsel of God during their life stages;*
- *providing the best possible teaching resources that enable teachers to teach for spiritual transformation;*
- *providing the best possible space and equipment as appropriate for age-group teaching and learning.*

ten best practices

The Teacher: The Point Person for Sunday School Ministry

Sunday School sometimes is thought of as only a teaching organization. In this book, we have broadened this understanding of Sunday School to identify it as a foundational evangelism and discipleship strategy. Teaching is a means to that end. It is not the end in itself. We teach so that lives may be changed by the power of God.

Moreover, the open Bible study group, which is the key element of Sunday School ministry, is the vehicle for engaging people in doing what a church does: evangelism, discipleship, ministry, fellowship, and worship. The Bible study group does not exist just a a teaching group. It is a group that focuses as well on discipling one another, caring for one another, and so forth. The Bible study group, or Sunday School class, then, is a multi-faceted group. All the facets need to be kept in balance for the group to accomplish it purpose and for it to be an enjoyable and profitable experience for all participants.

The teacher is the point person to ensure that this balance is maintained. Therefore, Sunday School teachers should not be selected solely on the basis of their Bible knowledge and ability to communicate. Those elements represent part of the task, but not all of it. This in no way is intended to minimize the teaching function. As we will see, this function is critical. The teacher must, however, see his role as more than presenting a 45-minute lesson. The teacher is the catalyst for leading the class to fulfill its purpose. He must understand clearly and fully embrace that purpose.

Teach the Bible Effectively

The first goal of the teacher is to teach the Bible with conviction and excitement. To do so, the teacher must also be a good learner, one who is committed to personal Bible study, lesson preparation, and participation in training events and leadership meetings.

The Bible is the text. Taught plainly and with conviction under the inspiration of the Holy Spirit, the Word of God is powerful in its effects. Help for teaching the Bible with effectiveness with spiritual transformation in mind is offered as this chapter continues.

to make your sunday school work

Embody the Lesson

The teacher serves as an object lesson that accompanies the taught lesson. This is not to suggest that the teacher must be perfect to be qualified to teach. All believers are on a spiritual pilgrimage, continuing to be transformed into the image of Christ. That being said, the teacher should be characterized by some non-negotiable traits.

- A clear testimony of a personal relationship with Jesus Christ.
- Actively shares his faith in Christ with others
- Models the Christian home.
- Practices the Christian disciplines.
- Gives evidence of spending time alone with God.
- Committed to the church through participation in worship, the practice of stewardship, and support for the mission and ministry of the church.

Birth New Classes

This subject is dealt with more completely in chapter 10, "Multiply Leaders and Units," but a brief word is appropriate when discussing teaching and teachers. Every class or open Bible study group should have as its goal the birthing of a new class or group every year. The teacher needs to take the initiative at this point in raising the need, challenging the current class, and urging a core group to be part of the new unit.

Reproduce Themselves

Every teacher should establish a goal to discover and mentor one new teacher each year. A gifted teacher who becomes selfish and is unwilling to send class members out to serve is voiding any lesson he has taught on responding to the call of God to serve. The highest compliment that can be given to any teacher is that the teacher is known for producing other teachers and encouraging class members to seize opportunities to serve under the call of God.

ten best practices

Essential Practices for Teaching People God's Word?

Simply stated, here are three essentials for Sunday School teachers who want to engage in Bible teaching that leads to spiritual transformation. These essentials are summarized in three words: prepare, encounter, continue.

- Before the teaching session, *prepare* the ministry environment for spiritual transformation.
- During the session, guide the learners toward spiritual transformation through an *encounter* with God's Word in a Bible study group.
- After the session, *continue* to guide learners toward spiritual transformation in daily living and family relationships.

Prepare

Begin with the ministry environment. A ministry environment includes the teaching-learning setting. Attention must be given to the physical setting—walls, chairs, and visuals, for example. But the ministry environment is much more. It includes also the relationships of those in the class or group. The teacher will want to create an environment in which everyone feels welcome and wanted—including the Holy Spirit.

What's the best way to make such preparation? Here are two tried and proven strategies—Sunday School leadership meetings and personal Bible study.

Prepare Through the Sunday School Leadership Meetings

Sunday School leadership meetings help teachers and other leaders to prepare through praying together and focusing on the three elements of Sunday School ministry. These elements were introduced earlier when we discussed the leadership meeting in chapter 3. Nevertheless, look at them again in this context.

- *Focus on the Mission (10 min.)*

During this portion of the leadership meeting, the department director guides teachers and other leaders to relate the work of their department and classes to the overall vision and mission of the church. Everyone finds out about churchwide and age-group events and emphases. Also, organizational issues, records, and other administrative concerns are addressed.

• *Focus on Relationships (25 min.)*

During this time, the needs of members and prospects are assessed and, as appropriate, plans are made for responding. Approaches are determined for being involved with members and prospects beyond the Sunday session, especially ways to involve members in evangelism and ministry. Fellowship activities and assimilation actions also may be planned.

Witnessing and ministry approaches should be reviewed. Churches using FAITH Sunday School Evangelism Strategy will use this time to review assignments, give reports, and make follow-up assignments.

• *Focus on Bible Study (25 min.)*

Teaching for spiritual transformation is facilitated when leaders work together to plan the best ways to bring participants into an encounter with God's Word in the Sunday morning Bible study group. As teachers and leaders plan together, what is planned in department time interfaces with what will be done in class time. Such intentional planning maximizes the impact of God's Word on the hearts of individuals and the group as a whole.

In addition, teaching methods can be previewed and adapted. New approaches can be created. Previous Bible study sessions can be evaluated and assignments made for the upcoming study.

Finally, the weekly leadership team meeting is a good time to pray for each other as leaders and teachers. That will do wonders to improve the Sunday morning Bible study experience!

Prepare Through Personal Bible Study

Beyond the Sunday School leadership meeting, the teachers must first prepare personally for God to use them to teach His Word. As teachers prepare for the Bible teaching session, they are to ask God to speak to them personally about their own walk with Him. As God creates personal conflict and conviction in their preparation to teach or lead, they may come to a point of fresh surrender to the Lord's leadership in their lives.

The depth of the ministry environment is directly related to the teacher's own depth of spiritual transformation. Therefore, teachers need to begin with prayer, making themselves available to God to depend upon Him. Then, they can engage in intercession on behalf of others and about needs within the

ten best practices

departments, classes, and their families. In addition they can pray for their fellow leaders.

Second, teachers prepare so that their learners can encounter God's Word. Using information and ideas from the Sunday School leadership meeting, teachers should do as much as they can to magnify caring relationships among participants. When teachers lead people to experience New Testament fellowship—sharing the common life found in Christ—during the Bible study session and throughout the week, then, like Jesus, they will find opportunities to communicate biblical truth in a variety of settings, dilemmas, and crises. The depth of relationship with the learner will affect how well that learner will be motivated to participate in the Bible study session.

Here are some factors for teachers to consider to help them prepare to lead their learners into an encounter with God's Word.

1. *Teachers need to learn to enjoy the people they teach.* If people hear their teachers affirm and accept them, they will more likely be responsive to the teachers' guidance from the authority of God's Word.

2. *Teachers need to make sure that ministry to the individual's needs takes place.* One practical reason to keep classes small is to be able to attend to individual needs. The wise teacher will organize the individuals in the class in such a way that participants can care for one another and can receive care.

3. *Teachers need to be prepared to teach people God's Word in, and through, their families.* The home is the first place where God desires Bible teaching for spiritual transformation to occur (Deut. 6:6-8). Because the Bible emphasizes the primary responsibility of parents and families in spiritual instruction, Bible teaching sessions and the resources used before, during, and after the sessions should support and encourage spiritual growth and understanding within the context of the home. For example, teachers should intentionally challenge participants to share what they learn with their family members.

4. *Teachers need to prepare to teach people in a variety of ways.* The role of the teacher is to guide learning in ways that facilitate the work of the Holy Spirit to transform learners' lives. This includes recognizing the ways in which learners learn best. Teaching people God's Word more likely will bear fruit when teachers relate to them with the teaching-learning approaches they prefer. Teachers must seek to connect not only with the learner's intellect but also with the learner's heart.

to make your
sunday school work

For more specific help in building a teaching ministry focused on spiritual transformation, see the book *Teaching the Jesus Way: Building a Transformational Teaching Ministry,* by Jay Johnston and Ronald K. Brown. For help with understanding appropriate teaching approaches and methodology for each age group, see the books in the Teaching for Spiritual Transformation series produced by LifeWay Church Resources.

Encounter

During the session, teachers are to guide people toward spiritual transformation through an encounter with God's Word in a Bible study group. This is accomplished through the following seven key elements that characterize the transformational teaching-learning process.

1. Acknowledge Authority

The key word related to this element is *control*. Teachers must discern as far as humanly possible what authority, power, assumptions, presuppositions, worldview, or rule guides or controls the life of each participant. Ultimately, teachers want to address the fundamental life questions common to all people: *Where did I/we come from? How do I/we fit in? Where am I/we going?*

Knowing where people are "coming from" will help teachers choose teaching approaches that will motivate the learners and engage them more readily in the Bible study session. Key questions for discerning the authority in participants' lives are such questions as these: *Where is your heart—what is the most important authority in your life—as you approach Bible study? What grips your life—including developmental issues associated with "growing up" or generational issues associated with living in this era? What assumptions—maybe prejudices—do you have about the Bible, this subject, or the people in the Bible study group?*

This element identifies an assumption that teachers must make for every session, specifically that every participant comes to a Bible teaching session with an authority—recognized or unrecognized—that controls his or her life. Knowing each participant and what controls his or her heart will give the teacher insight in how to guide the person to participate in the Bible study. The ultimate goal is to lead participants to accept the authority of God and His Word as the sovereign rule over all of life.

ten best practices

2. Search the Scriptures

The key word is *content*. Searching the Scriptures is what most people associate with Bible teaching—reading, examining, and communicating the content of the Bible. And this element of Bible teaching is probably what most Christians have done best. In searching God's Word, answer this question: *What did God say in the Scriptures to the first readers or hearers?*

To answer this question most effectively, Bible teachers should examine:

- *The linguistic factor*—the intended meaning of words and phrases, the relationship of words, and the kind of literature in a particular part of the Scriptures;
- *The historical factor*—the setting, including the customs of the time, the land, and the people of the Bible, the language of the Bible, and the archaeology of the Bible;
- *The holistic factor*—Scripture compared to Scripture in light of how the entire Bible treats that particular truth or concept.

Careful study of what the Bible said to its original readers leads to another question: *What abiding truth(s) for all generations is the Holy Spirit teaching from the Scripture?* Answering that question takes us to the third element in the transformational teaching-learning process.

3. Discover the Truth

The key word for this element is *concept*. The Bible is much more than a book of history. It has eternal truths and principles that relate to today's life issues and life questions. In other words, *How do we understand these truths and communicate them?* There are two different approaches that can be taken.

One, the teacher begins with a single "Biblical Truth" or "Central Bible Truth," studies the Scriptures, and then calls for the learners to apply the truth to their lives. The teacher's role is to communicate effectively the biblical truth and to create a climate for learners to engage the biblical truth. For the most part, the teacher controls the pace, sequence, and content of instruction to cover.

In the second approach, the teacher begins by selecting a passage and calling upon learners to read it and name the truths they identify in the passage. The teacher's role in this approach is to guide learners effectively

so they can discover personal biblical truths, then help them to apply biblical truth and principles to their daily lives. The teacher does not simply tell the learner the biblical content or truth but seeks to guide the learner to express what he or she thinks it says and means. Through individual study and through group discussion, each person is given an opportunity to respond and to take steps toward changing or transforming the way he or she thinks and acts.

Which approach is best for helping people "discover the truth"? The Holy Spirit can use either or both approaches effectively. A teacher may select elements from both teaching-learning approaches to create a blended plan that is right for the group. Or, the teacher may choose one approach based on his personal giftedness, the context in which the Bible teaching session is conducted, the preferred learning approaches of the participants, or the content of the study. The key is variety.

4. Personalize the Truth

The key word for the fourth element of the transformational teaching-learning process is *context*. Important questions to answer are these: *Based on the abiding biblical truth(s), what is God teaching me personally about thinking, feeling, and living today? What is God teaching people in their personal lives?*

In this part of the Bible study process, the teacher's understanding of the life context of the learners plays a critical role. Is the person lost or saved? If the learner is not a Christian, how can the truth be understood from his or her point of view? How does the person's cultural, generational perspective, age, or life stage influence how he or she will personalize this truth? If the teaching method is not connecting, perhaps due to a disability, what is another approach that can be used to help the participant to personalize the truth?

Again, here is where you as teacher are totally dependent upon the Holy Spirit's presence with you, in you, and through you in the teaching process. The learner also has to determine how open he or she will be to the Spirit's ministry. And that brings us to the next element.

5. Struggle with the Truth

The key word is *conflict*. Any time sinful humans encounter the truth of God's Word, there will be a struggle. Some questions to ask are these: *What*

ten best practices

conflict or crisis of belief is the Holy Spirit bringing about in my heart and life to challenge what I think and value and how I live? What life questions, problems, issues, or struggles compel me to seek answers and promises in the Bible? What aspect of my thinking and belief system needs to be changed?

Conflict is the work of the Holy Spirit. He may use what has been taught, how the learners were involved, or the teacher's own testimony. The teacher cannot create this internal spiritual conflict on his own, however. Real "application to life" intensifies when we allow learners to be honest with how God's Word creates conflict in their hearts, minds, and lives.

6. Believe the Truth

Its key word is *conviction.* These questions arise: *How is the Holy Spirit leading me to live and repent—to change my mind, my values, or the way I live—or to resolve the struggle or conflict in my life? What new truth is God leading me to receive and integrate into my life?*

Conviction is the point at which spiritual transformation becomes most intense, for conviction addresses the human will. At this stage—if the learner has been open to the leadership of the Holy Spirit—the learner is confronted by or convicted with, a change that needs to be made in his or her life in order to become a Christian or to become more Christlike. When a person accepts God's Word as truth and then repents, such repentance is without regret (2 Cor. 7:9-10). People who place their trust in God will not be disappointed (Ps. 22:5; Rom. 10:11).

7. Obey the Truth

Its key word is *conduct.* The "bottom line" question is this: *To what extent will I obey the Holy Spirit's leadership in what I think and value and in the way I live?*

In the Bible, the word *believe* carries with it more than intellectual assent. In the Bible, believers showed their faith by acting on their faith. In recent years, almost everyone has insisted that Bible study resources "apply the Bible to life." Yet, experienced Bible teachers realize that application means more than merely making a mental connection of biblical truth to a life issue. Faithfulness to obey God's Word is the ultimate application. People who are being spiritually transformed depend upon the Holy Spirit to

provide the power for living in obedience to God. Because their old human nature has been crucified with Christ, believers set their minds on Christ who strengthens them.

Review of the Seven Bible Teaching Elements

The seven Bible teaching elements of control, content, concept, context, conflict, conviction, and conduct rarely will be completed before the end of a 60-minute Bible study session. For the Holy Spirit to transform lives, however, all elements should be experienced by leaders and participants before, during, and after the session. In addition, the amount of time devoted to the seven Bible teaching elements will vary based on the different life situations. While some people may need these elements in specific, sequenced steps, other learners may prefer that the elements occur in a different sequence or repeatedly throughout the session. The elements can be repeated throughout a session or over a period of several lessons in a unit, much as a spiral advances upward through a series of repeated movements.

Continue

Because God uses His Word to transform lives after the session concludes, teachers continue their teaching ministry 24 hours a day, 7 days a week. They continue to guide participants toward spiritual transformation in daily living and family relationships. Actually, spiritual transformation into the image of Christ is a lifelong process. Teachers need to plan to lead learning that continues to facilitate the Holy Spirit's ministry for as long as the Lord allows a ministry to the person or his or her family.

Continue means helping the learners connect the everyday experiences with the larger picture of what God has planned for their lives. *Continue* also means getting the Word of God off the page and bringing it to life in the minds and hearts of the participants.

Learning occurs all the time. Some of the best learning experiences are spontaneous. Teachers can continue teaching by helping people connect new truths with what they already know. When people see that God's "abundant life" for them is spiritual transformation into Christlikeness, they will have a framework that the Holy Spirit can use to help them make sense of their day-to-day problems, questions, victories, and joys.

People desperately want to make sense of what is happening with God,

ten best practices

their friends, their family, their church, their careers, and their world. Sunday School teachers can continue their teaching ministry in many different settings—in the workplace, at school activities, in conversation with parents and other family members, on church trips, in one-on-one times. Encourage youth and adult teachers to enlist participants as class team leaders to help "continue" the teaching.

Based on the Bible study and in obedience to the Holy Spirit, teachers can use in conversations, cards, letters, or emails to members such questions as these to further explore after the session:

- What command did God present?
- What promise did God make?
- What truth did God teach?
- What attitudes, behaviors, or values will you make a part of your life?
- What relationships are you developing in your life that are a part of your journey of becoming a Christlike believer?

As teachers continue to teach, they will have opportunity to work with the families of participants. Much of what influences the people in Sunday School classes, especially the amount of support participants receive from their families and the kind of acceptance and affirmation they get from others, is beyond our control. Nevertheless, we must do all we can to connect with home, friends, school, or work. Teachers do have control over the environment at church or in their Bible study group. We must create positive ministry environments there and maintain seven-day-a-week instruction based on the truth that learning can occur anytime and anywhere. Love for teaching people God's Word has no limits (1 Cor. 13).

In light of what you have read, how can you as a general leader—

- be more aware of the kinds of preparation being done by classes and departments?
- enable your team to lead participants to encounter God consistently through life-changing Bible study?
- communicate that learning can and does continue?

to make your sunday school work

Prepare

The ministry environment

Sunday School Leadership Meeting

Personal Bible Study

Encounter

God's Word in a Bible study group

Acknowledge Authority (control)

Search the Truth (content)

Discover the Truth (concept)

Personalize the Truth (context)

Struggle with the Truth (conflict)

Believe the Truth (conviction)

Obey the Truth (conduct)

Continue

Teaching-learning in daily living and relationship

3 Essentials of Bible Teaching for Spiritual Transformation

Spiritual transformation is God's work of changing a believer into the likeness of Jesus by creating a new identity in Christ and by empowering a lifelong relationship of love, trust, and obedience to glorify God.

ten best practices

12345678910123455678

Choosing Curriculum for Sunday School

First of all, exactly what is curriculum? Essentially, curriculum refers to the course, track, or path on which a person runs, so to speak. Choosing *Bible study* curriculum means pursuing the course that *the Bible* sets for life—Christlikeness, transformation into the image of Christ. Sunday School curriculum is the continuous course, process, or system for Bible study groups to use to guide unbelievers toward faith in Christ and believers toward Christlikeness through the transformational power of the Holy Spirit. Curriculum sometimes can be a sprint, like a 100-meter dash—a short course. Ultimately, however, curriculum should be viewed as a marathon, for in the final analysis, the track of study the leader and learners choose shapes their worldview.

There are two aspects of curriculum: the curriculum plan and the curriculum resources. The curriculum plan sets the course for *wha*t is studied. The curriculum resources contain the curriculum plan and set forth *how* to study it.

Getting on the Right Curriculum Track

A curriculum plan, or "curriculum map" as some call it, is an orderly arrangement of Bible study content organized so that Sunday School leaders can engage the learner in the study of God's Word to meet spiritual needs through planned teaching-learning experiences.

An ongoing Sunday School ministry begs for an ongoing Bible study curriculum plan. What guidelines should you use to select or develop an ongoing curriculum plan for your church, and why will such a plan keep you on an exciting and fruitful track?

1. When choosing a curriculum plan, choose one that covers all of the Bible's content, not just selected or "favorite" parts.

"All Scripture," Paul wrote, "is . . . useful for teaching, rebuking, correcting and training in righteousness" (2 Tim. 3:16). That is, make sure that the curriculum plan is comprehensive of all of the Bible and all of life concerns that people face over a specified length of time.

2. Choose a plan that has a balance of biblical content, Bible study approaches, and life issues.

For example, the plan should contain a balance of Old Testament studies, the life of Christ, and New Testament epistles. The plan could contain a balance of approaches to studying the Bible, such as studying through a Book of the Bible, a character in the Bible, or a topic or life issue.

Why not just choose whatever people want to study or whatever the current "hot topic" or surfacing "felt need" is? By following a systematic, comprehensive plan, ongoing Bible study points repeatedly to the fact that the Bible, not developmental life needs and human issues, must guide and shape believers' lives. If a Sunday School leader selects studies that address only age-group needs and issues, then the leader risks supplanting the Bible's goal for believers with contemporary perceptions of age-group needs and issues. Occasional topical, issue-oriented studies are beneficial and are included in ongoing curriculum plans, but the ultimate goal of the Bible and of the Sunday School curriculum is to lead people toward faith in Christ and transformation toward Christlikeness.

While He was responsive to immediate physical, emotional, and spiritual needs, Jesus did not always teach on subjects the people wanted—their "felt needs." Jesus was aware that there were deeper issues of the human heart that went beyond the current issues of the day—ceremonial washing of hands, Sabbath laws, and getting caught in adultery. Jesus' curriculum plan focused on redemption, the cross, and transformation of human lives, beginning with the human heart.

Make sure that the curriculum plan has a balanced diet of biblical truth and life issues. Yes, the plan needs to address head-on where people are. Even so, a balanced curriculum plan will not only address the "hot topics" and "felt needs" but also studies that will place people on the path toward mature biblical faith, such as being in Christ, being empowered by the Holy Spirit, being a faithful witness, caring for a lost world, and developing a biblical worldview.

3. Confirm that the curriculum plan is properly sequenced so that learners can build on what they already know.

A systematic approach to Bible study facilitates the integration of biblical truth into the learner's life as a lifelong, ongoing process. Jesus built on what His hearers already knew and took them to a new level when He said, "You have heard that it was said . . . But I tell you. . . ." (Matt. 5:43-44).

Remember that spiritual transformation into Christlikeness is a lifelong process. Appropriate repetition of biblical content and life concerns in different ways and at different times strengthens learners. At the same time, open Bible study groups will always have new people joining the group—new learners who need the basics the veteran learners could help teach.

4. A planned, ongoing Bible study strategy is most conducive to creating a ministry environment that fosters strong relationships and regularly invites the lost to believe in Christ.

Ongoing groups have a fixed organizational structure that provides more stable leadership over a longer period of time. A ministry environment of grace and acceptance takes time for God to create.

In addition, one important aspect of creating such a ministry environment is helping to prepare the participants to hear God's message for a particular time. A planned, ongoing Bible study strategy is a wise discipline for the person who wants to hear God speak and is seeking to obey God's direction. By submitting to a disciplined, lifelong approach to listening to God through His written Word, we do not presume to know exactly what God would say to us. Instead, we demonstrate a commitment to love God and His Word—all of it; to trust God and His Word—all of it; and to obey God and His Word—all of it. Studying and then teaching an ongoing, well-designed curriculum plan demonstrates a heart that is ready to be transformed.

With regard to curriculum planning, or "curriculum mapping," God knows the timeliness of any study for any individual's life, as well as for one's time and circumstances. Through the leadership of the Holy Spirit, God will guide those He has placed in strategic places of leadership in discerning the lessons and messages He has for those who will receive them. Curriculum planners carry a tremendous accountability to seek God's direction actively and then to receive, and obey faithfully, His direction.

The Holy Spirit can work in the hearts of curriculum planners months and years in advance to design studies that are truly God's message for a particular time. Those who design comprehensive, balanced, and properly sequenced Bible study plans always will seek to hear God's voice to choose Bible studies that help believers come face-to-face with God's message in order for them to take it to their communities, culture, and world.

to make your sunday school work

Choose the Best Curriculum Resources

In regard to choosing the curriculum resources, make sure that the resources express the curriculum plan that meets these four principles just stated and accomplishes the ministry goals God wants you to fulfill. Materials produced by LifeWay Church Resources contain Bible study curriculum plans that are comprehensive, balanced, properly sequenced, and conducive to ongoing ministry. In all addition, LifeWay curriculum resources, whether print, video, audio, electronic, or multimedia —

- guide churches to fulfill the Great Commission through the five essential functions for church growth—evangelism, discipleship, ministry, fellowship, and worship;
- provide sound, reliable interpretation of the Bible from a conservative point of view;
- offer clear support for evangelism, including the FAITH Sunday School Evangelism Strategy;
- provide a variety of age-appropriate, timely, and relevant teaching-learning approaches, all of which lead learners toward faith in Christ and spiritual transformation into Christlikeness;
- supplement teaching-learning plans with resource kits and leader packs containing creative posters and teaching aids and with free online *EXTRA!* teaching supplements containing the latest news, research, and other ideas on this Web site: *www.lifeway.com*;
- provide choices of Bible study options that feature comprehensive, balanced, sequenced, and ministry-conducive curriculum;
- offer a variety of reasonably priced, easy-to-use, and attractive learner and leader resources in print, audio, electronic, and multimedia formats;
- feature biblical insights and teaching approaches written only by Southern Baptists experienced in Sunday School ministry in churches;
- provide financial assistance for various Southern Baptist ministries;
- offer an optional devotional and reading guide to deepen participants' daily commitment to love, trust, and obey God that are based on the Bible study participants study on Sunday;
- contain leader, teacher, and learner development features to engage

and equip persons in the full ministry of evangelism, discipleship, ministry, fellowship, and worship through Sunday School.

Why Use a Learner's Guide?

The teaching-learning process is a two-sided coin. On the one hand, people have certain expectations of Sunday School teachers and leaders. On the other hand, Sunday School leaders have certain expectations of the participants. Most people usually arrive for Bible study with little or no personal preparation for the Bible study experience or for ministry opportunities. That lack of preparation and anticipation is rooted in a wide range of issues, from low motivation for spiritual growth to time limitations. Can the most significant factor be traced to the leader's low expectations and lack of planning for participants' involvement before, during, and after the session?

To help people get the most out of Bible teaching-learning before, during, and after the session, Sunday School leaders should take advantage of the most strategic tool other than the Bible itself—the learner's Bible study guide.

Bible study learner guides are designed to:

- provide readers with features on how to become a Christian and live for Christ. What other resource, week in and week out, better communicates the primary purpose of an open Bible study group than a well-designed learner's guide that prominently features the plan of salvation?
- help people to develop Bible knowledge and Christian convictions based on sound biblical exposition. Where else can people learn more consistently what the Bible teaches on the Christian faith?
- encourage learners to develop lifelong Bible study skills and Christian disciplines by providing Bible study helps. What better way is there to help people learn to study the Bible, pray, and feed themselves spiritually than through a well-planned learner guide?
- provide attractive visuals that engage people in reflective questions and biblical insights. How often do people find photography and illustrations that beg them to examine and integrate God's Word?
- challenge readers to make a personal commitment to obey what God

to make your sunday school work

is teaching them. What tool will you provide after the session for God to use to reinforce the truths you teach on Sunday morning to help them to love, trust, and obey God in their daily lives?

- support a diversity of learning preferences. How will people learn it all during a single Sunday session? When will those who prefer to learn alone have their best opportunity to learn and obey the Scriptures?
- provide leaders with an economical tool for involving people during the session for Bible research and response. How much more does it cost in time and church resources to prepare or duplicate handouts in comparison to multi-page, full-color resources that are economically priced?
- assist people in preparing for Bible study sessions. Where is the easiest place for participants to discover what the Scripture passage is for the next session?

To strengthen the Bible study experience, provide a Bible study guide for each Bible study participant and prospect. Use the learner guide in the Bible study session as a tool for exploring the Bible passage. Show participants how to use the learner guide as a spiritual growth resource after the session. Finally, hold learners accountable for obeying what God teaches from Sunday to Sunday.

Determining Space and Equipment Needs

A church needs to provide the best possible space for small-group Bible study. Exquisite space with the latest equipment and furnishings may not be available, but any space can be made clean, appealing, and functional.

Classrooms should be made ready for Bible study prior to members' arrival on Sunday morning. The classroom should be designed and furnished for the age group that meets in it. That includes having proper-size chairs, adequate room for the participants, marker boards, and other items as needed. See the equipment and furnishings chart for each age group on pages 205-207.

Where chairs are used, they should be arranged to facilitate the teaching style appropriate for the age group and the lesson. For example, to

ten best practices

encourage discussion, arrange the chairs so that the class members can see each other.

Also give attention to the arrangement of the chairs in relationship to the entry points to the room. Avoid embarrassing late arrivers by placing chairs so people do not enter the front of the class. That is especially important when thinking about newcomers who may arrive late.

The classroom space needs to be well lit, bright, and freshly painted. A comfortable temperature should be appropriately maintained. The general appearance and feel of the room will indicate the leader's level of commitment to an effective Bible study ministry.

Analyze all space using the guidelines provided in the chart on page 204. Determine the total square footage of space that can be used in Bible study for all the age groups. In doing the analysis, consider that it is difficult to sustain attendance beyond 80 percent of the room's capacity in classrooms where members attend by choice. For example, 12 babies may be placed in an area with a capacity of 12, but adults generally will not attend a class that is regularly more than 80 percent filled.

Maximizing Use of Space

You will recall in the discussion about expanding the organization that space is a factor. Every unit must have some place to meet. What if your space is limited? Here are some suggestions for making the most of the space that is available.

Available Space

Take a "space walk" to look at and physically count all the space throughout the building. The most complete count will include recording the dimensions of the space. This may be simplified if architectural drawings are available for your review. Don't overlook any space; don't evaluate space yet.

Adjust Space

By examining how space is currently used, you may see adjustments that need to be made. The information in this chapter will help you to know how much space is needed for each age group. With this information in hand, you may determine the need to move some larger groups into larger rooms

to make your sunday school work

currently occupied by smaller groups. Perhaps more than one adult group can meet in opposite ends of a larger room.

Adapt Space

Some areas may not be ideal classroom space, but they may be adapted for use for an interim period of time. A kitchen, an office, a hallway, or a storage room are possibilities.

Adjacent Space

Don't limit your look to the inside of the building. Look around outside the building, as well. Identify some homes or buildings nearby the church building that may be used as space for a Bible study group.

Additional Space

Of course, adding space is an option, albeit an expensive one. When building new space, plan wisely with long-term objectives in mind.

Multiple Use of Space

An inexpensive and available way to reach more people, solve the space crunch, and avoid the struggles associated with a major building project is to make multiple use of spaces. Using space more than once is good stewardship of resources. Moreover, the more time options your church provides for small-group Bible study, the more opportunities you have to reach people because not everyone is available at the same time no matter what time you have Bible study when you have it only one time.

In cases where the church has more worship space available than small group space, the Sunday morning schedule may be:

Sunday School: 8:30—9:30 a.m.

Worship: 9:45—10:45 a.m.

Sunday School: 11:00 a.m.—12 noon.

If the worship space and small group space is essentially equal, the schedule may be:

Sunday School/Worship: 9:30—10:30 a.m.

Sunday School/Worship: 11:00a.m.—12 noon.

ten best practices

By using the latter schedule, one-half of the congregation is encouraged to attend Bible study groups before worship time; the other half is to attend Bible study groups following worship. In this arrangement, members need to commit themselves to a particular meeting time so they can be identified with a class.

A word of caution: don't act too hastily. Many issues must be considered before launching into multiple-use options: schedule, size of leader base, leader enlistment, organization and coordination of the Sunday Schools, and prospect assignments. Here is a simple timetable to implement a multiple-use and meeting times schedule.

1. Study needs and options—24 months in advance of anticipated beginning date.
2. Present the need and rationale to the church—18-20 months in advance.
3. Orient the church to the concept—12-14 months in advance.
4. Prepare a schedule and tentative organization—8-12 months in advance.
5. Allocate space; begin enlistment and training of workers—6-8 months in advance.
6. Ask members to choose the meeting time in which they prefer to enroll—4-6 months in advance.
7. Complete enrollment process and organization—2-4 months in advance.
8. Launch and maintain the multiple-space use and meeting time schedule.

to make your sunday school work

Meeting Space Specifications Chart

Advantages of Multiple Meeting Times

- Increase use of education space
- Provide for efficient use of buildings
- Maintain growth with little additional outlay of money
- Offer more service opportunities and utilize more people
- Make funds available for missions and expansion of other ministries
- Give members a choice of times, departments, and leaders
- Extend the outreach potential of Sunday School ministry
- Demonstrate responsible stewardship
- Conserve energy

Age Group	Space/Person	Maximum Enrollment	Room Size	Leader: Learner Ratio
Preschool				
Babies	35 sq. ft.	12	420 sq. ft.	1:2
Ones–Twos	35 sq. ft.	12	420 sq. ft.	1:3
Threes–Pre-K	35 sq. ft.	16	560 sq. ft.	1:4
Kindergarten	35 sq. ft.	20	700 sq. ft.	1:5
Children				
Grades 1-6	20-25 sq. ft.	24	480-600 sq. ft.	1:6
Youth				
Gr. 7-12 (class)	10-12 sq. ft.	12	120-144 sq. ft.	1:12
Gr. 7-12 (dept.)	8-10 sq. ft.	65	520-650 sq. ft.	1:12
Young Adults 18-24 yrs				
Department	10 sq. ft.			
Class	12 sq. ft.	25	300 sq. ft.	1:4
Dual Use	15-18 sq. ft.	25	375-450 sq. ft.	
Adults 25 yrs-up				
Department	10 sq. ft.			
Class	12 sq. ft.	25	300 sq. ft.	1:4
Dual Use	15-18 sq. ft.	25	375-450 sq. ft.	

Securing Equipment and Furnishings

Equipment is another factor that affects the climate or setting for Bible study. The type of equipment and furnishings needed will differ according to the age group being taught. Few churches are able to provide everything. Provide what you are able at the time. One annual goal may be to make improvements in providing equipment and furnishings for classrooms.

ten best practices

Recommended Preschool Equipment

Symbols: **x** - recommended; **o** - optional; *all* - specialized equipment purchased in limited quantity for use by all ages.

General	B	1	2	3	4	K	All	B-2	3-K	B-K
Rest mats or towels		x	o					x		o
Cribs (hospital 27"x42")	x	o						x		x
Adult rocking chair (2)	x							x		x
Solid surface floor mat (42" x 42")	x									
Wall cabinet (50" above floor)	x	x	x	x	x	x		x	x	x
Trash receptacles with lid	x	x	x	x	x	x		x	x	x
Diaper bag cubbies or hooks	x	x	x							
Vinyl changing pad		x	x							
Open shelf/closed back for toys (26"x36"x12")		o						o		o
Child safety gate										o
Water source for disinfecting	x	x	x					x		x
Slow cookers	x							x		x
Folding screen for nursing area	x							x		x
Rocking boat with enclosed steps		o								
Small counter top refrigerator	o									
Homeliving/Dramatic Play										
Horizontal unbreakable mirror 24" x 48" attached to wall	x							o		
Vertical unbreakable mirror 24" x 48" attached to wall		x	x	x	x	x			o	o
Wooden doll bed (16" x 28" x 8")		o	x	x	x	x		x	x	x
Child size rocker		o	x	x	x	x			x	x
Table (24"x36"x22")			x	x						
Table (24"x36"x24")					x	x			x	x
2-4 chairs (10")			x	x						
2-4 chairs (12"-14")				x	x				x	x
Wooden sink			x	x	x	x			x	x
Wooden stove			x	x	x	x			x	x
Chest of drawers						o				
Child size ironing board and iron*							o			
Music										
Cassette tape/CD player	x	x	x	x	x	x		o	o	o
Autoharp							x			
Rhythm instruments							x			

Recommended Preschool Equipment (cont)

Blocks	B	1	2	3	4	K	All	B-2	3-K	B-K
Cardboard or vinyl blocks		x	x					x		
Wooden unit blocks (various shapes and sizes)										
1. 29-70				x					x	x
2. 100-150					x	x				
Open shelf/closed back (26"x36"x12")			o	x	x	x			x	x
Art										
Table (30"x48"x22")			x	x					x	x
Table (30"x48"x24")					x	x				
2-4 chairs (10")			x	x						
2-4 chairs (12"-14")					x	x			o	o
Art Easel/ adjustable legs *			x	x	x	x			o	o
Drying rack			x	x	x	x				
Water source at child's height for clean up			x	x	x	x			x	x
Art shelf (36"x46"x16")						x				
Nature/Science										
Open shelf with closed back (26"x30"x12")				x	x	x			o	o
Water/table (1 per church)							o			
Table (24"x36"x24")						o				
2-4 chairs (12"-14")						o				
Manipulatives/Puzzles										
Puzzle rack				o	o	o			o	o
Table (24"x36"x24")						o				
2-4 chairs (12"-14")						o				

Maximum number of two tables per room in 2-4 year-old rooms.
*One option for art easels is to have one easel per every three rooms.

Recommended Equipment for Children, Youth, and Adult Departments

Equipment	Children	Youth	Adults
Chairs (age appropriate)	x^1	x^2	x^2
Coat rack	x	x	x
Resources cabinet	x	x	
Tables	x^3	x^5	o
Shelves	x^6	x	x
Book racks	x^7	x	o
Tackboard or bulletin boards	x^8	x	x
Wastebasket	x	x	x
Podium/table for teacher	o	o	o
Sink	o		
Autoharp	x		
Cassette player	x	x	x
TV/VCR combination	o	o	o
CD player	o	x	o
Piano	o	o	o
Chalk/marker board(s)	x	x^4	x^4
Tear sheets	x	x	x
Equipment	Children	Youth	Adults
Felt-tip markers	x	x	x
Other art/writing supplies	x	x	x
Picture rails	x^9		

[1] Recommended chair sizes for children:

    Grades 1&2: 12-13 inches

    Grades 3&4: 14-15 inches

    Grades 5&6: 16-17 inches

[2] Standard chairs 18 inches above the floor.

[3] Tabletops for children should be 10 inches above chair seats.

[4] 36x45 inches min. for hanging boards; freestanding and movable boards of comparable size or larger are preferred.

[5] Folding chairs for youth should be no more than 28 inches high.

[6] 14-19 inches deep, 42-46 inches high, and 3-4 feet long with shelves 12-14 inches apart.

[7] Bookracks should be 42-46 inches high and 30-42 inches long.

[8] Tackboards should be 24-30 inches in height and 6-10 feet in length with the bottom edge 24-30 inches above the floor.

[9] Picture rails should be about 30 inches above the floor on the front wall and 12 feet long.

to make your sunday school work

Best Practice Check Up
Teach to Transform

___ We lift up the Bible as the Word of God and use it as the textbook for Bible study through Sunday School ministry.

___ We provide Bible study curriculum materials appropriate for preschoolers, children, youth, and adults.

___ We provide space appropriate for Bible study with each age group.

___ We provide equipment and furnishings appropriate for Bible study with each age group.

___ We have a plan for obtaining, adding, or upgrading equipment and furnishings needed for Bible study with each age group.

___ Our leaders are committed to teaching for spiritual transformation, using the three essentials of Prepare, Encounter, and Continue.

___ Our leaders recognize the seven elements of teaching for spiritual transformation and are committed to practicing them in their teaching-learning settings.

___ We are focused on equipping parents to be the primary Bible teachers in their homes.

___ We have conducted a "space walk" to identify all available space that could be used as meeting places for our Bible study groups.

___ We have explored the option of other meeting times and multiple meetings times as possibilities for expanding our organization and increasing the potential of our Sunday School ministry.

ten best practices

BEST PRACTICE 9
Mobilize for Ministry

"Then the righteous will answer Him, 'Lord. when did we see You hungry and feed You, or thirsty and give You something to drink?. . . And the King will answer them, "I assure you: Whatever you did for one of the least of these brothers of Mine, you did for Me.'"
—Matthew 25:37,40, HCSB

Sunday School sounds like something that happens on Sunday. Earlier, in redefining Sunday School in this book, we challenged that thinking, however. We have retained the familiar nomenclature to build on the heritage it provides, but the nature of Sunday School as strategy requires us to think beyond historical time parameters. No strategy built on the Great Commission can expect to be accomplished if it is carried out one hour one day a week. According to Scripture, living for Jesus requires a lifetime investment.

That could never be truer than when we talk about the practice of ministry. Ministry in this context is people helping other people in Jesus' name to meet the needs of life that they cannot meet themselves. Obviously, ministry cannot be limited to one hour one day a week. The needs and hurts of people cannot tell time. Therefore, one objective of Sunday School ministry is to help class members to be poised and ready for ministry action much as a runner is poised and ready on the starting block, awaiting the starting signal.

to make your
sunday school work

0123456789101234567

Our model for ministry is Jesus. He came to minister (Mark 10:45). By His example, He exhorted His disciples to humble service (John 13:12-15). The apostle Paul established a principle of service based on Jesus as the model (Phil. 2:5). And in describing the judgment of the last days, Jesus pointed to how individuals responded to others in need as a practical determinant of their righteousness and acceptance into the kingdom.

Ministry, then, is the vocation—calling—of the believer. How can the church help believers to seize opportunities of service? How does Sunday School strategy equip and mobilize people for ministry?

We will take deliberate actions to mobilize people to meet the needs of individuals and families with compassion by —
- *remembering that the greatest need is to be in right relationship with the Lord;*
- *helping to identify ministry needs and informing leaders and members about ministry opportunities;*
- *equipping individuals and families to minister to others in need in all settings;*
- *leading members and their families to be involved in ministry and mission projects as a continuation of Sunday School Bible study;*
- *involving the church family in supporting missionaries and mission work through prayer and giving.*

Every class or Bible study group, no matter the age group, is to be organized for the personal care of all its members. The level of care will be determined by the need of the individual. Nevertheless, giving ministry to others requires commitment, training, supervision, and accountability

Sunday School, Ministry, and Evangelism

Since its beginning, the church seems to have struggled with the relationship of evangelism and ministry action, as if the two could be separated. James addressed this struggle in his letter (2:14-19). His conclusion was that saving faith that cannot be seen in compassionate acts of mercy toward others has lost its vitality (v. 17).

We have emphasized throughout this book the mandate of Jesus to His

1234567891012345678 ten best practices

church to be evangelists—"make disciples." Yet, who was more caring for others in the midst of need, hurt, and crisis than Jesus? His touch brought wholeness to the ailing. His tender words brought peace in the middle of a storm. His actions met the immediate need of the hungry.

In addressing those immediate needs, which to those individuals involved seemed to be the most critical needs, Jesus was also communicating something about a deeper need of life. His healing touch conveyed a message about the power and love of God to bring wholeness to a life being destroyed by sin. His word of peace in the storm represented the ultimate peace God can give to those in spiritual turmoil. His action to feed the hungry opened the door to introduce them to the Bread of life who would eternally satisfy.

We are surrounded by needy people who are suffering from loneliness, emptiness, family breakdowns, poverty, hunger, violence, prejudices, mental anguish, and physical pain. Everyone needs to know that someone cares. Our Sunday School classes can respond in a variety of ways, and they should. Even so, we must not become so involved in the physical ministry that we neglect the spiritual ministry. On the other hand, we don't want to be guilty of just teaching a Bible lesson as if that is our sole responsibility.

We can do both. We can focus attention on the greatest need of any individual, which is the need to know Jesus Christ as Savior and Lord. We teach the Bible to that end. At the same time, we will be extending ourselves to others in acts of loving-kindness. We do so not for our benefit, but for theirs. We do so because we believe that the gospel includes both the message of hope and actions of love toward needy people found in our classrooms, neighborhoods, and in the world beyond.

Organizing for Ministry

In earlier chapters, we noted ways that appropriate organization enhances the effectiveness of a class or group's efforts to reach people, evangelize people, and teach people. Organization is also directly related to the effectiveness of a class or group in care ministry.

An old truism says, "Everybody's business becomes nobody's business." Through a sound organization, every Sunday School member

and prospect becomes the responsibility of a specific person in a class or department group. Therefore, every person's hurt becomes somebody's responsibility. No one is overlooked.

Use the Record System for Ministry

Information about record systems was included in chapter 5 when discussing prospect discovery and accountability actions and in chapter 6 when discussing enrollment as an action of assimilation. The same accurate and complete record system has implications for ministry, also. To be accountable for helping others, we need to know their names, addresses, phone numbers, and spiritual conditions. We also need to know about other family members. All that information should be part of the records maintained on both prospects and members. Everyone is assigned to a particular group for ministry.

Use the Organizational Design for Ministry

Help for developing an organizational structure was given in chapter 2. The components of the organization of an open Bible study group are designed to encourage and enable ministry as well as general administration, outreach, and teaching. Also review chapter 3 on enlisting leaders. The leader-learner ratio suggested for each age group is intended to enhance ministry as well as teaching and learning. The dynamics and interpersonal relationships that are important to the exercise of caring ministry are difficult to achieve in larger groups.

If you choose to develop large Sunday School classes, you may need to take additional actions to ensure that ministry takes place. Remember that the ability to assemble a large group for Bible study time on Sunday morning (or whenever the open group meets) is not the final objective. Sunday School is a foundational strategy for leading people to faith in the Lord Jesus Christ and building on-mission Christians. The Bible study group is a vehicle for leading people to do what the church does. One principal function of the church is ministry.

In large classes, the development of ministry sub-groups or teams becomes even more critical. The leaders of the larger classes need to be team players who understand what Sunday School strategy is and are committed to carrying it out. Of course, that is something to be addressed during the leader enlistment process.

ten best practices

Large Sunday School classes can become entities within themselves that cease to cooperate with the ministry as a whole. They can become little congregations that rival a church. Furthermore, large classes can take other prospective leaders out of circulation. Members of a large class taught by a popular teacher may become consumers, not servants. They attend the class because they enjoy what they receive, but they fail to become engaged in self-giving actions that are expected of one who is following Christ's example of service.

For the most part, the larger class ought to be the exception rather than the norm. This is not to say you may not need to allow for a large class in some settings. For example, a large class may be an entry point for newcomers who at first seek anonymity. Nevertheless, make any large class a part of the intentional strategy.

For more details about organization and ways it supports the ministry that is taking place in each age-group department, see the various age-group books in the Sunday School for a New Century series available from LifeWay Church Resources.

An Approach to Ministry Using Ministry Groups

The approach being suggested is a leader-based approach in which class ministry group leaders are enlisted to care for a group of prospects and members. The number of ministry group leaders needed depends on the size of the class. This approach is similar to what countless Sunday School classes have used for many years.

What is a ministry group?
A ministry group consists of members or prospects of a Sunday School class who are grouped together for the expressed purpose of making regular contacts for prayer, communication, and the discovery and meeting of needs.

What is the optimum size for a ministry group?
The goal is to limit the size of ministry teams to a maximum of six

members and prospects. That represents a manageable number for the group leader to be able to make weekly contact. For example, if the adult class has 24 members and prospects assigned to it, then at least four ministry group leaders would be needed.

What does a ministry group leader do?

The primary responsibility is to care for the needs of those assigned to his or her group. The level of care is based on the needs of the individual.

The ministry group leader telephones or otherwise contacts all group members each week. Some ministry group leaders have mistakenly understood this to mean contacting only absentees. Those members who attend weekly also need the affirmation that comes from a contact. In addition, in the conversations, the ministry group leader may learn about other ministry opportunities that otherwise may be missed.

Calls, emails, and personal notes can be used to maintain contact with group members. The personal call is the best means because it allows for interaction and personal prayer. The call from the ministry group leader is not primarily a call to encourage attendance; it is a call to provide ministry. Regular attendance is frequently the outcome of ministry, but it is not to be the goal. We minister because we care.

The ministry group leader assures that a personal visit is made to every new member who is assigned to the ministry group. Part of the process of enrolling someone in a class is to assign the person to a ministry group. The ministry group leader and another group member make an initial visit to get to know the person and to encourage her to be a vital participant of the ministry group and the Sunday School class. Additional visits need to be made as ministry needs and special occasions occur.

Periodically, the ministry group leader sends personal notes or cards. A handwritten note offering encouragement or a timely birthday or anniversary card are ways of letting group members know that someone cares about them or is remembering them at a special moment in life.

Keep records of visits, calls, and contacts. Include information about ministry needs, prayer concerns, and ministry actions. Such records are a good way to track member birthdays, wedding anniversaries, and dates of death of loved ones, all of which are important contact and ministry opportunities.

Share prayer and ministry needs with the class. The ministry group is a way to manage ministry but the entire class needs to be involved as appropriate in responding to needs and in praying.

Maintain confidences. A ministry group leader may learn some things that are not to be shared with others. As appropriate, that information must be treated with confidentiality. Breaking confidences will hinder future ministry opportunities.

Report to the teacher, outreach-evangelism leader, or other appropriate class leader the results of ministry contacts. Regular reporting helps to maintain the accountability of the ministry group leader. The ongoing class leadership meeting is a good time to give such reports.

What is the relationship of the ministry group to discipling ministry?
As we affirmed in chapter 6, every new member should be assigned to an ongoing Bible study group—Sunday School class— as part of the strategy for helping to assimilate the person into the life and ministry of the church. The individual then is assigned to a ministry group in the class. The ministry group leader or another group member closely monitors the new believer in the early stages of his Christian experience. The group member offers to sit with the new believer or member in worship, provides encouragement in personal spiritual disciplines, and prays with, and for, the person. This process not only helps disciple the new member but becomes a spiritually enriching time for the group member who is engaged in the ministry.

What are the lines of communication?
Communication between the Sunday School class and the pastor and church staff must go both ways for greater effectiveness. When the pastor and staff learn of needs, they are to notify the appropriate class leader (teacher, outreach-evangelism, class ministry leader), who in turn will be certain that the appropriate ministry group leader is aware of the needs. When informed, the ministry group leader should make sure that the pastor and staff know about it. Furthermore, when any class member learns of needs of other class members, that information needs to be shared with the class leaders.

Ministry in Preschool, Children, and Youth Classes or Departments

The ministry group approach described above is primarily targeted toward Adult Sunday School classes. The approach is slightly modified for youth, who are able to participate in ministry. Ministry to children and preschoolers and their families primarily is conducted by the leaders of those departments.

Ministry to Preschoolers and Their Families

All the department (or class) leaders in a Preschool Sunday School department are to engage in actions that allow them to interact with the preschoolers and their families. This includes the teaching time on Sunday morning, and also ministry that occurs in other settings. Ministry may be needed in times of great joy, in times of crisis, or in the day-to-day moments of life.

Every member and prospect is to be assigned to a Preschool leader for regular contact. The assignments may be made based on (1) where teachers live; thus, the teacher would be responsible for ministry to preschoolers who live in his neighborhood; (2) attendance patterns, with each leader having responsibility for both regular and irregular attenders; (3) ministry needs, with leaders having assignments they are equipped to meet. Some combination of any of those factors may be used in making assignments.

Contacts need to be made with regularity either by mail, telephone, email or through a personal visit. A combination of methods is best. When making personal visits, the leader should visit accompanied by at least one other person, either a co-worker or spouse.

A contact needs to be made when a child is absent, when a ministry need is indicated, on special occasions, during churchwide special events, or when important information needs to be communicated. Contact also needs to be maintained on a regular, ongoing basis as a means of expressing genuine care and learning about needs. Valuable insights about preschoolers and their families can be learned during a home visit even with those who attend regularly.

ten best practices

Preschool leaders have several opportunities to get to know the parents of the preschoolers. In fact, the ministry of Preschool leaders may frequently be targeted to parents who need help and encouragement in developing their parenting skills and learning ways to be the primary Bible teachers of their preschoolers in home and family situations.

Ministry to Children and Their Families

Likewise with children, every child, both members and prospects, is assigned to a department leader for ministry. Ideally, enough leaders are needed so that no one person is assigned more than six enrolled children plus prospects. The leader is expected to get to know the children and their families. Building relationships is critical to effectiveness in ministry. A meaningful relationship with the child can open opportunities to minister to other family members who may not have been included in the ministry scope of the church. Developing relationships with parents may open the door to encouraging them to be the primary Bible teachers and disciplers of their children. Contacts with children should be made when a child is absent from Bible study, needs information about the department and church, or even just for fun. The contacts can be made by mail, email, telephone, or through a personal visit.

Children themselves can also be involved in ministry projects. This is an important dimension of the teaching and learning that takes place in the ongoing Bible study group with children. The children are able to see the practical meaning of what they are learning by putting the Bible truth to practice in real life situations.

Ministry to Youth and Their Families

Youth Sunday School leaders are charged with ministering to teens and to their families. The leader can provide a listening ear or a shoulder to cry on. He may also offer encouragement to Christian parents to fulfill their responsibilities as the primary Bible teachers and disciplers of their teenagers. Ministry to youth involves writing notes, making phone calls, eating meals at school, and going to ball games and other school events.

The class teacher is the primary leader for all that occurs in the youth class. Class leaders selected from among the youth in the class assist her. In the leader-based approach similar to that described above, enough ministry

to make your sunday school work

leaders will be selected for each to have a ministry group of members and prospects not to exceed six teens.

The ministry leaders help to create an atmosphere in which members and prospects can experience direct care and concern for life's needs. They help their group members to know about missions projects and missions needs through which they may make best use of their talents and spiritual gifts in the exercise of ministry.

Equipping for Ministry

We have focused primarily on doing ministry using the organizational component as the ministry base and leaders as ministry practitioners. This is not to suggest that other members in the class or department are exempt from ministry. To the contrary, everyone in a department or class is to be equipped and mobilized for ministry.

Equip Through Bible Study

As noted particularly in chapter 8 and foundational to the philosophy of Sunday School espoused in this book, the Bible teaching and learning that takes place through Sunday School ministry has as its goal spiritual transformation. That transformation begins by receiving by faith the salvation Christ has made possible. A person's new life in Christ is on the one hand final and complete; the believer is saved once and for all. On the other hand, it is the beginning of a life focused on spiritual growth and maturity that leads to obedience, trust, love, and glorifying God. Engaging in ministry becomes both a means to, and an expression of, a person's spiritual maturation. In addition, ministry becomes a way of expressing obedience, affirming trust, sharing love, and glorifying God. Bible study is critical to coming to know Christ and then for becoming more like Christ, the model of ministry.

Equip by Making Members Aware of Ministry Opportunities

As we have learned, one value of keeping records and developing a sound organizational structure is to provide channels for information to flow about ministry needs among those who are enrolled in the Sunday School class or are prospects for the class. Communication about ministry needs makes members aware of opportunities for ministry.

Ministry needs exist outside the class context. The class teacher and other class leaders can help members know about needs that exist in other areas of the church. Those needs may be for leaders with other age groups, children who need adult friends and companions, youth who need financial support for an outing, senior adults who need assistance in home maintenance, and so forth.

Class leaders can also help members to be aware of needs that exist in the community. In some cases, the needs may be areas of service in which an individual chooses to participate, such as volunteering to assist with distribution of staple goods through a local food bank. Or, the ministry need may be one that can be addressed through a class ministry project, such as leading a Vacation Bible School in an unchurched part of town.

Because the Great Commission has worldwide scope, Sunday School class leaders may make members aware of mission project opportunities in other areas of the state, or nation, or another country. A class may engage in a missions project on its own or support a project being carried out by the church at large.

Equip Through Skill Development

One great concern for many persons who are aware of ministry needs and have the desire to minister is what to do and what to say. Fear of saying the wrong thing may lead to silence. Fear of doing the wrong thing may lead to inaction. Both may be incorrectly interpreted as lack of concern.

Skill development is one area where the value of having a partnership with the church Discipleship ministry surfaces. Training may be provided that helps to equip members for ministry. Topics that may be covered address three major ministry categories.

Ministry in times of grief and loss. Grief is the universal human crisis that strikes all of us at some point. Grief comes from experiencing significant loss, going through major change, or enduring life transitions. Death, divorce, job loss, loss of a home, or a broken relationship may be events that bring on grief. Members need to be equipped to know how to respond to such situations with sensitivity, compassion, encouragement, and hope.

to make your
sunday school work

Ministry in times of emotional crisis. We are emotional beings. Our emotions sometimes get out of control and actually control us. While some emotional distress is severe and needs professional attention, members still can be equipped to render support and ministry to those who are in emotional crisis or family members of people who are in emotional crisis. Emotional crises may come while dealing with terminal illness, the struggle with depression, a feeling of failure, a desire to end life, or a codependent relationship.

Ministry in times of family crisis. Ministry opportunities abound in this category. Some crises are extremely personal; others reach beyond the family unit. Neither can be ignored. Neither will just go away. People need to know that someone cares about them. The family crises that need caring ministry are teen pregnancy, abortion, homosexuality, drug abuse, spouse or child abuse, aging parents, and arrest and incarceration.

Even some otherwise happy events can lead to stress buildup, which can become ministry situations. Families planning weddings deal with many demands on their time. The birth of a child can be a traumatic experience, especially if the birth is accompanied by health problems. Or, moving into a new house may be a joyous occasion but the challenge of parting with the familiar can result in mixed emotions. Members are to be helped to see how they can respond to such needs in ways that provide help without being intrusive.

Equipping Families to Minister to Families

Parents are the primary Bible teachers and disciplers of their children. They are to live out in the family setting what it means to be a follower of Jesus Christ. One way that can be done is by leading the family to minister to others. That may be introduced by encouraging families to participate as a family in giving support to a child or family through a church- or community-sponsored emphasis during the Christmas holidays. That beginning may grow into a year-round practice of ministering together as a family to another family, working as a family in a community project, or going as a family on a missions trip.

ten best practices
123456789101012345678

A Concluding Word About Ministry Through Sunday School

The reaching, teaching, and witnessing that go on through Sunday School do not occur in a vacuum. Members and prospects are real hurting people. They may have brought the hurt on themselves or they may be victims of others. Our response is not to place blame but to go beyond the walls of our own comfort zones to extend help in Jesus' name. That is ministry. It is a major element of Sunday School strategy that comes from our commitment to the command of our Lord and our desire to live like Him and for Him.

to make your sunday school work

Best Practice Check Up
Mobilize for Ministry

___ Our annual plans include a goal for every Sunday School class or department to take the initiative to involve members in ministry to life needs of members and prospects.

— We have evaluated our record-keeping system in light of the need to provide valid information for classes and departments to engage in ministry actions to specific individuals and families.

___ We have evaluated our organizational structure for its effectiveness in encouraging and enabling classes and departments to minister to specific individuals and families.

___ We have developed ministry groups in the adults and youth areas as an approach for ensuring that the ministry needs of every member and prospect are addressed by a particular class, ministry group, and person.

___ We have enlisted enough leaders with preschoolers and children to ensure that the ministry needs of every member and prospect are addressed by the appropriate preschool or children's departments.

— We are helping members in classes and departments to be sensitive to ministry needs of other members and prospects, including the most important need of being in right relationship with the Lord.

___ We are training all class and department leaders to both teach and model the biblical message of engaging in ministry to others.

___ We are working in consultation with our Discipleship ministry to provide skill development training that will further equip and mobilize ministry to members and prospects in times of critical need.

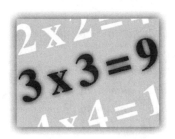

BEST PRACTICE 10
Multiply Leaders and Units

"While they were worshiping the Lord and fasting, the Holy Spirit said, 'Set apart for me Barnabas and Saul for the work to which I have called them.' So after they had fasted and prayed, they placed their hands on them and sent them off."

—Acts 13:2-3

This best practice is closely related to two of the best practices we have already discussed: "Organize with Purpose" (chapter 2) and "Build Kingdom Leaders" (chapter 3). You may find it helpful to review those chapters in conjunction with your reading and application of the information in this chapter.

The focus of this chapter is on the need for an intentional, ongoing plan to multiply the leadership base and the number of teaching-ministry units. The word *multiply* is purposefully used as opposed to the word *add*. Obviously, both words suggest an increase in number. To multiply, however, suggests a more rapid and greater quantitative increase by multiples.

We will develop and implement an intentional process for continually multiplying leaders and units by —
  • *communicating the key relationship multiplication of leaders and units has to the overall mission of Sunday School as strategy;*

to make your sunday school work
01234567891101234567

• *teaching every believer to be in service and on mission and to multiply themselves;*

• *developing potential leader training ministry that helps members to explore their leadership potential and possibilities;*

• *making leader enlistment and multiplication of units an ongoing process rather than annual actions;*

• *encouraging and supporting the initiative of existing Bible study groups to reproduce themselves through new open Bible study groups that increase the opportunity to evangelize and disciple more people;*

• *encouraging and supporting the efforts of leaders to identify prospective leaders and to guide them toward service for Christ and His church;*

• *engaging the church to start a new Vacation Bible School or a new Sunday School or to help plant a new church mission.*

Focus on the Purpose for Multiplying Leaders and Units

Keep clear focus on the purpose of any Bible study group. Sunday School is designed as the foundational strategy for leading persons to faith in the Lord Jesus and building on-mission Christians through open Bible study groups that engage persons in evangelism, discipleship, ministry, fellowship, and worship. That same purpose is to influence our efforts to multiply leaders and units.

• The Spirit of the Sovereign Lord is on us to target persons who are poor, brokenhearted, captive, and mourning. As the Lord's servants, we are to share hope, bind up those who are brokenhearted, show how those imprisoned can find release, and share the basis of comfort to all those who are mourning (Isaiah 61:1-3).

• Bible study groups exist to help the church enlarge the possibilities for reaching more people (Isaiah 54:1-2).

• Bible study groups and the leaders of those groups are to focus on the Great Commission (Matthew 28:18-20).

• Bible study groups are central in training other persons to be strong in grace and to teach them to teach others (2 Timothy 2:1-2).

Give Priority to Reaching Unchurched Persons.

The priority for reaching unchurched persons will be evidenced in both attitude and action. An objective of Sunday School ministry is to find every way possible to identify, enroll, cultivate relationships with, and seek to assimilate persons into the ministry of the church. Because new open Bible study groups will generally provide a higher percentage of success in reaching persons, a church that wants to reach more people needs to establish as a priority allocating personnel, resources, space, and energy to actions that result in the multiplication of leaders and units.

• *Priority of personnel.* Sunday School actively seeks to enlist and to train persons who are developing a passion for building relationships with persons for Christ's sake; for helping persons to study, discover, and apply God's Word; and helping new participants to feel part of the work of the church.

• *Priority of resources.* Sunday School needs to designate finances for communicating with prospects and members of new Bible study groups, purchasing additional Bible study curriculum for leaders and learners and other resources that help to assimilate new participants into the church, and training new leaders. A church may need to set aside funds to remodel or adapt space for a new unit. In addition, age-appropriate equipment and supplies for a new unit may need to be evaluated.

• *Priority of space.* Every Bible study group needs age-appropriate space in which to meet. Space in the church facilities needs to be accessible to all participants. Persons with little or no church background are to be made to feel as comfortable as possible. Clean and appropriately furnished space helps to create an atmosphere for making newcomers feel both comfortable and welcome.

• *Priority of time and energy.* More time and energy may be required for multiplying leaders and units than it takes to sustain those that have been organized for a year or more. The investment of time and energy will be well worth it when seeing the joy in the faces of new leaders in service for Christ and in that of people who have come to know Jesus as Savior and Lord.

to make your
sunday school work

Multiplying Leaders and Units Is an Intentional Part of the Strategy

Creating new Bible study groups is to be seen as a natural and necessary part of the total Sunday School strategy that focuses on open Bible study groups. A new Bible study group can be started with a small core of committed leaders, including a teacher and outreach-evangelism leader. This core group needs to approach the new class or group as an opportunity to be part of an intentional effort to reach people for Christ through Bible study who are not being reached currently.

The plan needs to be thought of in terms of multiplication, not division. If the core group begins the new class or group discouraged about being separated from the friends they have in the class from which they have come, they will not be able to engender the excitement that needs to be associated with starting a new, Bible study class. If they see it as an opportunity to exercise their spiritual gifts, take intentional actions that are in obedience to the command of our Lord, and lead people to faith in the Lord Jesus Christ, then starting a new class will become an exciting venture.

Multiplying Leaders and Units Is an Ongoing Action

Multiplying leaders and units should not be seen as an option but as a holy obligation and a key action of Sunday School strategy. Strive to instill in every class the desire to see leaders come from the class and at least one new teaching unit birthed by it during the year. Multiplication of leaders and units is in itself a testimony to the increase that God has given through the ongoing ministry of the class. Multiplying leaders and units ought to be an occasion for rejoicing. A commissioning service may be designed to call attention to the accomplishment.

Here are some reasons for making multiplication of leaders and units a priority:

1. The birth of new units creates excitement.

2. The creation of new units enlarges the organizational base of Sunday School ministry, thus enabling growth to take place naturally without sacrificing the quality of the ministry.

3. New units grow more quickly than older established units. New Bible study groups generally have more motivation for reaching people because they usually are smaller groups that want to grow, they tend to have a focus

on a clearly defined group, and they are led by leaders who have a commitment to the effort. Leaders in new units tend to make more contacts to prospective members and tend to follow up absentees more consistently than do classes where relationships and attendance patterns have become more crystallized. Leaders and members of new units tend also to discover and seek to enroll persons for the class at a higher percentage than established groups.

4. New units are easier for newcomers to penetrate. Group dynamics work both for and against most Sunday School classes. The same actions that growing classes take to build relationships and increase attendance generally cause people in those classes to bond and grow closer. As more people are added to the group, persons in the class may find it more difficult to build relationships with new people. Similarly, new members may find it difficult to fit in and feel part of the group unless people in the group make concentrated efforts to assimilate them. New open Bible study groups give leaders and members the opportunity to focus on building relationships with people who are new to the group.

5. New leaders and members of new units tend to be more aggressive in evangelism and ministry. Leaders and members of new Bible study groups frequently:

- make ministry visits in homes of prospective members and absentees;
- send cards, letters, and email messages to members and prospects;
- seek to enroll prospective members;
- take actions to assimilate persons into the class;
- plan and conduct events that include unchurched prospects and make effort to invite them to the events;
- prepare to make evangelistic contacts to present the gospel and win people to Christ.

6. New units provide opportunities for more people to serve in leadership positions.

to make your
sunday school work

A Process for Multiplying Leaders and Units

Many churches may use the beginning of a new church year as they are enlisting leaders and evaluating the current organization as the time for focusing attention on multiplication of leaders and units. That timing certainly is appropriate. Let it be understood, however, that the multiplication of leaders and units is an ongoing action that can be done at any time.

Identify a Target Group

Although every believer and every church is to be on mission to reach anyone and everyone, according to the message of the Great Commission, realistically, each Bible study group needs to focus on a specific target group. The target group may develop around such influential factors as age range, gender, school grade, marital status, life status, or transitional point (such as newly married, recently retired, recently widowed, new parent, and so forth).

Seek Sponsorship

A successful new Bible study group needs a support system. Leaders need the encouragement that comes from knowing that others are praying for them. Such support comes naturally when multiplication of leaders and units is part of an intentional strategy wherein the leaders and the core for the new unit come from an existing class.

An existing class can help the new class to discover, contact, and enroll prospects. Members from an existing class can "adopt" members and prospects from a new class and provide prayer and ministry, particularly until the class grows and can stand on its own. Leaders from an existing class can work alongside one or more leaders from a new class as mentors, especially providing help in planning, teaching improvement, evangelistic outreach, and administration.

Enlist and Build the Leadership Team

New leaders are needed to birth new units; new units require leaders. The two are so closely related. Look at the suggestions given in chapter 3 for discovering and enlisting new leaders.

Enlist at least two leaders and two prospective members as the core group for starting a new unit. The core group may be larger for adult coeducational classes and single adult classes. The core group needs to meet together several times prior to the start date to plan for the first session.

Promote the Start Date and Location to the Target Group

Promote the specific date, time, and place the new Bible study group will meet. Such an intention assumes that ample preparation time has been given to the process so that information can be conveyed to the target group as well as to other existing groups that may be affected by the birthing of new units. Ask core group members to invite prospective members to attend a get-acquainted social gathering a couple of weeks prior to the start of the new class or group.

Invite and Enroll Members

Enrollment gives the Bible study group a tangible list of persons with whom they can minister and pray for regardless of the attendance pattern of the enrolled.

Conduct the First Session

The sequence of these elements can be varied based on the target group. The first sessions should be well planned and coordinated with all leaders.

• *Party.*—Provide time for fellowship among leaders, members, and other attenders. Serve light snacks as appropriate for the age of the participants. Plan group-building and get-acquainted experiences. Use name tags to help everyone learn names.

• *Praise.*—Ask some leaders and members to tell how they understand that God is working in their lives. Do not embarrass new participants (particularly unchurched persons), who may find it awkward to talk about spiritual things. As part of the worship time, read a Psalm or other Scripture passage that will be part of the Bible study for the day and provide music or lead group singing.

• *Prayer.*—All persons have concerns for which they need God's intervention. Some new attenders may not be familiar with the idea of bringing concerns before God confident that He hears, understands, and answers our prayers. As the leadership team learns about individuals in the group, it will become apparent who is comfortable praying aloud in a group. Prayer time

can be a vital group-building experience as well as a meaningful time of worship. While this time is important, leaders will want to be sure that plenty of time is given for Bible study.

   • *Participation.*—Approximately two thirds of the total session should be designated for Bible teaching.

When Should We Start a New Adult or Young Adult Class?

   • Classes with too wide an age span (more than 10 years);
   • More than 25 enrolled in the class;
   • Room in which the class meets often is filled;
   • Single adult prospects but no single adult class provided;
   • Young adult prospects but no class provided;
   • Adult prospects in a particular age segment but no class provided;
   • Unenrolled adult church members;
   • Classes with more prospects than members;
   • Classes with more absentees than members present.

When Should We Start a New Youth Class or Department?

   • All youth in one class or department;
   • More than 60 youth enrolled in one department;
   • More than 12 youth enrolled in a class;
   • A school grade with prospects but little or no attendance;
   • Class or department with less than 50 percent enrollment attending;
   • A school grade with more prospects than youth enrolled.

When Should We Start a New Children's Class or Department?

   • Grades 1 through 6 in one class or department;
   • Grade 1 in class or department with another grade;
   • Grade 6 in a class or department with another grade;
   • Class or department with more than 24 enrolled;
   • Class or department with less than 60 percent of enrollment attending;
   • A school grade with prospects but none attending.

When Should We Start a New Preschool Class or Department?

- Birth through age 5 in one class or department;
- Babies in same department with other ages;
- Kindergartners in same department with other ages;
- Class or department of younger preschoolers with 12 or more enrolled;
- Class or department of threes, fours, and pre-K with more than 16 enrolled;
- Class or department of kindergartners with more than 20 enrolled;
- Class or department where only "babysitting" is done;
- More prospects than preschoolers enrolled.

Models for Multiplying Units

Most ways of beginning new groups fall into one of the following models. Some local variations may be made depending on the specific target group, experience of the leadership team, or situations that are unique to the culture, region, or setting in which the Bible study group is being started.

Restructure Existing Class or Department

Generally, a new unit should be started when an existing Bible study group reaches an enrollment or attendance that exceeds the number of persons who can adequately be cultivated and assimilated, and when additional prospects have been discovered. The new group may be started by creating two or more groups from the existing group. For example, a single department for fifth and sixth graders may become two separate departments, one for fifth graders and one for sixth graders.

Multiplication of units also may occur by enlisting specific attenders and targeting nonattenders from one or more existing classes. A new group may be created that focuses on the new target group. For example, one department of adults may have three existing classes: coed ages 31-35, coed ages 36-42, and coed ages 43-49. Assigned to the classes in this department are many men whose wives attend but the men do not. In addition, several other men in these age ranges are members of the church but are not attending a Bible study group. To address those needs, the department can be restructured to create a class for men and a class for women and to broaden the tar-

geted age groups of the coed classes. Hence, the department would now consist of these classes: coed ages 31-38 (because many of the women will be attending the women's class), coed ages 39-49 (because several attenders agree to be part of the men's or the women's class), a class for men ages 31-49, and a class for women ages 31-49. Plans may be made for a future class in the department that targets new parents who likely would come from the coed class targeting ages 31-38.

No matter how the class or department is restructured, use terminology that communicates the process in a positive manner. Avoid such words as *split* or *divide*.

Assign a Leadership Team to an Unchurched Target Group

Another approach to multiplying leaders and units is to enlist a new leadership team to start a new class that targets a specific group of nonattenders. The leadership team will consist of a Bible study leader and an outreach-evangelism leader to identify and enroll prospects and to encourage nonattenders to participate. A third leader may be a class coordinator or apprentice who helps to arrange the facilities, obtain resources, and assist with ministry, fellowship, and worship opportunities.

A new class or group may be started to target non-attenders in other existing classes. Additional prospects need to be identified as well if the class is to reach its full potential. The goal of any Bible study group is to have the members of that group engaged in reaching others, even to the point of being multipliers themselves. Hence the need for continuing to discover prospects.

Identify Unreached Persons and Begin a Nontraditional Bible Study Group

A target group may be identified that consists of people who cannot or likely will not attend Bible study at the church or on a Sunday morning. Such groups may include:
- Homebound adults
- Shift workers
- Business men and women who travel on weekends
- Residents of multi-housing units

- Professionals who work on weekends, such as firemen or nurses
- People in life transition stages (new parents, recently divorced, college students)

As stated much earlier in discussing open Bible study groups as the key element of Sunday School ministry, a "Sunday School" class is not defined by when or where it meets but by its purpose. Therefore, a Bible study group may be created that meets at a nontraditional time and place in order to reach a particular target group. Examples of such target groups may include, but are not limited to, the list given above. A leadership team needs to be enlisted to be responsible for teaching, reaching, and ministry to members of the target group.

Locations for this Bible study group may be

- a home or apartment
- a business office
- a recreation site
- a residential institution where members receive care, live, or work

The Bible study group can be designed to be an ongoing open Bible study group. It could also be a short-term open Bible study group designed to build relationships and eventually to lead members to become involved in an ongoing group.

The Class Teacher and Creation of New Bible Study Groups

Creation of new units needs not be initiated by the pastor or Sunday School director. If birthing new units is part of the overall strategy that is communicated during leader enlistment, then the class leadership team led by the teacher should feel the freedom to take the initiative to create a new unit as they assess needs and evaluate current growth in the existing class.

In fact, positive leadership from the existing Sunday School class's teacher and leadership team will go a long way in eliminating, or at least minimizing, the trauma that sometimes accompanies the creation of new units. Creating a new unit ought to be seen as a goal accomplished and not punishment for overachievement.

The Class Teacher and Enlistment of New Leaders

As noted in chapter 8, the class teacher is to be challenged to reproduce himself each year by discovering and mentoring one new leader. How tragic it is when a gifted teacher becomes selfish and unwilling to send class members out to serve. On the other hand, how great a compliment it is to have the reputation of being a leader who produces other leaders.

When a class teacher notices a class member who is constantly well-prepared, freely enters into discussion, relates well to others, and demonstrates spiritual maturity, the teacher may want to enlist that person as an apprentice (See a brief description of apprentice on page 98.) If the person agrees to serve, the teacher makes a commitment to spending time with the apprentice in a mentoring relationship. The teacher will help the apprentice to develop relationships with other key leaders; assist in class leadership functions; participate in teaching during a class session, and eventually substitute for the teacher when she must be absent. This apprentice then may be enlisted according to the normal church enlistment processes to assume a teaching leadership role in an ongoing Bible study group. In some cases, the new leader may become the leader of a new unit being birthed by the class.

Best Practice Check Up
Multiply Leaders and Units

___ We have included in our annual plan an ongoing emphasis on the multiplication of leaders and units.

___ Because the multiplication of leaders and units is a critical part of our ongoing strategy, we have placed a priority on personnel, financial resources, space, time, and energy devoted to enlisting leaders and beginning new units.

___ We are constantly encouraging existing leaders and classes to identify target groups for whom new Bible study groups may be started.

___ Our leader enlistment process is designed to be an ongoing process rather than a once-a-year process.

___ Our leaders and members know the guidelines we use for evaluating our need to create new units.

___ We regularly focus attention in existing groups on the need for new leaders and challenge members to consider the call of God upon their lives.

10
123456789101012345678

ten best practices

APPENDIX A
Sunday School and Church Functions

In the New Testament, the church is characterized by five essential functions that grow out of the Great Commission: evangelism, discipleship, ministry, fellowship, and worship. These functions are evident in the church practices described in Acts 2:42-47.

As believers, we need to be characterized corporately and individually by those same five functions if we are to fulfill the calling of Christ. Sunday School as strategy provides the primary framework for involving families and individuals in the comprehensive work of the church and for following the Great Commission.

Sunday School and Evangelism

We are not saved from our sin and separation from God merely for our own benefit. We are to join Him in His work of reconciling the lost world to Himself. The key to accomplishing God's work is obedience to Jesus in telling others about the good news of salvation in Christ.

When we share the good news, everyone who hears it is changed. The lost person becomes accountable for hearing the good news and for responding to the opportunity to receive salvation and new life through personal belief. The Christian becomes more like Christ through faithfulness to the Lord's command.

0123456789101234567
to make your
sunday school work
567

Sunday School as strategy focuses on obedience to Christ in the work of evangelism.

Leaders and members are constantly to be reaching people for Bible study. They must be dedicated to seeking, discovering, and inviting spiritually lost people to participate in open Bible study groups. Leaders and members work one-on-one to reach the unreached and to teach them the good news sometimes in settings away from church.

Classes and departments that are not leading people to faith in the Lord Jesus Christ are stale and stagnant. One great threat to the effectiveness of the strategy is the tendency of Bible study groups (classes and departments) to become closed groups, focused on the needs and interests of their members to the exclusion of those who do not know Christ or the fellowship of His people.

Some Bible study classes become so focused on "deeper Bible study" that they assume a common level of foundational Bible knowledge, possibly unintentionally excluding those who are new to the study of God's Word. Or, a Bible study class may become so focused on the fellowship within the existing group that members erect social barriers to "outsiders" who need to be reached.

Sunday School as strategy is marked by evangelistic Bible teaching through ongoing Bible study classes and other Bible study groups that are always open for anyone to participate.

That means providing foundational Bible study for preschoolers and younger children from which they will be encouraged to respond positively to the message of salvation as soon as they are able to do so. It means providing an environment in older children's, youth, and adult Bible study groups that encourages unsaved people to come to faith in Christ and encourages believers to lead others to Christ. It means seizing every opportunity the Holy Spirit provides to present the gospel through Bible teaching.

Sunday School as strategy provides a churchwide evangelism training network to equip members to become passionate soul-winners.

Sunday School is a systematic way of organizing, equipping, and mobilizing individuals to reach and witness to others in their networks of relationships. Participants are encouraged to pray for spiritually lost people throughout the world and especially for people they know. They are urged to take seriously the responsibility of witnessing to others through ongoing evangelistic visitation, both as a group activity and as an individual mandate. FAITH Sunday School Evangelism Strategy described in chapter 4 is a comprehensive process for accomplishing the reaching dimension of Sunday School ministry. FAITH includes both witness training and weekly opportunities to engage in evangelistic and ministry visitation.

Sunday School as strategy uses organizational expansion to encourage evangelism.

Multiplying new Sunday School classes and departments and other Bible study groups is a priority because new units consistently seek, discover, and involve more lost people than do existing units.

to make your
sunday school work

Sunday School Strategy
and Evangelism Check Up

On a scale of 1 to 5 (1 being low; 5 being high), how would you rate your Sunday School in leading people to faith in the Lord Jesus Christ? How would you rate yourself?

SS   Me

___   ___   Making a commitment to personal evangelism

___   ___   Praying for spiritually lost people to come to know Jesus Christ as personal Savior and Lord

___   ___   Seeking, discovering, and inviting spiritually lost people to become involved in a Bible study group

___   ___   Enrolling unreached people

___   ___   Seeking, discovering, and enlisting members to serve in leadership positions related to outreach and evangelism

___   ___   Appropriately teaching the Bible for evangelistic results

___   ___   Making an investment in teaching others about Christ in one-on-one settings away from church

___   ___   Constantly organizing and training individuals in personal evangelism

___   ___   Always viewing ongoing evangelistic visitation as a group activity

___   ___   Always viewing evangelistic visitation as a personal responsibility

___   ___   Starting new Bible study units

___   ___   Conducting special evangelistic Bible study events

Sunday School as foundational strategy focuses on leading people to faith in the Lord Jesus Christ.

ten best practices

123456789101012345678

Sunday School and Discipleship

Discipleship is a process that begins after conversion and continues throughout a believer's life. Evangelism initiates this process; fellowship and ministry grow out of it.

Discipleship is not an option for the believer. Every Christian needs to grow in his or her understanding of, and obedience to, God and His Word (Eph. 4:11-16). Thus Bible study is a part of discipleship.

God has provided the Bible as the authoritative written revelation of Himself to humanity. The apostle Paul reminded believers through his words to Timothy that the Scriptures "are able to make you wise for salvation through faith in Jesus Christ. All Scripture is God-breathed and is useful for teaching, rebuking, correcting and training in righteousness, so that the man of God may be thoroughly equipped for every good work" (2 Tim. 3:15-17).

Sunday School as strategy provides for foundational discipleship that places people in Bible study groups where they can grow in their understanding of God's Word and in their obedience to His commands.

Growth in a person's understanding of the Bible is a necessary goal of Bible study and Bible teaching. Knowledge, however, cannot be the end of Bible study and Bible teaching if we are to make disciples. Neither is it enough simply to understand a biblical truth and be able to apply it to an area of life.

The need is for Bible teaching that facilitates the Holy Spirit's work of spiritual transformation in the lives of learners. Believers are urged to integrate a biblical worldview into their minds, hearts, and lives through participation in ongoing, systematic Bible study.

Sunday School as strategy encourages members to strengthen their Christian walk by participating in other discipleship opportunities.

Genuine discipleship involves guiding people to integrate biblical truth into the total fabric of their hearts, minds, will, and actions. Participation in a church's Discipleship ministry greatly enhances a believer's spiritual growth. Involvement in missions education ministries, music ministry, and other church ministries provides focused opportunities to grow in Christlikeness. Sunday School leaders are responsible to keep other church leaders aware of the discipleship needs of individuals in their Bible study groups.

Sunday School as strategy recognizes that Bible study is most effective

when it occurs in the context of the learner's total life, especially family relationships, and when it considers the generational perspective, age and life-stage characteristics, and preferred learning styles of the learner.

Personal and family Bible study are a responsibility for every believer. Not only does the individual benefit from extended Bible study opportunities, that person's family also is strengthened. God did not give us His Word to study as an addendum to our lives. Rather, His Word is to be upon our hearts.

Sunday School as strategy affirms the home as the center of biblical guidance.

As such, Adult Sunday School ministry helps to equip Christian parents to fulfill their responsibility as the primary Bible teachers and disciplers of their children. For too long, churches have focused on Sunday morning Bible study as sufficient while neglecting the equipping of Christian parents to fulfill their role as the spiritual instructors of their children. God desires for godly parents to teach His commands to their children as an integral and natural part of daily living (Deut. 4:9b).

Sunday School as strategy encourages Bible study in ongoing groups, short-term groups, and through special Bible teaching events as effective ways to address specific life concerns, spiritual issues, church functions, and doctrinal issues and to promote outreach and evangelism.

Such special Bible study events as January Bible Study can strengthen discipleship. Additional short-term Bible studies that focus on specific topics or issues can address particular discipleship needs in a person's life. Participation in training toward leadership, evangelism, or another area of ministry or missions enhances a believer's recognition and use of his or her spiritual gifts for Christ's purpose.

10

ten best practices

1234567891012345678

Sunday School Strategy
and Discipleship Check Up

On a scale of 1 to 5 (1 being low; 5 being high), how would you rate your Sunday School in discipling others through Bible study? How would you rate yourself?

SS	Me	
___	___	Lifting up the Bible as the absolute truth and authority of God's Word, and using it as the textbook of the Sunday School
___	___	Regularly attending ongoing Sunday School classes, departments, and other Bible study groups
___	___	Providing training for all Sunday School leaders
___	___	Providing Bible study curriculum materials appropriate for preschoolers, children, youth, and adults
___	___	Providing space, equipment, and furnishings appropriate for Bible study with preschoolers, children, youth, and adults
___	___	Working to provide a ministry environment in Bible study that facilitates spiritual transformation
___	___	Encouraging involvement in the church's Discipleship ministry
___	___	Providing opportunities to be involved in special Bible study events beyond Sunday morning
___	___	Providing tools to help parents fulfill their role as the primary Bible teachers and disciplers of their children

Sunday School as foundational strategy guides people to integrate biblical truth into the fabric of their hearts, minds, will, and actions.

Sunday School and Ministry

Ministry is the discovery and use of spiritual gifts and abilities to meet the needs of others in Jesus' name. Ministry naturally follows discipleship in the process of Christian development. We need to be reminded, however, that the functions of the church actually are in operation simultaneously. Even so, Christian ministry flows from the life of a person who has received Christ into his or her life and is following Christ's example.

Through the Holy Spirit, God gives Christians spiritual gifts and empowers Christians to use those gifts in His service. Paul made it clear that the gifts were given "for the common good" (1 Cor. 12:7). Paul explained to the church at Ephesus that they were to "prepare God's people for works of service" (Eph. 4:12). Ultimately, those works of service or ministry are for the purpose of leading others to faith in Jesus as Savior and Lord.

Sunday School as strategy is committed to ministry.

Acts of caring ministry are an essential part of building and maintaining unity and fellowship in any Bible study group. Ministry must not, however, be limited to those who already have been reached. It is important for Sunday School leaders to make Bible study participants aware of ministry needs.

God's people desire to serve Him and others. Acts of ministry sometimes go undone and people suffer needlessly simply because others are uninformed. Sunday School leaders must keep the ministry function of the church before its members to encourage them toward missionary service to their world.

Sunday School as strategy organizes people for effective ministry.

Sunday School equips people for service individually and collectively. The strategy's structure for doing ministry takes into consideration the gifts, abilities, and resources available to those performing the ministry, as well as the needs of those who will receive the ministry.

Sunday School as strategy supports all church ministries and intentionally encourages its members to be good stewards, fully involved in the church's overall mission.

This support is accomplished through Bible study that builds disciples and through working with other church ministries to train and develop Christians to be faithful servants to Christ.

ten best practices

Sunday School as strategy equips people for ministry, mobilizes them, and sends them into service.

Leaders identify and magnify opportunities for member involvement in ongoing, caring ministry actions through their Sunday School classes, departments, and other Bible study groups. Direct assignments to members help to involve them in specific ministry actions in one-on-one or family-to-family ministry situations.

The needs of specific groups offer special opportunities for ministry. For example, new parents can benefit significantly from acts of service that help them to establish relationships with a church. Ministry to homebound individuals is a way to send members into service as ministering teachers. Sunday School strategy can ensure that people with special physical or educational needs receive Great Commission ministry.

to make your
sunday school work

Sunday School Strategy and Ministry Check Up

On a scale of 1 to 5 (1 being low; 5 being high), how do you rate your Sunday School in ministry? How do you rate yourself?

SS   Me

____   ____   Calling people into the ministry of caring service

____   ____   Identifying ministry needs and informing people about ministry opportunities

____   ____   Assisting individual Christians in identifying their gifts and abilities for ministry

____   ____   Organizing for effective ministry to members, prospects, and family members

____   ____   Equipping people for ministry through ongoing Bible study and special training opportunities

____   ____   Developing, maintaining, and using information systems to identify and address individual ministry needs

____   ____   Involving individuals and groups in ongoing ministry actions through their Sunday School classes, departments, and other Bible study groups

____   ____   Involving individuals and groups in ongoing visitation for the purpose of ministry

____   ____   Involving individuals in specific one-on-one ministry opportunities through specific assignments

____   ____   Involving individuals and groups in the ministry of intercessory prayer

____   ____   Involving individuals and groups in ministry to specific groups in the church and community

Sunday School as foundational strategy organizes, equips, and mobilizes its people for ministry.

10

123456789101234567 8

ten best practices

Sunday School and Fellowship

Christians share a common belief in Christ and a unity of purpose that is rooted in God's love for us and our love for Him and one another. Jesus prayed that He, His disciples, and all those who would believe in Him through their message may be one (John 17:1-26). God wants for His people to join with other believers and to share their common life in Christ. The baptism that Jesus commanded His disciples to perform as a part of the Great Commission is a symbol of being sealed in belief and in belonging.

Sunday School as strategy recognizes that genuine fellowship uses diversity to build unity rather than to separate.

People are different, and believers have diverse gifts; but "in Christ, we who are many form one body, and each member belongs to all the others" (Rom. 12:5). Paul recognized that Christ gave believers a variety of gifts to "prepare God's people for works of service, so that the body of Christ may be built up until we all reach unity in the faith and in the knowledge of the Son of God and become mature, attaining to the whole measure of the fullness of Christ" (Eph. 4:12-13). The church as the body of Christ must be unified and harmonious to accomplish Christ's purpose.

Sunday School as strategy seeks to build relationships through the ongoing work of classes, departments, and other Bible study groups.

It places people in groups and calls for Bible teaching that facilitates the building of relationships in a ministry environment of grace, acceptance, support, and encouragement. The small group provides opportunities for participants to interact with God's Word, the study leader, and one another.

Sunday School as strategy includes classes, departments, and other Bible study groups that provide additional opportunities for people to build fellowship beyond the time the group is gathered for Bible study.

Some additional gatherings may be social functions that allow members to become better acquainted with each other. Nonmembers may be invited to the gatherings as a way to cultivate relationships with them. Other effective efforts at building fellowship are those providing times for members to pray or to work together. For example, ongoing visitation for the purposes of outreach, evangelism, and ministry provides opportunities to bring unreached people into fellowship with Christ and His people. In addition, this effort strengthens the unity of believers as they serve Christ together.

to make your
sunday school work

Sunday School Strategy and Fellowship Check Up

On a scale of 1 to 5 (1 being low; 5 being high), how would you rate your Sunday School in establishing and building relationships with God and His people? How would you rate yourself?

SS   Me

___   ___   Establishing an environment that encourages a sense of belonging

___   ___   Encouraging new believers to unite with the church through baptism

___   ___   Providing Bible study groups for preschoolers, children, youth, and adults

___   ___   Creating an environment of grace, acceptance, support, and encouragement in ongoing Bible study groups

___   ___   Providing opportunities for Bible study participants to interact with God's Word, the teacher, and one another during Bible study sessions

___   ___   Providing opportunities to build relationships through social activities beyond Sunday morning

___   ___   Providing opportunities to build relationships through ongoing outreach, evangelism, and ministry visitation

___   ___   Providing opportunities to build fellowship through such special emphases, as Single Adult Day, Student Sunday School, and Senior Adult Day

___   ___   Maintaining contact with members and prospects who are away from home and those who are serving in leadership positions in age groups other than their own

___   ___   Praying together

Sunday School as foundational strategy guides people to establish and build enduring relationships with God and with His people.

10

123456789101123456678

ten best practices

Sunday School and Worship

Worship is the act of knowing and loving God in spirit and in truth (John 4:23). The essence of worship is recognizing Christ as the Almighty God of heaven and earth and responding to Him with adoration.

All Great Commission work grows out of worship—love and devotion, recognition and response—of God. Without the honoring of Christ through a genuine understanding of who He is and what He has done for us, we labor in our own power and are likely to be driven by our own purposes.

Sunday School as strategy involves people in worship by leading them to acknowledge who Jesus is and to express love for Him both personally and corporately.

Participation in classes and departments or other Bible study groups provide opportunities for people to worship through prayer and praise; stewardship of time, abilities, and resources; and other forms of expressing devotion to Christ.

Sunday School as strategy emphasizes the need to seek God's power and presence by seeking Him.

Leaders benefit from time set aside daily in their own lives to remember who God is and to seek Him through personal prayer and Bible study. Sunday School leaders encourage participants in Bible study classes, departments, and other Bible study groups to do the same. They strive to establish an environment in study sessions that leads people to encounter and respond to the life-changing God through the study of His Word in the fellowship of His people. Such an environment encourages people to open their lives to God. When people do that, amazing things happen: evangelism becomes a priority; discipleship deepens; fellowship grows; and ministry expands freely.

to make your
sunday school work

Sunday School Strategy and Worship CheckUp

On a scale of 1 to 5 (1 being low; 5 being high), how would you rate your Sunday School in involving people in worship? How would you rate yourself?

SS   Me

___   ___   Acknowledging Jesus as Lord of all and responding by expressing love for Him

___   ___   Joining regularly with other Christians to encounter God and encouraging one another through the church's corporate experiences of worship

___   ___   Seeking God's power and presence by seeking Him personally through daily prayer and Bible study

___   ___   Establishing an environment in classes, departments, and other Bible study groups that leads people to encounter the life-changing God during and beyond Bible study sessions

___   ___   Growing in commitment to evangelism as a priority

___   ___   Growing in commitment to building fellowship through involvement in Bible study with others

___   ___   Growing in commitment to discipleship through studying and obeying God's Word

___   ___   Expanding in commitment to ministry and to missions

Sunday School as foundational strategy emphasizes the need to seek God's power and presence by seeking Him.

Sunday School Strategy and Other Church Ministries

The premise of this book is that Sunday School is the foundational strategy for helping a church do the work of the Great Commission. What does this mean about the place of the various ministries that can be found in the life of almost any church?

A key to understanding the relationship of Sunday School as strategy to other church ministries is the word *foundational.* A foundation is an underlying base or support. It is the basis upon which something stands.

Perhaps the most common illustration is to think in terms of a building. Jesus used that imagery to emphasize the importance of building one's life on His teachings (Matt. 7:24-27). A solid foundation is critical to the stability of any structure. It comes first because the rest of the structure is supported by it. The framework for the rest of the building is attached to it. No wise builder begins with the walls. Obviously, the roof is not constructed first.

To say that Sunday School is the foundational strategy is not to make it exclusive or better than other ministries. It is to say that as the foundational strategy, Sunday School can give stability and provide essential support to other ministries. A church that wants to develop a comprehensive approach for doing and being that which is unique to the church as the people of God can lay a solid foundation by giving attention to the growth and development of Sunday School.

Obviously the church will have additional ministries: missions ministry, music, discipleship, youth, and deacon ministry, to name a few. Sunday School does not take the place of any of those, but can provide support by encouraging members to be participants. As members become involved in various ways, they discover the ministries to be ways to grow in Christ, to use the spiritual gifts with which they have been endowed, and to move the church toward greater fulfillment of its mission and objectives.

Even when considered as an institution, the church is a body made up of many parts or ministries. The effectiveness of the church is dependent on each ministry doing what it has been called out to do, working with all other ministries for the common good. Some ministries may be more visible than others, but visibility is not necessarily the sign of importance. Even so, church ministries are not competitive with one another, for no ministry has value apart from what it does to contribute to the work of the church.

The effective use of Sunday School as foundational strategy can help a

church avoid duplicating its efforts; hence, a church is able to use its resources—especially people resources—with greater effectiveness.

For example, Sunday School provides the foundational structure for outreach and evangelism. A church using Sunday School as its outreach and evangelism strategy will focus attention on improving the effectiveness of visitation by members in classes and departments. Only when the foundational effort is firmly in place can additional structures be developed. The same can be said for care ministries and prayer ministries.

Sunday School becomes the way to take the great assignment given to the church and break it down into manageable pieces. It is a way of involving people judiciously, of using resources wisely, and of multiplying efforts strategically.

ten best practices

APPENDIX B
Sunday School Growth and Evaluation Plan

Enrollment

Open enrollment means that we enroll people in Sunday School anywhere and at any time as long as they agree to be enrolled.

Current Enrollment: _____
Recommended Goal: Increase from year to year

Follow-up is the key. When enrolling someone with the open-enrollment method, follow up on the person immediately.

Prospects

A prospect is defined as anyone who is not attending Bible study anywhere.

Current Prospects: _____
Recommended Goal: 1:1, or 1 evangelistic prospect cultivated for every member on roll

To be in a good growth posture, a church needs to have one prospect for every person enrolled in Sunday School.

to make your
sunday school work

Units or Classes

A Bible study class or unit reaches its maximum size in 12-18 months. It can also become closed to new people.

Current Status: _____

Recommended Goal: 1:20, or 1 class for every 20 people enrolled. Specific age-group ratios also apply; see age-group books in the *Sunday School for New Century* series

New units keep growth alive.

Leaders

A leader is defined as someone who leads the teaching, reaching, or ministry related to members of a Sunday School class or department.

Current Status: _____

Recommended Goal: 1:5, or 1 worker to every 5 members

Space

If and when you fill up parking, worship, or education space, growth will stop from occurring.

Current Status: _____

Recommended Goal: 1:1, or 1 space for each unit

You need a meeting space for each Bible study unit. Some units may meet offsite (telephone class, students-away class, nursing-home classes, classes meeting in homes). Every church has three types of space: worship, parking, and education. If any one of those spaces is at 80 percent capacity, then consider the space full. When Preschool space is full, church growth will plateau.

Ministry Contacts

The Sunday School roll is also a target for weekly ministry opportunities. The class must be organized for this to happen.

Current Status: _____

Recommended Goal: 1:1, or 1 contact for every member each week

ten best practices
123456789101234 5678

The Sunday School roll is not merely a list of persons who should attend Sunday School but is a target for weekly ministry opportunities.

Leaders in training

Every leader needs to participate in some type of leadership training during the year.

Current Status: _____

Recommended Goal: 1:1; every worker needs some training each year

Sunday School Leadership Meetings

The meetings are about we seek during meetings to prepare to meet the needs of people targeted by that class or department.

Current Status: _____

Recommended Goal: 75% of workers

Sunday School Attendance

If attendance is below 40 percent of enrollment, there probably is a need for stronger ministry through Sunday School.

Current Status: _____

Recommended Goal: 40-60% of Sunday School enrollment

Several factors impact attendance:

- Enrollment: Attendance tends to average between 40 to 60 percent of enrollment. Increase the enrollment and the average attendance potential increases.
- Weekly contacts: Attendance will increase based on an increase in number and types of contacts made.
- Ratio of workers to members: Attendance is impacted by increasing the number of workers and decreasing the ratio of workers to members.
- Number of units: Attendance is increased by starting and strengthening new units that target unreached groups.

Persons in Discipleship

Discipleship classes are closed groups that are designed for Christians. They focus on applying God's Word and exist to help build on-mission Christians.

Current Status: _____
Recommended Goal: 50% of Sunday School enrollment

Worship

The ratio of Sunday School attendance to worship reflects the effectiveness of assimilation done by the Sunday School. The higher the ratio of Sunday School attendance to worship, the more effective the assimilation and the greater the opportunities for evangelism, discipleship, fellowship, and ministry.

Current Status: _____
Recommended Goal: Sunday School average attendance at least 90% of the average worship attendance

Offerings

The projected Sunday School attendance, multiplied by the per-capita giving number, will determine future offerings.

Current Status: _____
Recommended Goal: Sunday School attendance multiplied by per-capita giving

FAITH Teams

Count the number of FAITH Teams in your Sunday School. The number should equal the number of Bible study units.

Current Status: _____
Recommended Goal: 1:1, or 1 Team for every unit

Baptisms

One half of the net enrollment gain usually will be lost persons; half of those persons will be baptized and assimilated into the church in one year.

Current Status: _____
Recommended Goal: _____

ten best practices

1234567891012345678

Sunday School Growth/Evaluation Plan

Planning Sheet For _____

	Formula Goal	Current Status	Evaluation	1st _ Goal	2nd _ Goal	3rd _ Goal	4th _ Goal
Enrollment	Increase from previous year						
Prospects	1:1						
Units	1:20						
Workers	1:5						
Space	1:1						
Ministry Contracts	1:1						
Leaders in Training	1:1						
S.S. Leadership Meeting	75% of workers						
S.S. Attendance	40-60% of workers						
Persons in Discipleship	50% of S.S. Enrollment						
Worship Attendance	S.S. Attendance 90% of worship						
Offerings	Attendance x per capita giving						
FAITH Teams	1 per unit						
Baptisms	Increase from previous year						

If your current status is within the range of the formula goal, evaluate your Sunday School with a plus (+). If your current status is outside of the range of the formula goal, evaluate your Sunday School with a minus (–). The minuses are areas you need to concentrate on improving, while the pluses are areas in which you are doing well. To plan for future growth, set an enrollment goal for the year and calculate where you need to strengthen your ministry to accommodate the growth.

to make your
sunday school work
0123456789101234567

APPENDIX C
Prepared by God to S.E.R.V.E.

Leaders know who they are in Christ Jesus. They know how God molded and gifted them for His use. They trust that God can use every experience to prepare them for ministry. They trust that God has prepared them to serve for His glory, not their gain.

God has prepared you for His purposes to bring honor to Him. The Bible says to use the spiritual gifts God gave you to serve others.

According to 1 Peter 4:10, the goal of all God's gifts is service to others. "Each one should use whatever gift he has received to serve others, faithfully administering God's grace in its various forms."

Servant leaders are leaders who serve. The acrostic S.E.R.V.E. is an outline for how God has prepared you for His purposes.

S *piritual gifts.*—Those gifts God gives through His Holy Spirit to empower you for service

E *xperiences.*—Those events God allows that mold you into a servant leader

R *elational style.*—Behavioral traits God uses to give you a leadership style

V *ocational skills.*—Those abilities you have gained through training and experience that you can use in service to God

E *nthusiasm.*—That passion God has put in your heart for a certain ministry to others

ten best practices

1234567891012345678

Your relationship with Christ as well as those five areas—spiritual gifts, experiences, relational style, vocational skills, and enthusiasm— become the raw materials God uses to mold you into a servant leader.

Spiritual Gifts

Leaders know how God has gifted them for service in the body of Christ, the church. Leaders serve out of their spiritual giftedness. They seek to lead from their God-given place in the body of Christ. The church works best when its members know how God has gifted them spiritually and when all members, empowered by their spiritual gifts, are in places of service. Spiritual gifts are the key to understanding how God intends the church to function.

A spiritual gift is a "manifestation of the Spirit" (1 Cor. 12:7). It is not a special ability that you develop on your own; that is a skill or talent. You do not seek a spiritual gift. Even so, you should prayerfully seek to understand how God already has gifted you for His purposes.

God gives you your spiritual gifts for a special purpose in the church when He graces you with salvation through Christ. Understanding spiritual gifts begins with knowing the biblical nature of the church.

Both 1 Corinthians 12:7 and Ephesians 4:12 help us to understand why God gives gifts to the church. "Now to each one the manifestation of the Spirit is given for the common good" (1 Cor. 12:7). Ephesians 4:12 further describes this purpose: "To prepare God's people for works of service, so that the body of Christ may be built up."

Spiritual gifts are for the common good of the church. God gifts members of the church to equip and build up the body of Christ. Spiritual gifts are not for pride but for service. Servant leaders allow God's spiritual gifts to motivate them to serve.

Important to any study of spiritual gifts is God's work in the life of the believer and the church. You do not decide you want a certain gift and then go get it. God gives the gifts "just as he determines" (1 Cor. 12:11). Spiritual gifts are part of God's design for a person's life and for the life of the church. The Bible says that "God has arranged the parts in the body, every one of them, just as he wanted them to be" (1 Cor. 12:18).

Your goals as a servant leader are to discover how God in His grace has gifted you for service and to lead others in the same joy of discovery.

A spiritual gift can be defined as "an individual manifestation of grace from the Father that enables you to serve Him and thus play a vital role in His plan for the redemption of the world."[1] For this study, we will use this definition: A spiritual gift is an expression of the Holy Spirit in the life of believers that empowers them to serve the body of Christ, the church.

Romans 12:6-8; 1 Corinthians 12:8-10,28-30; Ephesians 4:11; and 1 Peter 4:9-11 contain representative lists of gifts and roles that God has given to the church. A definition of those gifts follows. Check two or three gifts that seem to fit how God has made you.

- *Leadership*—Leadership aids the body by leading and directing members to accomplish the goals and purposes of the church. Leadership motivates people to work together in unity toward common goals (Rom. 12:8).

- *Administration*—Persons with the gift of administration lead the body by steering others to remain on task. Administration enables the body to organize according to God-given purposes and long-term goals (1 Cor. 12:28).

- *Teaching*—Teaching is instructing people in the truths and doctrines of God's Word for the purposes of building up, unifying, and maturing the body (1 Cor. 12:28; Rom. 12:7; Eph. 4:11).

- *Knowledge*—The gift of knowledge manifests itself in teaching and training in discipleship. It is the God-given ability to learn, know, and explain the precious truths of God's Word. A word of knowledge is a Spirit-revealed truth (1 Cor. 12:28).

- *Wisdom*—Wisdom is the gift that discerns the work of the Holy Spirit in the body and applies His teachings and actions to the needs of the body (1 Cor. 12:28).

- *Prophecy*—The gift of prophecy is that of proclaiming the Word of God boldly. It builds up the body and leads to conviction of sin. Prophecy manifests itself in preaching and teaching (1 Cor. 12:10; Rom. 12:6).

- *Discernment*—Discernment aids the body by recognizing the true intentions of those within or related to the body. Discernment tests the message and actions of others for the protection and well-being of the body (1 Cor. 12:10).

- *Exhortation*—Possessors of this gift encourage members to be involved in, and enthusiastic about, the work of the Lord. Members with this gift are good counselors and motivate others to service. Exhortation exhibits itself in preaching, teaching, and ministry (Rom. 12:8).

ten best practices

- *Shepherding*—The gift of shepherding is manifested in persons who look out for the spiritual welfare of others. Although pastors, like shepherds, do care for members of the church, this gift is not limited to a pastor or staff member (Eph. 4:11).
- *Faith*—Faith trusts God to work beyond the human capabilities of the people. Believers with this gift encourage others to trust in God in the face of apparently insurmountable odds (1 Cor. 12:9).
- *Evangelism*—God gifts his church with evangelists to lead others to Christ effectively and enthusiastically. This gift builds up the body by adding new members to its fellowship (Eph. 4:11).
- *Apostleship*—The church sends apostles from the body to plant churches or be missionaries. Apostles motivate the body to look beyond its walls to carry out the Great Commission (1 Cor. 12:28; Eph. 4:11).
- *Service and Helps*—Those with the gift of service and helps recognize practical needs in the body and joyfully give assistance to meeting those needs. Christians with this gift do not mind working behind the scenes (1 Cor. 12:28; Rom. 12:7).
- *Mercy*—Cheerful acts of compassion characterize those with the gift of mercy. Persons with this gift aid the body by empathizing with hurting members. They keep the body healthy and unified by keeping others aware of the needs within the church (Rom. 12:8).
- *Giving*—Members with the gift of giving give freely and joyfully to the work and mission of the body. Cheerfulness and liberality are characteristics of individuals with this gift (Rom. 12:8).
- *Hospitality*—Those with this gift have the ability to make visitors, guests, and strangers feel at ease. They sometimes use their homes to entertain guests. Persons with this gift integrate new members into the body (1 Pet. 4:9).

List here the gifts you have begun to discover in your life:

1._____
2._____
3._____
4._____

to make your
sunday school work

God has gifted you with an expression of His Holy Spirit to support His vision and mission of the church. It is a worldwide vision to reach all people with the gospel of Christ. As a servant leader, God desires that you know how He has gifted you. That will lead you to where He would have you serve as part of His vision and mission for the church.

God has gifted you for service in Christ's body, the church (1 Cor. 12:7). His goal is for you to prepare others for service in the church (Eph. 4:12). As a servant leader, you are to use your spiritual gifts for the common good of the body. God gifted you for His glory, not your gain. God gifted you to build up His church, not your ego.

After prayer and worship, I am beginning to sense that God wants me to use my spiritual gifts to serve Christ's body by . . .

I am not sure yet how God wants me to use my gifts to serve others. But I am committed to prayer and worship, seeking wisdom and opportunities to use the gifts I have received from God.

Experiences

Leaders trust that God works in their lives to bring about His plan for their lives. Experiences become God's crucible to mold you into His image. Servant leaders are confident that events happening to them and around them are part of God's sovereign work in creation.

God can take what already has happened in your life to help accomplish His will. God can mold and make you into a tool of His grace. God can break into your life to make you a new creation for His purposes.

Henry Blackaby calls events like Paul's conversion "spiritual markers." He says that a spiritual marker "identifies a time of transition, decision, or direction when I clearly know that God has guided me."[2] Spiritual markers remind you that God is at work in your history. Remembering them helps you to see God's work in your life and how He is unfolding His plan for your life.

10

ten best practices

1234567891012345678

You have events in your life when God has made His will clear to you. God broke into history, and you know God spoke to you. He may have confirmed a decision you made. He may have revealed something new about who He is.

Take a moment to describe briefly in the space below some of your most important encounters with God. Write as if you are telling a friend about those life-changing moments. Start with your salvation experience. Don't worry if you do not have a dramatic story. God works in everyday events to shape you into His likeness. Spiritual markers can be any life experience, from a burning bush to a child's gentle touch.

Let me tell you about my most important encounters with God . . .

Relational Style

Every person has a natural style of how he or she relates to others. Every style has its strengths and weaknesses. God can use any relational style that is submitted to His will to serve His purposes.

How you relate to others is basic to how you serve as a leader. To know your relational style is to know how God has molded you to serve people through your relationships with them. Servant leaders know how they naturally relate to others and how others relate to them.

Because leadership involves influencing others for the common good, knowing how God has molded your temperament is key to knowing your leadership style. Knowing the style of others allows you to meet their relational needs. Moreover, understanding the relational needs of other people helps you to communicate with them and to lead them more effectively.

God will help you to understand your role as a servant leader as you assess the strengths and weaknesses of your relational style. A four-category model has been proved over time and has strong scientific support. The primary source for understanding this model is Ken Voges, an author of *Understanding How Others Misunderstand You.* Voges uses the letters DISC to represent the four primary relational styles.[3]

- **D** stands for the "dominance" style—Works toward achieving goals and results; functions best in active, challenging environments.
- **I** stands for the "influencing" style—Works toward relating to people through verbal persuasion; functions best in friendly, favorable environments.
- **S** is the "steadiness" style—Works toward supporting and cooperating with others; functions best in supportive, harmonious environments.
- **C** represents the "conscientious" style—Works toward doing things right and focuses on details; functions best in structured, orderly environments.

Using the descriptions above that best describe you, personalize your DISC style by completing the following statements:

Because of my special, God-given style of relating to others, I tend to work toward . . .

and I function best in . . .

But I also see these additional qualities of my God-given personality:

The most important part of the above written activity is to reflect on these questions: How does my relational style relate to servant leadership? How can my own God-given temperament be used by God to make a difference in my church and community?

As you think about those questions, note the following chart that summarizes possible strengths and weaknesses of each leadership style.

Dominant		**Influencing**	
Strengths	*Weaknesses*	*Strengths*	*Weaknesses*
Direct	Too controlling	Gregarious	Forgets the goal
Active	Hates routine	Enthusiastic	Poor follow-through
Decisive	Hates details	Extremely flexible	Overlooks details

10

ten best practices

1234567891012345678

Steadiness		Conscientious	
Strengths	*Weaknesses*	*Strengths*	Weaknesses
Cooperative	Fails to confront	Detailed	Inflexible
Deliberate	Dislikes change	Conscientious	Rigid
Supportive	Too compromising	Cautious	Indecisive

Note that each style has both strengths and weaknesses. No single style can meet every need. God intentionally created a variety of styles, none being more important or more needed than another. All gifts and strengths are important to the overall servant ministry of a church. At the same time, each strength, when out of control, can become a weakness. And weaknesses should not become excuses for failure. A person and a church constantly must strive to accomplish without excuse the ministries received from God.

Such diversity of styles within the church may at times produce conflict, but it provides the important balance needed to accomplish what God gives the church to do. It reminds us of the important lesson that God needs each one of us and that we need each other.

Churches function best when members accept the relational styles of others and seek to meet the needs of those persons, never compromising the message of Christ. Relationships remain strong when members follow God's pattern for living together as His body with all its diversity (1 Cor. 12:14-26).

God's Word offers clear teaching on how we are to serve one another in love. Colossians 3:12-14 says, "Therefore, as God's chosen people, holy and dearly loved, clothe yourselves with compassion, kindness, humility, gentleness and patience. Bear with each other and forgive whatever grievances you may have against one another. Forgive as the Lord forgave you. And over all these virtues put on love, which binds them all together in perfect unity."

Remember that your natural relational style is not an excuse to sin. God's indwelling Spirit balances your natural tendencies with God's temperament. Regardless of your style, the fruit of the Spirit (Gal. 5:22-23) is always a vital part of a servant leader's relationships. God's Spirit molds your temperament for His glory.

to make your sunday school work

Vocational Skills

Our English word *vocation* comes from the Latin word *vocare*, which means "to call." A vocation, then, is what one feels called to do with his or her life. In previous generations, a sense of divine calling was part of a person's place in the world. A vocation was part of God's plan for a person's life. God called and you responded by gaining the skills necessary to live out that calling.

Vocation has come to mean any profession or occupation. A vocational skill is any ability you have learned that enhances your calling in life. In today's secular world, people often prefer to use the word *career*. A career is your choice. Instead of looking for God's plan, the world teaches you to choose what you want to do and then to plot a course of training to accomplish your career choice. A career, then, is what you choose for yourself.

In the New Testament, Paul encouraged the Christians in Ephesus to "live a life worthy of the calling you have received" (Eph. 4:1). He was not talking about their jobs. He encouraged them to adopt a lifestyle consistent with who they were in Christ. Calling, as presented in the Bible, is one's position in Christ, not one's position in the world.

Whatever your vocation, your calling is to live worthy of the salvation God gives you in Christ Jesus. In Colossians, Paul wrote, "Whatever you do, work at it with all your heart, as working for the Lord, not for men. . . . It is the Lord Christ you are serving" (Col. 3:23-24). Whatever you do, God calls you to live as a child of God and to bring honor to God through your actions. It matters less what you do in life than it does what you do with your life.

For the sake of this study, let us define vocation as what you do to provide for your needs in society, recognizing God's work in your life to lead you to that choice. Calling is God's call to salvation in Christ Jesus and to a special mission in your life for His purposes.

Vocational skills are those skills you have acquired to do your career or hobbies. Make an inventory of your skills. Use the following table to create your skill inventory:

ten best practices

Name of Skill	How I Use This Skill in My Vocation
1.	
2.	
3.	

God enabled Paul to use his vocational skills for his life's calling. God can do the same for you. Take time to imagine how God can use the skills you listed above for His work of spreading the gospel. For example, if one of your skills is carpentry, you can use that skill to build shelves in your church's preschool rooms or for a local mission or ministry. Be creative as you consider how you can use your skills for the glory of God.

Name of Skill	How God Can Use This Skill in His Mission
1.	
2.	
3.	

Enthusiasm

The word *enthusiasm* comes from a Greek word that literally means "in god." The Greeks believed that a god could enter a person and inspire or enthuse him. Enthusiasm takes on the meaning "God in you." While the Greek word for enthuse is not found in the New Testament, the emphasis on God's presence that energizes the believer is a recurring theme (John 14:20; 20:21-22; Matt. 28:18-20; Acts 1:8).

The Bible is clear that God's Holy Spirit is the source of passion for God's mission within the believer. Paul declared it is "Christ in you" that is "the hope of glory" (Col. 1:27). We do not generate hope on our own. God energizes us with His living Holy Spirit. Jesus promised that the Holy Spirit will be the Counselor and "guide you into all truth" (John 16:7,13). He is our counselor and guide as we follow the Lord. Passion and enthusiasm for ministry come from God.

Scripture tells about people who were enthusiastic about what they did. That is not a self-generated thrill. Enthusiasm is a God-given desire to serve Him by meeting the needs of others. Servant leaders have a God-given passion to serve.

A servant leader's joy comes when he sees God at work and he is a part of it. Servant leadership is a God-given passion for the success of God's plan. Servant leaders find joy when God's will is done.

Your God-given enthusiasm is sometimes your only source of joy in ministry. As you lead, you will face obstacles and disappointments. People will criticize you. Sometimes they will question your motives. But the sincere desire to know God's will and the passion God puts in your heart for His work absorb those negative reactions and allow you to move forward with your ministry. Your enthusiasm is the beginning of a fruitful life in Christ.

What has God burned in your heart to do for His mission on earth? Take a moment to consider what that may be. Prayerfully write your responses to the following statements. Complete them with honest, heartfelt statements.

The one thing I do for God that makes my heart beat fast is . . .

If I could do one thing for God, it would be to . . .

ten best practices

123456789101 2345678

My S.E.R.V.E. Profile

Believing God has prepared me for servant leadership. I am discovering that He has molded me in the following areas. (Pull together what you have written on the previous pages to complete the following statements.)

- *God has gifted me with the spiritual gifts of:*

- *God has allowed these experiences to guide me for His purposes:*

- *God has created me to relate most often to others naturally in this way:*

- *God has given me the opportunities to develop these vocational skills that can be used in His service:*

- *God has burned in my heart the enthusiasm to serve in this area of ministry:*

End Notes

"Prepared by God to S.E.R.V.E." has been adapted from C. Gene Wilkes, *Jesus on Leadership: Becoming a Servant Leader* (Nashville: LifeWay Press, 1996), 31-84. This resource can lead you to apply biblical principles of servant leadership to all areas of ministry and includes more detailed spiritual gifts and relational style surveys.

[1]Ken Hemphill, *Serving God: Discovering and Using Your Spiritual Gifts Workbook* (Dallas: The Sampson Company, 1995), p. 22.

[2]Henry Blackaby and Claude V. King, *Experiencing God: Knowing and Doing the Will of God* (Nashville: Convention Press, 1990), p. 104.

[3]Ken Voges and Ron Braud, *Understanding How Others Misunderstand You* (Chicago: Moody, 1980).

APPENDIX D
Other Evangelism Training Resources

got life?™

Developed by Ken Hemphill and Frank Harber, *got life?*™ is a unique evangelism tool that connects with the modern culture. This creative program combines a gospel presentation with hard-hitting apologetics. The material may be used with large or small groups. Included are multimedia resources such as CD ROM, Flash, video, and more. *got life?*™ resources may be ordered from HeartSprings Media, P.O. Box 1655, Keller, Texas, 76244.

Share Jesus Without Fear

Written by William Fay and Ralph Hodge, *Share Jesus Without Fear* is a natural, nonthreatening way to share the gospel. The method is simple: A witness asks the individual to whom he is witnessing five questions and relies on the Holy Spirit to do the convicting and the convincing. This approach eliminates the pressure, the argument, and the fear of failure that often accompanies a witnessing endeavor. *Share Jesus Without Fear* resources are available from LifeWay Church Resources. See page 2 for information on ordering resources from LifeWay Church Resources.

The Net

The Net, produced by the North American Mission Board, is a mentor-apprentice strategy that helps a believer share his or her faith in the twenty-first century. Easily customized, *The NET* teaches individuals to tell effectively the story of how Christ changed their lives. This user-friendly, easy-to-learn strategy requires no certification. *The NET* resources are available from North American Mission Board and LifeWay Church Resources. See page 2 for information on ordering resources from LifeWay Church Resources.

ten best practices

12345678910 12345678

An Overview and Use Plan

This book can be used effectively as a training tool for leaders in your church's Sunday School ministry. Every leader would benefit from having a copy of the book for evaluation, goal-setting, and planning toward the use of Sunday School as a strategy for engaging people in fulfilling the Great Commission of Christ. Each leader should read and work through the entire book individually. The Sunday School Leadership Team would benefit further by meeting together to thoroughly explore how best to implement best practices for Sunday School as strategy. That might be done at a retreat of one or more days, or perhaps in a series of meetings over the course of several weeks or months leading toward the launch of a new year of Sunday School ministry.

Following is a plan for a general overview of the main points in *10 Best Practices to Make Your Sunday School Work.* Each of the steps is designed to be accomplished in approximately 10 minutes. They may be used in a single 2-hour overview session, individually as a mini-session, or in any combination that suits the needs of your church. Keep in mind that an in-depth treatment of the material in this book will require a significant investment of time, attention, and involvement by all Sunday School leaders.

1. Ask leaders to share an important affect Sunday School has had on their lives. When several have responded, suggest that Sunday School has always been a life-changing enterprise. Use information from pages 5-7 to lecture briefly on the history of Sunday School. Highlight the importance of the Bible, volunteer leaders, and evangelism as constants through the ages. Guide leaders to consider how those constants are represented in their experiences with Sunday School ministry and in the church's use of Sunday School currently.

2. Write on a chalkboard the definition of Sunday School that appears at the top of page 5. Discuss each of the phrases in the definition in relation to

your church's current practice. Ask: Is our church using Sunday School as its foundational strategy for leading people to faith in the Lord Jesus Christ and for building on-mission Christians? Review information on pages 9-13 to help leaders understand the biblical basis for using Sunday School as strategy.

3. Assign each of the strategic principles for Sunday School for a New Century (pages 14-17) to a different leader to review and summarize. Guide leaders to identify ways they recognize each of the strategic principles are represented currently in the church's Sunday School ministry.

4. List on a chalkboard the ten best practices from page 8. Use information on page 17 to explain the intended context for understanding "best practices." Explain the significance of the sequence in which the practices are listed.

5. Review the information about "Commit to the Strategy" from page 17. Guide leaders to identify implications each of the bulleted statements has for their work.

6. Continue to review each of the remaining best practices following the same instructions given in step number 5. To cover each within a 2 1/2-hour session, spend only about 10 minutes on each best practice. Remember, this is only an overview.

7. Conclude the overview by leading the group to make a commitment to Sunday School as strategy. Then determine a follow-up plan to further exploring the implications of each best practice for your church and develop actions for implementing the best practices in your setting.

123456789101012345678
ten best practices

Index

Advancement day, 75

Age grading, 63-71

Annual planning, 24-34

Assimilation, 155-164

Bible study groups; open, 14,41-45; short-term, 43-45; ongoing, 42-45

Bible study events, 45-48

Bible teaching, curriculum resources, 195-200; essentials of teaching-learning, 185-194; equipment and furnishings, 204-207; foundational, 147-150; and evangelism, 147-152; parents as Bible teachers, 172-179; for spiritual transformation, 181-182, 184-194

Budget planning,48-51

Christian Growth Study Plan, 112-113

Church functions and Sunday School, 237-251; implications for organization, 61-63

Curriculum, choosing, 198-200; learner guides. 199-200;

Discipleship (ministry) and Sunday School, 242-244

Discipleship (church function) and organization, 61; Principle of Foundational Discipleship, 15

Enlistment of leaders, 79-88

Enrollment, 158-162; suggested ceilings, 68-71,76,77

Essentials of teaching-learning, 185-194

Equipment and furnishings, preschool, 205-206; children, youth, adult, and young adult, 207

Evangelism, through Bible teaching, 126-128,147-152; FAITH Sunday School Evangelism Strategy, 126-131; and organization, 62, Principle of Foundational Evangelism, 14-15

FAITH. Sunday School Evangelism Strategy, 126-131

Fellowship, and Sunday School, 247-248

Foundational principles, of Sunday School ministry, 14-17

Great Commission, 10-11

History, of Sunday School, 5-8

Home and family, Principle of Family Responsibility, 15-16; Sunday School partnering with, 171-180

Kingdom mission, 9-10

Leaders, as models, 79-80

Leader Commissioning Service, 53-57

Leadership, enlistment of, 79-88; discovering leaders, 81-89; leader:learner ratios,72-75,83 ; leader training, 116-122; model visit, 93-94; multiplying as element of strategy,235-236; position descriptions, 94-106; potential leader training,115-116;Principle of Biblical Leadership, 16-17; security issues in, 124-126

Leader-learner ratios, 68-71,76,77

Learner guides, 199-200

Leadership Planning Team, 26,89

Leadership Meetings, 100-109

Ministry and Sunday School, 244-246, 174-179; families and, 174-179,220

Ministry groups, 213-215

Multiplying leaders, 226-229 *see* Leader enlistment

to make your
sunday school work

Multiplying units, 226-240; guide-lines, 240; models, 231-233

New member orientation, 157; *see* Assimilation

New units, *see* Multiplying units

Ongoing Bible study groups; 42-45

Organization,60-74; age-grading, 63-71; and purpose, 60-61

Outreach-evangelism leader, 91-92,95-97

Open Bible study groups, 14,41-45

Parents as Bible teachers, 172-179

Pastor and Sunday School, 16,90,108

Planning, annual, 24-34; monthly, 38-40; weekly, 100-109; budget, 48-51

Position descriptions, 88-100

Potential leader training, 109-110

Prospect, assignments of, 140-141; discovery, 136-139; files, 139-140

Recordkeeping,164-169

Robert Raikes, 5

Security issues, 116-119

S.E.R.V.E., 257-268

Short-term Bible study groups, 43-45

Space, 201,204; maximizing use of, 201-202; multiple use of, 202-204

Special education, 71-74

Spiritual transformation; definition of, 181-182, Principle of Spiritual Transformation, 16; teaching for, 184-194

Steps to Organizational Progression and Growth, 76

Stewardship, 168

Strategic plans, examples of, 34-37

Sunday School, biblical foundations of, 12-13; and church functions, 11, 237-251; definition, 13-14;

FAITH Sunday School Evangelism Strategy, 126-131; and families, 15-16,171-180; foundational prin-ciples, 14-17; and the Great Commission, 10; history of, 5-8; and kingdom mission, 9-10; lead-ers of, 94-106; multiple meeting times, 202-204; and other church ministries, 251-252; as strategy, 13-14, 41-42

Sunday School director, 90-91,108-109

Sunday School Growth and Evaluation Plan, 253-257

Sunday School Strategy Growth Worksheet, 77

Sunday School Launch Event, 52-53

Sunday School Planning Team, 89

Teacher, characteristics of evangelis-tic, 152-153; and leader enlistment, 81-86; and multiplication of units and leaders, 233-234; responsibili-ties, 96-97

Teaching *see* Bible teaching

Training, evangelism 126-131; lead-ership, 54,109-116; potential leader, 109-110-

Vacation Bible School

Visitation, 134-136,142; evangelistic and ministry, 142-144; files, 139-140; flow of assignments, 141; making assignments, 140-41

Worship, organization and, 63; and Sunday School, 249-250

ten best practices

1234567891012345678

CHRISTIAN GR🌐WTH STUDY PLAN

In the **Christian Growth Study Plan (formerly Church Study Course)**, this book *10 Best Practices to Make Your Sunday School Work* is a resource for course credit in five (5) Leadership and Skill Development diploma plans. To receive credit, read the book, complete the learning activities, show your work to your pastor, a staff member or church leader, then complete the form on the next page. The form may be duplicated. Send the completed form to:

**Christian Growth Study Plan
One LifeWay Plaza
Nashville, TN 37234-0175
FAX: (615)251-5067**

For information about the Christian Growth Study Plan, refer to the current Christian Growth Study Plan Catalog. Your church office may have a copy. If not, request a free copy from the Christian Growth Study Plan office (615/251-2525).

to make your sunday school work

0123456789101234567

115351

TEN BEST PRACTICES TO MAKE YOUR SUNDAY SCHOOL WORK
COURSE CREDIT INFORMATION

Please check the appropriate box indicating the courses you want to apply this credit. You may check more than one.

☐ Developing the Administrative Skills of the General Church Leader (Sunday School) (LS-0048)
☐ Developing Administrative Skills (Sunday School) (LS-0052)
☐ Planning and Administering Associational Ministry (Sunday School) (LS-0066)
☐ The Sunday School Ministry (Church Leadership) (LS-0090)
☐ Administration of Special Education Ministries (LS-0104)

PARTICIPANT INFORMATION

Name (First, Middle, Last)

Social Security Number (USA ONLY-optional) | Personal CGSP Number*

Home Phone | Date of Birth (MONTH, DAY, YEAR)

Address (Street, Route, or P.O. Box) | City, State, or Province | Zip/Postal Code

Email Address for CGSP use

Please check appropriate box: ☐ Resource purchased by church ☐ Resource purchased by self ☐ Other

CHURCH INFORMATION

Church Name

Address (Street, Route, or P.O. Box) | City, State, or Province | Zip/Postal Code

CHANGE REQUEST ONLY

☐ Former Name

☐ Former Address | City, State, or Province | Zip/Postal Code

☐ Former Church | City, State, or Province | Zip/Postal Code

Signature of Pastor, Conference Leader, or Other Church Leader | Date

*New participants are requested but not required to give SS# and date of birth. Existing participants, please give CGSP# when using SS# for the first time. Thereafter, only one ID# is required. **Mail to:** Christian Growth Study Plan, One LifeWay Plaza, Nashville, TN 37234-0117. Fax: (615)251-5067.

Revised 4-05